# MUSICAL COMPOSITION

# MUSICAL

# COMPOSITION

## CRAFT AND ART

**ALAN BELKIN**

Yale UNIVERSITY PRESS

NEW HAVEN & LONDON

Published with assistance from the foundation established in memory of Philip Hamilton McMillan of the Class of 1894, Yale College.

Yale University Press books may be purchased in quantity for educational, business, or promotional use. For information, please e-mail sales.press@yale .edu (U.S. office) or sales@yaleup.co.uk (U.K. office).

Set in Meridien and Futura type by Newgen North America.
Printed in the United States of America.

Library of Congress Control Number: 2017956623
ISBN 978-0-300-21899-2 (paperback: alk. paper)

A catalogue record for this book is available from the British Library.

# CONTENTS

# ACKNOWLEDGMENTS

First and foremost, my thanks to Andrew Schartmann, who encouraged me to write this book and to propose it to Yale University Press. He also made numerous detailed and perceptive comments on the first draft of the text.

Matthew Lane also spent many hours carefully commenting on the entire book in great detail; his numerous suggestions were always specific and constructive.

Maxime Samarov read the book from cover to cover and had many useful things to say, both musical and pedagogical.

Sylvain Caron commented perceptively on several chapters.

Michel Edward and Eric Jones-Cadieux gave me useful suggestions for examples from film and video-game music. Eric also took care of the many copyright requests and permissions for the twentieth-century examples.

Thanks to Maxime Goulet for explaining to me various particularities of music for video games, and also for giving me some intriguing ideas for exercises relevant to composers aiming to compose for video games and for films.

I am grateful to Nikolaï Miletenko and Thomas Goss for carefully proofreading the manuscript. Thanks to Fred Kameny for the index.

My best friend, Charles Lafleur, was a constant source of encouragement and thoughtful reflection while this project was underway. Both are enormously appreciated.

Thanks to Sarah Miller, Ash Lago, Harry Haskell, and the rest of the team at Yale University Press for their help in bringing this project to completion.

There are too many people to name who have contributed to my ideas about composition and composition pedagogy over the years, but I really must at least mention my teachers at Juilliard, David Diamond and Elliott Carter, who set me on such an interesting path.

Obviously, whatever weaknesses remain are mine alone.

# INTRODUCTION

Teaching musical composition today has become a very complicated endeavor, owing to the students' unprecedented variety of needs, interests, and backgrounds.

Overall, there are three broad categories of students studying musical composition at the undergraduate level: those aiming to compose concert music; those aiming at a career writing functional music for film, theatre, TV, video games, publicity, and so forth;[1] and those whose main interest lies in theory or musicology, but who nonetheless want to have some insight into a composer's point of view.

Making the teacher's problem even more complex, above and beyond these disparate needs, the concert music of the past century has seen an unprecedented level of stylistic fragmentation. A composer of concert music could be writing in a hyper-complex style, like that of Brian Ferneyhough, or applying electro-acoustic techniques to harmonic spectra, like Tristan Murail, or else writing somewhat minimalist, tonal music, like John Adams. Even popular music today encompasses many different styles. How can one teach composition in a way that effectively addresses all these different needs?

Existing composition textbooks either focus exclusively on the classical repertoire or else simply catalog various more or less recent stylistic trends, with short chapters devoted to each one.

Arnold Schoenberg's *Fundamentals of Musical Composition* remains the best model of the former type, and it still contains much useful material, as well as a host of examples, with many useful comments by the author.[2]

The other kind of book focuses on what is distinct and unusual about each new style. While certainly of interest to a contemporary composer, this approach is of limited use to someone who wants to acquire more widely applicable basic skills, since these books do not focus on what the various styles have in common, but rather on what differentiates them. Also, such a compendium of the latest styles can become somewhat dated rather quickly.[3]

In this book I attempt to reconcile the varied needs listed above with an approach that is style-neutral, and that focuses on craft.

Despite their obvious differences, most kinds of music heard today[4] share certain formal requirements that grow out of how music is perceived. For example, even though film music normally follows an extramusical, narrative story line, a film composer still needs to know how to compose a convincing transition between music of differing characters. Music for an ad campaign needs an effective beginning, so as to quickly attract the listener's attention, and so on. As these examples show, there is a pressing need to teach composition today in a way that is stylistically flexible, but at the same time helps the young composer to master the skills required to respond to the music's formal requirements.

Over thirty-five years of composition and composition teaching, I have tried to find, and to focus on, general principles that are not limited to one style of music. The result is this book. The common principles laid out here have rarely, if ever, been explicitly discussed as such, and certainly not all in one place, in a logical pedagogical sequence, with exercises and examples. This is the book I wish had been available to me as a student.

Some of the ideas here germinated out of passing remarks by my own composition teachers, David Diamond and Elliott Carter. Most of them, however, came simply from regular observation of great music that I admire. In a sense, they were attempts to answer questions I myself had about what exactly makes great music work as well as it does. Other notions gradually became clear to me during years of trying to teach many different kinds and levels of students as constructively as possible.

These principles are certainly not of my own invention. Despite the fact that they are almost never referred to in composition textbooks, most successful composers have clearly been aware of them on some level for hundreds of years: they are everywhere to be seen in the best music of the western tradition.

## ASSUMPTIONS

Even attempting to focus on general principles in a way that is applicable to multiple styles, I do make certain assumptions in this book about the nature of music. Some of them can of course be debated, but it is impossible to teach composition at all without at least some minimal consensus about what the word implies.

I assume that powerful emotional communication is an important goal of music. I also assume that some means are more effective than others in reaching this goal. Often the difference between a successful piece and a weak one is that in the latter there are aspects of the music that distract from, or even contradict, the desired musical character. This is because beginning students do not always realize the significance of all of their choices. For example, imagine the beginning of Beethoven's Fifth Symphony played very slowly, an octave lower, on a marimba. The enormous dramatic drive of the famous "fate motif" would completely disappear, even though the pitches and the note values would be correct. This may seem like a trivial example, but long experience with student work has shown me that dimensions of the music like register, tempo, dynamics, and timbre are often not accorded enough attention, although they contribute enormously to the quality of the final expressive result. If the young composer makes the wrong choices in these areas, the music's character will suffer greatly. In this book, I will try to pay more or less equal attention to pitch and to these other aspects of the music.

Another critical assumption here is that music's evolution over time is more than simply a question of duration. The musical frame—the beginning, the middle, and the end—greatly influences the way the music is structured.[5] In other words, what the composer needs to do at any given moment depends a lot on where the music has arrived in its temporal trajectory. A beginning has different requirements than an ending, and so forth. Also, during the piece, the music must develop, and that requires constantly balancing novelty and variety. Over longer time stretches, some contrasts will need to be more marked, so the composer also needs to be able to move between musical characters with various degrees of smoothness. In a word, the composer needs to be at ease with the techniques of transition.

Be it as background for a story in a film, or in an hour-long symphony, all the kinds of music here discussed need to respect these minimal formal requirements.[6]

## PERCEPTION

These formal principles are based, as much as possible, on how music is actually perceived. While this is not a textbook about the psychology of perception, a composer must, at least implicitly, take a position on these issues: composing is all about audible choices. All the principles here discussed will refer to aspects of the music that are clearly audible. Some are more refined than others, and some may not necessarily be easily audible at first hearing, but I have avoided spending time on anything that a sensitive music-lover cannot discern through attentive listening. Of course, a professional musician will perceive things somewhat differently than an amateur, but much of the difference is mainly a matter of knowing the names for what is happening. For example, a musician might speak of a perfect authentic cadence, where the untutored music-lover would just sense some kind of relatively strong punctuation.

## FORM AND FORMS

Some books on composition, like Schoenberg's, start from the well-known standard forms, such as ternary form, the rondo, and the sonata. While I also use simplified versions of these forms for the composition projects in this book, this is for pedagogical reasons. Eventually the mature composer will leave these textbook models behind, since no single description of any of these forms can be really adequate. A careful look at multiple examples of any one of these forms in the literature will always reveal wide-ranging disparities in the details of how they are actually realized. Indeed, books that attempt to discuss these forms in detail, even when limited to one single historical period, always list multiple variants of each. Only the most naive of composers would assume that all sonatas, or all binary forms, are alike. For a mature composer, these forms are just useful conventions for solving certain basic problems, but the details will always depend on the musical ideas contained therein. As the young composer moves gradually from learning the craft toward the more artistic aspects of musical composition, more and more of the work will consist of a search for the right form for any given piece.

For example, the transition section of the prototypical sonata form can be realized in many ways, all depending on the character of the ideas being connected. Some transitions are quite dramatic and sudden; others are so smooth as to be virtually unnoticeable. The decision in each case can only be made according to the character of, and relationship between, the specific musical ideas in the piece. A mature composer will often experiment with different transitions in order to find the most effective one. This is another reason for the craft-centered approach adopted here: a composer who is at ease with many techniques and degrees of transition will more easily be able to find the right solution for each situation.

To make this point about the variety of the standard forms clearer, each of the chapters containing a major composition project (Variations, Rondo, and Sonata) contains a little section at the end called "Elaborations," mentioning a few variants of the form in question. Such variants may also be mentioned occasionally elsewhere, but not as systematically.

## QUANTIFYING

A novel aspect of this book is the idea of quantifying various aspects of the music—say, from 1 to 5 or 1 to 10. This kind of rough quantification makes it easier to figure out what needs to be done to solve a given problem. For example, quantifying degrees of harmonic accent helps to fix harmonic problems. In the same way, understanding that a given formal problem is a result of too strong a contrast between two ideas makes it easier to see how to attenuate it: the composer will play with the newer elements in order to gradually attenuate one or more of them until the passage feels right.

When it comes to such formal problems, I have noticed that most unsatisfactory musical composition shows one of two kinds of defects, which I call bumps and holes. A bump draws the listener's attention to something undeserving of notice; a hole is a place where the music is inert, but where it should instead be attracting attention. With the quantifying approach, once we notice a bump or a hole, the next step is to determine in what aspect of the music (harmony, orchestration, etc.) it occurs, and then roughly how much adjustment it will take to correct the problem. A composer using this method would quickly see, for instance, that the passage leading up to a climax is too short, which makes the climax arrive too abruptly, creating an awkward bump. Quantification enables one to gauge such problems with more precision, to get from "Something feels wrong here!" to "How much more or less (of x) do I need here?" It also makes it possible to approach technical problems incrementally, by making finer and finer adjustments.

## WHAT THIS BOOK IS NOT

A useful textbook requires a clear focus. It is therefore worthwhile to clarify what distinguishes this book from other, related musical texts.

My goal is not to provide a compendium of recent compositional trends. However, the fact that most of the musical examples in this book are taken from the standard repertoire of tonal music should not be taken as implying that these trends are unimportant or uninteresting. Rather, it comes from the fact that no serious musician can be unfamiliar with this repertoire. It is enormous, it is the basis of western musical culture, and it also lurks behind most of the popular music and most of the functional music heard all over the world today. This music is also by far the most easily accessible online, in both score and sound, for free.

The people using this book who are aiming at writing music for video games, commercials, or films have a particularly strong need to know about tonal music in some depth, since it is ubiquitous in these domains. (I have included occasional examples here and there in the book from film music and music for video games, for students aiming to work in those areas.)

Serious concert music in some of the more current styles may sound quite different from the classical repertoire on the surface, but once again, the principles set out here are also applicable to many of these kinds of music.

For example, music with any pretense of intelligibility must include some kind of punctuation. The need for multiple levels of punctuation is ubiquitous, since it is an outgrowth of the ways in which human attention and memory always function. In tonal music this need is usually addressed by the familiar tonal cadences. In, say, the music of Pierre Boulez, such formulas are nowhere to be found. Nonetheless, Boulez's music does include punctuation; it is just accomplished by other means.

This will be true of all the principles discussed here: once the student has properly understood a core principle, it becomes easy to see it at work in other styles. I will from time to time refer to more recent examples of nontonal concert music to reinforce this point, and although I have not attempted to represent all current styles in the examples, many of the exercises can be realized in various diverse styles, if the instructor so desires.

*Musical Composition* also makes no pretense to being a history of musical form. Despite its emphasis on general principles and the many classical-repertoire examples, this book is not intended as a theoretical nor as a musicological study of the classical repertoire. My goal is not pastiche, nor is it historical precision. Of course, serious theoretical and musicological studies of specific repertoires do have great value and interest, and there exist several excellent books of this sort, especially for music of the Classical period. I will refer to them in due course. But their job is to catalog what composers have done, not to tell others how to do compose.

This book is also not an analysis textbook. The questions asked by a composer sometimes differ from those asked by a theorist. Specifically, the student often needs to focus on why the composer has chosen one particular gesture as opposed to another, and also on why it happens when it does, rather than earlier or later. For a theorist, the answers to these questions would be considered interesting, but perhaps too speculative. However, it is impossible to compose anything without making such choices, and some choices are necessarily going to be more convincing than others. We are mainly interested here in why, in a given situation, one choice is better than another.

Another aspect of analysis, already mentioned, where the emphasis is different for composers, is the relative importance accorded to timbre, tempo, articulation, and register. In much theoretical work, these issues are considered secondary; indeed, there are few well-developed analytical techniques to discuss them in detail. But these aspects of the music have enormous influence on musical character and movement, so the professional composer has to think about them in some depth. Compositional skill must include all of these dimensions, not just pitch and rhythm.

## CRAFT

It should be clear by now that I think that musical composition is best seen as a craft, whose principles can be explained and learned. Rightly understood, craftsmanship is not about memorizing formulas, but about knowing how each aspect of the music works on the listener (and the performer) to achieve a specific expressive goal. It means being at ease with all the tools available for achieving these goals.

Such a craft-based approach must inevitably remain somewhat open-ended. Looking at great music, simply asking how this or that effect is achieved, can lead to surprising discoveries. For example, I first observed what I call "announcing" (see chapter 20) when looking at the fugue from Bach's Fantasy and Fugue in G minor for organ, BWV 542. I then started seeing this technique in many other situations, not just in Bach. This led me to formulate a general principle: point the listener to important events, prepare them in advance, build up expectation for them. I have never seen this principle described elsewhere, and yet it is extremely common in great music. It helps to create the sense of inevitability we feel when listening to a masterpiece.

## PEDAGOGY

I have tried to provide for many and varied pedagogical needs in the exercises in this book. Of course, the instructor is free to choose the ones most relevant to a given student or group.

In a few chapters I have added one or two advanced exercises, for students whose preparation is more thorough than that of the average undergraduate student. I have also included several exercises potentially of interest to students in film and video-game music. As already mentioned, many of the exercises lend themselves to being realized in more than one style, and the instructor should not hesitate to adapt them as needed. I have also occasionally provided model solutions that are not limited to a classical tonal language.

For some of the shorter exercises, I have included and discussed poorly realized versions before examining better solutions. These less satisfactory efforts are typical of the kinds of mistakes often made by beginners, and can be useful as examples of what to avoid.

All the exercises must be listened to in class, ideally performed by the students themselves. If this is not possible, the teacher can play them at the keyboard. At a minimum, students should be required to provide a decent computer simulation for class use. I have added some tips about how to make quality simulations in Appendix B.

When working out the shorter exercises, it is a good idea to think in terms of more than one possible solution; listening to several students' versions of the same exercise can be a learning experience for everyone. The differences between the versions should be discussed in some detail. It is always worth trying to find out why something works, or why not. This "why" is an essential question, since it allows the students to transfer knowledge gleaned from other students' experiments to their own work.

One pedagogical idea I have found particularly useful, when looking at pieces from the standard repertoire, is to experiment with them, modifying various aspects of the music, one by one, to gauge their effect. This is also a good approach to discussing student work. For example, try a given passage in a different register or another timbre, or vary the dynamics, the tempo, or the articulation. Some changes will have little or no effect, but others will make an enormous difference in the result. Why do these changes affect the result to the degree they do?

Many such changes will not be black-and-white, but rather differences of degree. In orchestration, for example, there can be many degrees of contrast. A piccolo is closer to a flute timbre than to the sound of an oboe. A tuba is closer to a trombone than to a cello. The same kind of nuanced thinking is also useful when applied to register, harmony, contrasts between musical ideas, and so on.

For changes that affect the result dramatically, experiment with quantitative adjustments, for example, a less drastic change of register or of timbre. An experienced composer spends a lot of time on this kind of fine tuning; this is a good way to develop the necessary sensitivity.

There is also a separate pdf document for instructors (available on my website, alanbelkinmusic.com), with suggestions for teaching each chapter of the book.

## PREREQUISITES

A solid grounding in tonal harmony—at least one semester—is the minimum requirement to use this book. This grounding should include a knowledge of the common tonal chord progressions and cadences, as well as a thorough understanding of the way a bass line creates direction, in addition to furnishing a good counterpoint to the top line. The student should be at ease with basic roman-numeral analysis of the harmony.

Counterpoint and orchestration studies are also desirable, but they can be pursued at the same time as this course. Composition, by its nature, cannot ignore any of these dimensions of the music. Indeed, the practical application of many of the notions learned in these disciplines is only evident when composing whole pieces of music.

## THE LAYOUT OF THE BOOK

In *Musical Composition* I propose a novel, verb-based approach. I have carefully chosen a small list of verbs representing general formal functions, such as presenting, progressing, and connecting, that are also applicable to a wide range of styles. Thinking about musical processes as verbs encourages the student to see them as goals to achieve while composing the music, which need to be intentionally addressed.

The book begins with four preparatory chapters, focusing on motives and phrases, and then on singing and playing. The latter two subjects—in effect, a discussion of the differences between vocal and instrumental music—are rarely dealt with in composition textbooks, despite the immense importance for the young composer of knowing the subtleties of their respective constraints and possibilities.

After these preliminary chapters, the verb-based chapters are interspersed with practical composition projects. The latter chapters can be recognized by their names: each one is named after a standard musical form.

Whereas a theoretical or a musicological study would attempt to be comprehensive regarding all the existing variants of a given form, here the focus is on skill, on doing. Since a student cannot possibly compose all the various kinds of sonata forms, we have to choose one specific type.

To compose music is first and foremost to create something. The immediate goal may be modest, but the criteria that allow us to say why a Beethoven symphony is great should be the same ones used to evaluate a student composition. Although the expectations are much more limited, the goal is the same: to communicate strongly and significantly.

The material in this book can be efficiently covered in two semesters, the first ending with the variation project (chapter 10), and the second with the sonata project (chapter 19).

Chapter 20, on artistic refinements, and Appendix A, on sketching, can be approached when the rest of the book is done, or somewhat earlier on, as the instructor wishes. Sketching in particular may be useful for the sonata project.


## ACCESS TO EXAMPLES

When the examples are short, and from the standard repertoire, I have provided them here. When they are too long, or when it was impossible to obtain copyright permission without paying substantial fees that would have materially increased the price of the book, I have discussed them without quoting them. However, even for these latter examples the audio is always easily available online. A good college or university music library should have the scores as well.

Students are encouraged to first look online at imslp.org for scores, and at YouTube.com for audio.

Examples without attribution are by me. Audio for these examples can be found at alanbelkinmusic.com.

# MUSICAL COMPOSITION

# 1 MOTIVE

A motive is the smallest significant musical unit, a very short musical pattern that is characteristic and memorable. Internal contrast is a motive's most important characteristic. A chromatic scale, played in completely equal rhythmic values, on one instrument, is not very interesting as a motive. It is too neutral, it has no specific character, and it is not particularly memorable, since it lacks any kind of defining internal contrast. This is a basic principle of perception: we remember what stands out from the surroundings, even within a small motive. But if we take the same chromatic scale and play it with a simple repeating rhythmic pattern, through these repetitions we draw attention to the internal contrasts, thus imbuing the motive with a more distinct character and providing the listener with a focal point. If the scale or mode has some intervallic variety, that will also help to make it memorable—the contrasting intervals will stand out.

These internal contrasts help to create interest for the listener, since they make the motive not just trivially predictable. In this way, a motive engenders a little question in the listener, resulting in a mild form of suspense.

Normally one note is insufficient for a motive, but one could imagine using timbre or articulation as a way to characterize it. For example, one short staccato note, played by timpani plus harp, rather loud, has a definite character, because the timbre is unusual and distinctive, due to the inherent contrast between the two instruments. Repeating the note would add even more character.

The famous motive in the film *Jaws* starts out as one note, then becomes a minor second, with an accent on the second note, perfectly expressing the increasingly menacing feeling composer John Williams wants to evoke. The accent on the second note contributes a simple, but notable, contrast as well. Note also the low register, the legato articulation (at the start), and the thick, aggressive timbre: all these elements contribute greatly to strengthening the motive's character.

Contrasts within a motive can be in the pitch pattern, the rhythm, or both. More rarely, they can also include timbre, dynamics, articulation, register, and so forth. A famous example of a timbral motive occurs in the first movement of Mahler's Sixth Symphony, where a simple major triad changes its third to become a minor triad. The rhythm here is neutral—just two whole-note chords—but Mahler powerfully underlines the harmonic change by having the three notes of the chord played by three oboes and three trumpets in unison. By cross-fading their dynamics—the trumpets decrescendo while the oboes crescendo—the major-to-minor change is made more poignant. The change of timbre, when combined with the change of harmony, has an expressive force that the harmony alone cannot provide.

An enormous advantage of using motives is that it focuses the listener's attention on clear, easily remembered patterns. When we notice patterns, we easily develop expectations. A great deal of music's effect on us has to do with the way the composer creates expectations, and then fulfills or frustrates them.[1] Indeed, much of this book will focus on working with patterns and expectations, at various levels in the form, and on what the composer can do with them to create the richest experience for the listener.

Motives focus and intensify musical character. A good composer aims at expressive force; it is hard to be forceful with neutral, unmemorable material. Choosing the right inner contrasts in an important motive can give greater intensity to the desired character.

Figure 1.1 shows a few repertoire examples of striking, memorable motives. The first example, the beginning of the first movement of Sibelius's Second Symphony, is a simple rising scale. What gives the motive most of its individuality is the portato articulation, the repeated quarter notes, and their rhythmic grouping: two repeated notes acting as upbeats followed by three more repetitions on the same pitch, after the barline.

The second example is the first idea from the third movement of Brahms's Third Symphony. Here the motive is the dotted figure followed by a longer note, creating contrast. Also, Brahms often arranges the phrase so that one presentation of the motive rises and the next descends, creating a surging, wavelike contour, which is further accentuated by little crescendi and diminuendi.

The third example is richer, and more complex. It is taken from Beethoven's String Quartet in F major, Op. 59, No. 1, at the start of the first

1) **Allegretto**

2) **Poco Allegretto**

3) **Allegro**

4)

Figure 1.1. Memorable motives

movement. There are actually two motives in this phrase: first is the step-wise quarter notes followed by the long note; second is the eighth-note fig-ure, with its rather complex contour, including both slurred and staccato notes, followed by the rising sixth and its downward resolution. As we can see, both of these motives contain internal contrasts, and they also set each other off, giving Beethoven a great deal of interesting material to work with. (Note that the bowing slurs in the example do not correspond to the motivic boundaries.)

The fourth example, the subject of the Fugue in E minor from book 1 of Bach's *Well-Tempered Clavier* is all in equal note values, apart from the last two eighth notes. Here several patterns in the contour create motives: a simple arpeggio, a back-and-forth movement between a scale and a pedal tone (the high E), and the final zigzag figure: two notes up, and then a leap followed by two notes down. Despite the even sixteenth notes, this still pre-sents the listener with a rich trove of memorable material. This is one reason it makes a good fugue subject.

All of these memorable motives provide potential for development.

## MOTIVIC VARIANTS

Once we use motives, we immediately face one of the most important problems of musical form: balancing novelty and variety.

Repeating a motive ten times, unchanged, is boring. Music meant to be listened to with full attention needs repetition to be coherent, but large amounts of unvaried repetition quickly lose the listener's interest.[2]

On the other hand, too much variation becomes incoherent, going beyond what a normal human brain can easily remember and comprehend.

Between literal repetition and extreme variation there is a continuum of similarity between motivic variants, and the composer will need to use many degrees on this continuum to make a convincing piece of music.

## DEGREES OF SIMILARITY

We can make a rough scale of degrees of motivic transformation, say, from 1 to 5. One here signifies almost literal repetition, say, just transposing the motive up one scale step, so that the only change is a semitone becoming a tone, or vice versa. Five, on the other hand, would represent something that is audibly unrecognizable, such as a transposed retrograde inversion of the motive in a different tempo. This scale of motivic similarity will be useful in judging the varying degrees of novelty required at different moments in a composition.

The more we are immediately struck by the similarity to the original,[3] the more we are talking about local variants: not much motivic transformation. These are most often found within the same section as the original, or else at a place later on in a larger form where we need a very clear reminder of something previously heard. The further we get from instantaneous recognition (moving closer to 5 on our scale of similarity), the more the new variants lead us off in new directions, sometimes toward a major contrast. Of course, all the degrees of similarity can be useful at some point, especially during a longer piece, but the most vivid contrasts should be saved for special moments. Otherwise, they become the norm, and the subsequent requirements for major contrasts will only increase. Also, constant heavy demands on the listener's attention quickly become fatiguing.

Note that ease of recognition is also to some extent a function of where the variant appears. For example, the *Jaws* motive mentioned above moves quickly from legato to staccato. This would normally be a somewhat more remote variant, but since the staccato version arrives as part of an acceleration, in the same phrase as the legato version that starts it, and on the same exact pitches, the listener has no problem making the association.

Figure 1.2 proposes a motive and shows its common variants. Note that the way a motive is harmonized can be part of the pattern; for instance, an

Figure 1.2. Motivic variants

appoggiatura motive requires accented dissonances resolving stepwise. Although we will not detail the harmonization for every version here, note the two different harmonizations in the first system. In the first, all the notes of the motive are consonant, whereas in the second, the first and third notes are appoggiaturas. If the original presentation of this motive were the appoggiatura version, the closer variants would also need to be harmonized the same way. In this case the harmonic choice becomes part of the motive itself.

The original motive is characterized by a zigzag contour and a dotted rhythm. Let us look at the variants in more detail.

We can class these variants into close (nos. 1–4), medium (nos. 5 and 6), and distant (nos. 7–11) forms of the motive. In the discussion below, the numbers in parentheses, from 1 to 5, will apply our scale of similarity, classifying the transformations by their degree of resemblance to the original. To recapitulate: 1 is easily and immediately recognizable, and 5 strikes the listener as a strong contrast, rather than as being related.

Variant 1 (1) is simply a transposition, obviously a very close relative of the original. Variant 2 (1) enlarges the final leap from a fourth to a sixth. This also does little to change the character of the motive, since the ear seems to perceive leaps not so much as distinct intervals, but just as "not steps." Variant 3 (2) is inverted and transposed. Since the rhythm is such a prominent aspect of this motive, and the contour is the same, just moving in the opposite direction, the relationship to the original remains quite clear. Variant 4 (1) simply repeats the motive in sequence, which, if anything, enhances the familiarity for the listener. Variant 5 (3) changes the contour of the motive. This variant is definitely farther from the original version, although still recognizable, owing to the rhythm. Variant 6 (4) changes the two stepwise intervals of the original into leaps, which is somewhat distracting for purposes of recognition.[4] Variant 7 (5) reads the original motive backwards: retrograde. Here too, recognition is seriously jeopardized: since the rhythm is drastically changed, we are immediately struck by the difference from the original. Variants 8 (4) and 9 (4) respectively double and halve the note values of the original. (Variation 9 also changes the size of the leaps, but that is a minor detail compared to halving/doubling the tempo.) Variation 10 (5) uses repeated notes where there were none originally, which strongly deforms the character of the original.[5] Likewise, exchanging the accent patterns (strong/weak beats) of the motive, as in variant 11 (5), is a drastic change.

Notice that changes in the articulation of a motive can substantially distort its character, since articulation is really an aspect of rhythm. For example, staccato dots effectively shorten the duration of the notes.

As mentioned above, close motivic variants are more useful within the same section of the piece, as ways of developing a melodic line while staying focused on one idea.

Medium variants create more work for the listener: we hear similarity, but we also notice that something significant has changed, and that is potentially distracting. These medium variants are sometimes found during transitions, while gradually transforming one idea into another.

The distant variants strike us more by their difference from the original than by their similarity, and therefore they are not much use for creating continuity. However, they can sometimes be used to generate contrasting material, far away in the form, but with a subtle resemblance to a previous idea.


## DOUBLE MOTIVES

We have already seen an example of a motive with two distinct components in the Beethoven quartet theme referred to above (see Figure 1.1). The top staff of Figure 1.3 shows another example of such a double motive.

Figure 1.3. A double motive

We can call the slurred eighth-note pattern *a*, and the three repeated notes *b*. In the original motive, *b* occurs between two statements of *a*. However, with this kind of double motive it is possible to continue a phrase for quite a long time just by alternating *a* and *b*, as long as they are not always in the same order. On the second staff we see an example of how this can be done. Here we see *a* followed by *b* twice, followed by *a* three times, and then by a return to *b*. Reusing the two units in varied orders supplies much more variety than would be possible with a simple motive, while still clearly remaining close to the original.

## NEUTRAL LINES

As we have seen, motives help focus the listener's attention and intensify the musical character. However, even in a simple piece with only one motivic idea, the motive will rarely be present at every moment. The music can sometimes seem too dense; it needs to breathe.

Similarly, in contrapuntal textures, if all the voices are equally active, the music loses focus, since we cannot pay equal attention to multiple, motivically dense lines at the same time. Also, barring a certain kind of very intense ending, it is hard to finish a piece without somehow calming down the questioning effect created by the use of a motive in the first place.

Schoenberg refers to the process of smoothing a motive down at an ending by the rather grim name of "liquidation."[6] The idea is that the distinguishing characteristics of the motive are diluted to the point where it becomes neutral. A common example of this is the way, at important cadences in many Mozart piano concerti, the composer ends the phrase with a trill over an Alberti bass. This is a cadential cliché, and that is the point: the listener's attention is now free to move on, since a cliché, by definition, is something very familiar, which attracts less attention.

But such neutral, nonmotivic lines are not limited to endings. Even within pieces with well-defined motives, the composer sometimes will have more neutral moments while connecting statements of the main motive(s). In fact, in the classical repertoire, it is hard to find much music without such occasional neutral bits. Common examples include a fragment of a scale in a neutral rhythm, or common suspension and passing tone formulas. By lowering the level of intensity, these neutral parts of the line allow the music to relax momentarily, to breathe.

## MOTIVIC WANDERING

Sometimes motivic development is more complex.

In Figure 1.4, measure 1 introduces the main motive in the right hand. It is a double motive, with two components: the rising three-note scale followed by a leap, and then a back-and-forth pattern on the second beat. Both components are repeated in the second half of the bar. In measure 2 the first beat uses a retrograde inversion of the first element. In principle, this is a more remote variant that would score perhaps a 4 or 5 on our scale of motivic contrast. Why does it not sound unfamiliar here? Because the equal

Figure 1.4. Bach, French Suite No.6 in E major, BWV 817, Allemande

note rhythm is unchanged, and because, as we have already seen, changing the size of a leap does not much change the character of a motive. The second beat of the second bar simply changes the direction of the stepwise movement, which now goes down. The third and fourth beats, as well as the first and second beats of measure 3, obviously refer to the original form of the motive. The last two beats of measure 3 and the first two beats of measure 4 reverse the order of the double motive components. After that, the back-and-forth pattern of the original motive changes somewhat in measures 5 and 6, but it remains recognizable. Measure 7 includes bits of neutral scale, and the peak of the section is attained in the second half of the bar, announcing the cadence formula in measure 8.

This then goes back again to the main idea, now in the left hand. Meanwhile, the right hand introduces a contrasting motive (eighth note plus two sixteenths) as a counterpoint. But this rhythm does not last and soon leads to an even more contrasting, syncopated motive, in the second half of measure 9. This certainly would score a 5 on our scale of contrasts.

If we go by our previous principle that, within a section, motivic transformations should not go far afield, this "wandering" should cause a problem. Why does this new, syncopated motive not disrupt the musical flow? To understand why it works here, we need to examine how Bach places it in a context where, by creating enough clear associations with what immediately precedes it, it does not shock the listener. He takes care to audibly connect the syncopated motive with other processes already underway.

How? First, as already mentioned, the left hand in measures 9 and 10 quotes the original theme. The eighth-note pulse of the syncopated motive has been anticipated by the eighth notes right after the cadence in measure 8. (As we will see in a later chapter, cadences and peaks can be suitable places to introduce new elements.) Also, the other hand fills in the beats where the right hand is absent, so the syncopation does not interrupt the overall rhythmic momentum. Finally, Bach integrates the presentation of this new motive into a gradually rising line, formed by the highest notes— measure 9: D♯, E; measure 10: F♯, G♯, A♯, B. Incorporating new material into an existing progression helps mitigate its novelty. At the top of this rising line, the sixteenth-note momentum returns to the right hand, and when the last syncopation arrives in measure 11, it leads to a simple scalar descent into the cadence in measure 12, which seems to neutralize all this characteristic material. The rise at the start of measure 12 also incorporates a leap, recalling the original motive. The accelerated harmonic rhythm also sets off the cadence from what precedes it.

Significantly, immediately following the double bar, Bach brings back a literal version of the original motive, but transposed to B. Having moved gradually farther away from the original motive-forms, it is now essential to recall them very clearly, so the music does not simply wander off with no perceptible direction. The rest of the piece uses all the motives already presented, but introduces no new material.

By arranging various details in the texture to prepare the way, and then by returning clearly to the original form of the motive after the double bar, Bach introduces new elements in a way that proves intriguing, rather than gratuitous. This kind of motivic wandering, sometimes even involving variants that are in principle rather remote, requires special sensitivity to the overall balance of details of familiarity and novelty in the musical texture. But the basic principle behind all these techniques remains the same: the listener needs regular doses of easily familiar material to be able to follow the musical argument without undue strain.

## MOTIVIC ORNAMENTATION

There is one more motivic technique that can also lead the listener quite far afield: ornamentation. Unlike the gradually wandering motives just discussed, this kind of change tends to happen all at once, but once presented, the variants usually are stable for a much longer time. This procedure depends entirely on the listener immediately perceiving the relationship between a simple line and its more complex variants.

Figure 1.5 shows the same original motive discussed in Figure 1.2, but here each succeeding bar presents an ornamented version, rather than a close variant. Notice that all these spinoffs incorporate the pitches of the original version, but that each one sounds like a distinctive motive on its own. This kind of treatment, while it may occasionally occur during motivic wandering, is much more common when the composer is ornamenting an entire phrase or a section already heard. Using more than one of these

Figure 1.5. Motivic ornamentation

ornamental variants in a row would quickly become incoherent, but using just one of them, consistently, for an entire section of a piece creates its own unity. The difference in this case is that the connection with the original form is only felt once, at the start; the original does not subsequently return. This procedure is very common in variation form, where such variants can provide material for many variations, all based on the same skeleton, but each with its own new motive. In such cases, the composer makes an entire variation from each ornamented version of the motive.

## EXERCISES

**1** Listen to excerpts from well-known films, ads, and video games, identifying the motives used and their transformations. What gives each motive its character? Do not limit the analysis to pitch and rhythm; look also at tempo, articulation, timbre, and so forth. Classify the degree of transformation on our scale of motivic similarity from 1 to 5.

**2** Invent short motives to evoke the following characters: nostalgic, angry, funny, anxious. Specify not only pitch and rhythm, but also tempo, timbre, register, dynamics, and articulation. Experiment by changing these other (nonpitch) dimensions to create several entirely different characters for each motive.

**3** Invent motives to suggest specific characters, such as melancholy, heroic, or nervous. Check to see if other listeners agree about the character of each one. Could changing some aspect of the music make the character stronger?

**4** Invent a motive to be associated with a specific person in a film. Compose variants of the motive that suggest different moods, while still remaining recognizable. Classify the degree of transformation on our scale of motivic similarity from 1 to 5.

**5** Take each of the three motives shown in Figure 1.6 and extend it into a phrase, using only close variants. Aim to create a specific musical character in each case.

Figure 1.7 is a poorly realized example, for trumpet, to give a clearer idea of some of the potential pitfalls to avoid. The original motive is given in the first measure, and the rest of the phrase constitutes a (rather weak) development of it. The main problem with this solution is that, after listening to the whole phrase, no obvious pattern sticks in the memory. The fact that the second bar starts with the characteristic leap of a fourth is good, but the scale takes us too far afield. The next bar refers to the same fourth but, by placing it on an upbeat, with no notes on the downbeats, changes the rhythmic character to the point where we are more struck by the difference from the original than by the similarity. (This would

1)

2)

3)

Figure 1.6. Exercise 5

Figure 1.7. Exercise 5: a poorly realized example

be a 4 or 5 on our similarity scale.) The last beat of measure 3, with its completely irrelevant repeated-note motive, sounds out of place. The scale returns in measure 4, but again there is little audible association with the original idea in measure 1. Finally, the doubly augmented version of the motive at the end is again so different rhythmically from the original that there is no "ah, yes" experience of recognition. The result is a phrase completely lacking in focus.

Figure 1.8 shows the same phrase, improved. While the neutral scale figure from Figure 1.7 is retained, it is now completed by a clear reminder of the original motive, inverted, at the end of the second bar. Then, in the third bar, the rhythm again clearly refers to the source motive. Even the augmentation at the end works better, because it is not such a drastic change from the energetic, rhythmic character of the beginning. The overall impression is much more concentrated and memorable, and as a result the musical character emerges more clearly. With the possible exception of the very end, none of the variants used here would merit more than 3 on our scale of similarity.

Figure 1.8. Exercise 5: an improved version

**6** Continue the accompaniments below. Apart from composing phrases, developing accompaniment figures is a good exercise in working with motives, since they do not require much motivic variety. In fact, too much variation in an accompaniment can distract the listener from the main line. Accompaniment figures must remain coherent, but also must provide at least some melodic interest, if they are not to be reduced to simple copy-and-paste formulas.

Figure 1.9 is a model phrase for trumpet and strings. Examples 2 and 3 provide poor and good realizations, respectively, of the original (example 1). Let us examine them in more detail.

Figure 1.9. Exercise 6: two possible solutions

Example 2 has various problems. Note that most of them result from using motivic variants that are not immediately recognizable (they would get 4 and 5 on our scale of motivic relationships), and are therefore distracting.

First, the stepwise sixteenth-note motive has been changed into leaps in measure 2. The harmony in measure 2 suggests a seventh chord on the two last beats, but the seventh (E) is nowhere resolved. In measure 3 the harmony on the second and third beats in the strings sounds bare; the third is missing, and the neighbor-note motive is gone. Between measure 3 and measure 4 the sixteenth notes create a repeated note, which sounds foreign to the original motive. In measure 4 the repeated-note motive is completely gone, replaced by awkward melodic leaps. Between the second and third beats of measure 4 the harmony suggests two unresolved 6/4 chords. The last eighth note in the accompaniment in measure 4 suggests a seventh chord (taking the trumpet into account), with the seventh doubled, that is harmonically not rich. Finally, in the last measure, again the repeated-note figure is missing, and the momentum dies away completely. Some of these motivic changes might conceivably be appropriate if they were in the foreground, but they attract too much attention here while we are supposed to be focusing on the trumpet line. The harmonic problems also distract the listener in ways that add nothing to the overall effect.

Example 3 shows how to sculpt the motive and the harmony for a more coherent result. In measure 2 the motive stays on the same notes as in measure 1, changing only the middle voice on the second beat. In measure 3 the motive evolves up a step. To make the harmony richer, the middle voice becomes mildly contrapuntal in the middle of the bar. However, both the neighbor and repeated notes remain, thereby keeping the link to the original motive clear. In measure 4, for the first time the upper string parts don't have a rest on the first beat. (Although example 2 did this as well, the repeated-note change to the main motive there was a distraction.) The reason for this is that the trumpet line reaches its most intense point across the barline from measure 3 to measure 4; having a bit more activity in the strings supports that little climax, as does the more active upper part, which leaps from B to E at the end of measure 4. The last bar keeps up the rhythmic momentum and creates a link to the following phrase, by turning the A major chord into a dominant seventh of D.

Of course, there are many other possible solutions to this exercise, both good and bad. The point is to get the modifications of the motive to make sense in terms of the shape of the phrase, and not to weaken the overall momentum of the piece. As we will see in a forthcoming chapter, an effective accompaniment should add harmonic and melodic richness, and reinforce, not weaken, the musical character.

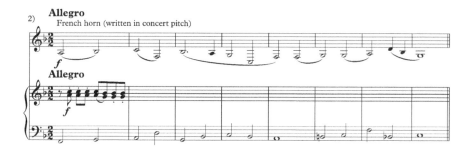

Figure 1.10. Exercise 6: piano accompaniments to complete

The three beginnings in Figure 1.10, to be realized by the student, are also for one soloist, now accompanied by the piano. The student should try to create interesting and coherent accompaniments for each example, based on the given starting motives. The given bass line will help to keep the harmonic organization clear. Be sure to keep the motivic variants on the low end of the scale of similarity.

# 2 PHRASE

While a motive is like a significant word—the core of an idea worth developing—a phrase is analogous to a more complete thought, comparable to a clause in a sentence. In vocal music, a phrase of music normally corresponds to a phrase of text. Phrases in instrumental music are to some extent limited by the technique of the instrument. For example, the tuba cannot play a very long phrase legato, since it requires so much air. However, if there are breaks in the rhythm, a tuba phrase could include more than one breath.

Phrases with a quasivocal character are common in instrumental music, but many other kinds of gestures are also possible, in ways that are idiomatic to each instrumental family. For example, a violin can easily play a leaping, staccato phrase that would be unsingable.

Our division of music into phrases is not arbitrary. The human attention span is quite short: after just a few seconds we need to make a special effort to maintain concentration. Ideas that can be expressed concisely and are clearly delimited are easier to remember and to understand. Imagine the first page of a newspaper with no columns, no paragraphs, no variety of typefaces, and no punctuation, and you can see why we need to divide information into digestible chunks. Also, music works on us largely via expectations we develop when we (mostly unconsciously) compare motives and phrases. Comparing phrases is much easier for the listener if the length of the musical statement remains within the limits of short-term memory.

The length of a phrase depends on its musical character, and also in part on where in the work it occurs. For example, when repeating music the listener has already heard, the composer may decide to shorten phrases to avoid monotony, or else to make phrases longer, taking them in new directions, to create a sense of formal development and intrigue.

## STRUCTURE OF THE PHRASE

A phrase is structured like a musical work in miniature. The beginning must attract the listener's attention. The phrase develops and evolves, either by carrying the opening motive to a local peak, or else by proposing a prominent motivic contrast. The phrase closes with some kind of punctuation.

Let us examine each of these components in more detail. The beginning is usually one motive, sometimes two, or perhaps a double motive of the kind discussed in chapter 1. A phrase with more than three different motives can create a problem of focus, since it is hard to remember a lot of varied information, presented within a very short time. Sometimes, at the start of a large form, presenting two or three motives in succession will make the listener curious about their shared destiny, but normally three seems to be the limit; four or five motives in a row easily become incoherent.

In a vocal phrase, the motivic content may be more neutral, simply following the rhythm and shape of the words. There may also be a few bars of introduction, to allow the accompaniment to start before the voice. But the objective remains the same: to get the listener quickly involved.

Once the listener's attention is engaged, a phrase needs to develop in a coherent way. If it centers on one idea, it will undergo some sort of incremental progression, since staying at the same level of intensity is monotonous. Examples of such incremental progressions include gradually rising peaks in the melody, accelerating harmonic rhythm, fragmentation of the motive into smaller chunks, and increasingly dissonant harmony. Sometimes the progression may be downward, for example, if the phrase starts at its highest point.

The progression within the phrase will usually lead to a modest, local culmination, or else it will descend from the (opening) high point. The peak is usually attained only once within the phrase, although occasionally it may be repeated for emphasis, perhaps with some other aspect of the music becoming more intense the second time. Again, the point is not to maintain the same level of intensity all through the phrase.

If the phrase contains more than one idea, such progression is less necessary, since the contrast in itself will pique the listener's curiosity. On such a small scale, the composer has no time for more than one idea to evolve; that will happen in subsequent phrases.

The phrase will eventually reach some kind of punctuation at its end. Many degrees of punctuation are possible, depending on the position of the phrase in the overall form. (Punctuation will be discussed in more detail in chapter 5.) If the music is tonal, the phrase will usually end with a familiar cadential progression. In other harmonic styles, rhythmic or textural changes can also create varied degrees of punctuation.[1]

Let us examine various phrases, with different characters and varied structures.

Figure 2.1 is the opening phrase from the last movement of Mahler's Third Symphony. This slow, conjunct phrase is vocal in character. There is little motivic contrast, in keeping with the quiet mood. The melody initially outlines a fourth, from A to D, before expanding up to a fifth (E, in m. 3), then pushing even higher, to F♯. This progression toward a local peak gives the line a clear sense of evolution, of direction. The quicker harmonic rhythm, starting in measure 3, also creates more momentum under the phrase's high point. Notice that the punctuation in measure 4 is not very final at all: while the melody descends to the tonic, the bass keeps moving.[2]

### Langsam. Ruhevoll. Empfunden.

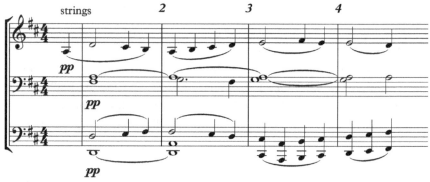

Figure 2.1. Mahler, Symphony No. 3, last movement

Our next example (Figure 2.2) is the beginning of the second movement of Beethoven's String Quartet in C major, Op. 59, No. 3. This smooth legato phrase is also somewhat vocal in its inspiration. The first, loud pizzicato note in the cello signals to the listener that something significant is ahead. The cello then creates regular pulsation, on a dominant pedal, until measure 5, when the movement to the tonic, combined with the silences in all the other voices, creates a fairly strong cadence. Note how in measure 3 the main line moves into the inner parts, in violin 2. The first violin at this point recedes into the background, until the end of measure 4. Despite this subtle change, there is still the sense that, overall, this phrase is one single

**Andante con moto quasi Allegretto**

Figure 2.2. Beethoven, String Quartet in C major, Op. 59, No. 3, second movement

gesture, owing to the smooth, steady eighth note rhythm and the registral overlap. Adding the viola at the same time as the second violin fills out the texture, making the phrase more intense. In a sense, this can be seen as the climax of the phrase, more so than the high C in measure 1. Note also how the cello line continues in measure 5 after the arrival on the tonic, instead of stopping completely. As we will see in chapter 5, it is rarely a good idea to have all the elements in the music come to a full stop at the same time, except at a very important final cadence. The cello line here maintains the music's forward momentum.

Our third example comes from the beginning of the second part of Bartók's Third String Quartet (Figure 2.3). The phrase here is delimited not by a classical tonal harmonic cadence formula, but by the slowing rhythm in the cello.[3] The first four bars, with the trill in the second violin, set up the nervous character in a sort of introduction, triggered by the pizzicati in the other instruments. The little viola upbeat in measure 4 introduces the core of the phrase, the line formed by the pizzicato cello chords. This line rises and falls from measures 5 to 11; the peak occurs in measure 7. The continuing trill in the second violin adds a certain unease in the background. Cadence is achieved by slowing down the cello rhythm to quarter notes, and by adding the viola, also pizzicato, to fill out the cello chords. The continuing trill, and the fact that the violin picks up the viola motive, once again create momentum toward the next phrase.

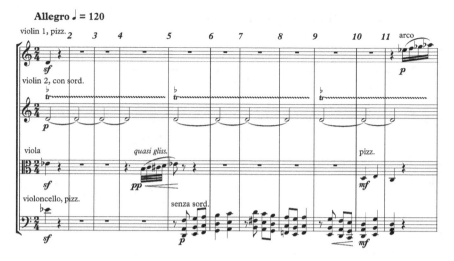

Figure 2.3. Bartók, String Quartet No. 3, Sz. 85, second part. © Copyright 1948 by Hawkes & Son (London) Ltd. U.S. copyright renewed. Reprinted by Permission of Boosey & Hawkes, Inc. © Copyright 1929 by Universal Edition A.G., Wien/UE 34310 for world except for territory of USA.

Our fourth example (Figure 2.4) is the beginning of Domenico Scarlatti's keyboard Sonata in D major, K. 336. The first four bars sequence the motive from measure 1 down three times. Then a contrasting motive leads to the light cadence in measures 6–7. The generally falling shape of the phrase is balanced by the quickly rising bass in measures 5–7, which also speeds up the harmonic rhythm, creating more direction toward the cadence. The character is playful, especially with the sudden burst of rhythmic energy in measure 5.

Figure 2.4. Domenico Scarlatti, Sonata in D major, K. 336

A final example, of a phrase based on two contrasting ideas, can be heard at the start of György Ligeti's Sonata for Violoncello Solo (Figure 2.5). The opening consists of two pizzicato chords that each glide by the interval of a second, first upward, then downward. Then, in measure 2, the composer presents a singing melody, arco. It has a generally descending contour,

**Adagio, rubato, cantabile**

Figure 2.5. György Ligeti, Sonata for Violoncello Solo, beginning. © Copyright 1990 Schott Music GmbH & Co KG, Mainz, Germany. All Rights Reserved. Used by permission of European American Music Distributors Company, sole U.S. and Canadian agent for Schott Music GmbH & Co KG, Mainz, Germany.

following a small local peak on the C, which has arrived on the fourth beat of measure 2. These two ideas are subsequently repeated and developed, which confirms our perception of them as a larger unit.[4] Note how the cadence on the final, cadential D is prepared by the low C two beats earlier (the lowest note in the phrase) and also by the E♭, leading into the D by semitone, typical of the Phrygian mode.

## LESS STABLE STRUCTURES

All of our examples up to this point have been taken from the beginnings of their respective movements. The reason for this is that, when presenting an idea for the first time, it is advantageous to use straightforward structures, so that the listener only has to absorb a limited amount of material, clearly presented. However, more fragmentary structures often arrive later in the movement.

Figure 2.6 is from Debussy's "La soirée dans Grenade," from *Estampes*. At the start of this excerpt, Debussy has already presented a first melodic idea, which is winding down in measures 15–16. The cadential note in the melody, which we expect at the beginning of measure 17 (a C♯), is momentarily delayed, arriving only when the new motive in the right hand enters a bit later: this means that the bass arrives on the first beat of measure 17 alone. This melodic syncopation weakens the punctuation, and also creates momentum to continue. Measures 17–18 present a striking new variant of the preceding idea, now in sixteenth notes rather than in triplet eighths, which is immediately repeated in measures 19–20, rising a bit higher at the end, to make a little local climax. This in turn is again interrupted, in measure 21, by a return to something previously heard (from mm. 5–6, not included here). Measures 17–20 are thus clearly set off from their surroundings, but they

Figure 2.6. Debussy, "La soirée dans Grenade," from *Estampes*

do not end with any clear melodic or harmonic cadence. This sort of cross-cutting effect would be confusing at the beginning of a movement, but here it acts to renew the listener's interest. (The music from mm. 17–20 comes back later in the piece, and the material from mm. 5–6, found here in mm. 21–22, also returns toward the end of the piece.)

The soundtrack of the movie *Avatar*, by James Horner, provides another example of this kind of phrase. The phrase that arrives around forty seconds after the start has a rather fragmentary structure.

After the preceding music, made mostly out of sound effects, the violas, in measure 14 of the score, begin a nervous rhythm, which, however, proves to be only an accompaniment figure. The main body of the phrase is announced by short rolls in the cymbals and in the bass drum. Sustained chords in the winds and the strings (apart from the viola, which keeps up the same rhythmic motive) enter in measure 20, and a crescendo leads to a trumpet motive, arriving in measure 22. After a breath in measure 24, the sustained harmony returns with another crescendo, leading in turn to the entry of the voice, in measure 33. This new section is somewhat more elaborately worked out, and seems like the culmination of all the fragments heard up to this point.

All this is part of a larger introduction, and it illustrates a specific kind of instability: small fragments building up to a significant focal point.

This kind of structure creates tension and uncertainty; when something more stable eventually arrives, it feels like a resolution. Since this music comes at the beginning of a film, it functions well, creating curiosity and interest.

We will have more to say about such complex phrase structures in chapter 16, "Exploring."

## EXERCISES

All the following exercises should be written for specific instruments, and should include all necessary performance indications: tempo, articulations, and so forth.

**1** Complete the melodic phrases in Figure 2.7 above the given bass lines. Do not introduce new motivic material. Aim at stable structures that coherently develop one or two motives and then arrive at clear punctuation.

Figure 2.7. Exercise 1

**2** Compose single phrases, each based on one of the harmonic progressions below. Invent a motive, and develop it throughout the phrase. Ensure that the melody and the bass form good counterpoint as well as solid harmony. You may use inversions of the given chords. These should be presented as two-part skeletons; no middle voices are required. However, you should specify the instruments and write idiomatically for them.

- I V VI IV II V I
- I III IV V I V I
- I IV II V VI III IV V I

**3** Using one of the motives invented for the exercises in chapter 1, compose two or three different complete phrases in various moods, but all based on the same motive. Imagine someone in a film, whom we identify with the original motive, appearing in various emotional states.

**4** Write phrases of various lengths, as described below. Treat all of them as opening phrases: aim for clear, memorable presentation of the idea(s). Finish them with varying degrees of punctuation.

- Write a slow melodic phrase, in mostly equal note values, without strong motives, like the Mahler example above (Figure 2.1). Include a sketch of the bass line and the harmony.
- Write a phrase for solo oboe, based on only one motive.
- Write a phrase for piano, alternating between two different motives.
- Write a phrase that includes a short introduction, as in the Bartók example above (Figure 2.3). The introduction should introduce one motive as a fragment, before the main body of the phrase, perhaps as an accompaniment figure.

# 3 SINGING

Two fundamental musical impulses, found in all cultures, are singing and dancing. While strongly rhythmic music grows out of the latter, the impulse to sing also lies behind much musical activity.[1]

Every able-bodied human has a voice, and uses it for communication. This communication includes words, but it also includes other dimensions, beyond the words, for example, vocal register, tone, speed, and loudness. An actor preparing for a role has to think about all these things, since these choices drastically affect the meaning of the words themselves. Think of the phrase "you love me." This could be a question, an affirmation, or even a sarcastic rejoinder, to mention just a few possibilities. Without knowing the tone, the "melodic" contour of the phrase, the tempo, and so forth, it is impossible to know the intended meaning, and to formulate an appropriate emotional response.

All these dimensions are heightened in song. Not coincidentally, they intensify our emotional responses. So while singing uses words, it is also very much about the emotions behind them. Singing may take many forms, from community chants to lullabies, but it always has this emotional component.

## WRITING FOR THE VOICE

When writing for voice, the composer needs to keep in mind its individual characteristics. There are many types of voices, above and beyond the two basic categories of male and female. Unlike instruments, which have more or less standard ranges, each singer is unique. Two singers, both sopranos, may not have the same ranges. Their lowest and highest notes may differ quite a lot, as may the part of the range where they are most comfortable.

When accepting a commission from a specific singer, there should be some discussion about her or his individual voice.

The composer needs detailed information about the specific singer's range—not just about the extremes, but also about where the "break" between registers occurs. Singers work to equalize the sound around the break, but it is best not to go across it quickly and repeatedly in a short span of time.

In general, voices are most comfortable in the middle of their range. The highest and the lowest registers should accordingly be used sparingly and consciously, for effect. It is hard to sing loud in the lower register, and not easy to sing very quietly in the upper part of the range.

Apart from range, voices are also classified by character. For example, a dramatic soprano and a coloratura soprano have very different characteristics, and music that is perfect for the former might be impossible for the latter to perform convincingly.

Singers need to breathe, so the best vocal writing allows for appropriate pauses. In a large-scale vocal work, it is also important to allow singers some longer periods where they do not sing at all, to avoid straining the voice.

## SETTING WORDS TO MUSIC

Although singing goes well beyond words, it normally includes text, and therein lies an important challenge for the composer and the performer. When writing for the voice, the composer should start with the text whenever possible.

First, the composer has to find a text that is emotionally stimulating and somehow seems to call for music. It's important to reread the text multiple times, to get a feel for it in detail. A serious literary analysis of the text can be useful as well. Although this is not something we will cover in this book, if you are interested in knowing more, there are many books on the subject.[2]

Once the text is chosen, to make it comprehensible, the composer has to let the words dictate several important aspects of the music, specifically the relative durations (long and short note values), the accents, and the rise and fall of the line. Even when the rhythm and the shape of the melodic line faithfully follow the words, the text may not always be easy to understand. If the rhythm and the melodic shape do not follow the words, the text can become more difficult, or even downright impossible, to follow. Such badly set text can be very distracting, as the listener will nonetheless try to make sense of it, despite the obstacles.

The reason sung text is hard to understand is because singers make their sustained sounds on vowels, not on consonants. This means that the normal balance between vowels and consonants in speech is drastically distorted in favor of vowels during song. This is why a singer with a microphone is easier to understand: the microphone amplifies the consonants enough to make them clear.

Further, not all vowels are equally easy to sing. The vowels that allow the best vocal sound production are the ones produced with the mouth wide open, Think of the Italian word *amore*, compared to, say, the *ooo* sound in the word *soup*. Try singing "soup" very loudly, and then try "amore." The difference is enormous.

This means that the composer must sometimes make decisions based on the sound of the words, in addition to their meaning. Not all texts are equally suitable for music. Abstract texts with lots of long words are often hard to set effectively, barring special programmatic situations, where they are justified by something extramusical. In any very emotional utterance, the text must allow for climactic, full-voiced expression, and therefore requires open vowels at key moments.

A first step, when setting any text, is to go through the words, marking the syllables where the important accents fall, phrase by phrase.

Here is an example, using a text from Shelley. The accented syllables are indicated below with the sign >.

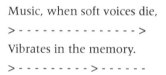

> Music, when soft voices die,
> \> - - - - - - - - - - - - - - - >
> Vibrates in the memory.
> \> - - - - - - - - - > - - - - - -

One could make a case for adding another mild accent on the word "soft" in the first line. Often poetry allows for more than one reading. But no normal reading of the text would accent, say, the word "when."

The next step is to do the same thing with the contour. The composer should speak the text, slowly, but with normal intonation, and observe where the voice naturally goes up and down, then transpose that contour into the musical line. In this example, "hi" indicates a higher note, and "lo" indicates a lower one; "-" indicates no special intonation.

> Music, when soft voices die,
> hi - - - - - - - - - - - - - - lo
> Vibrates in the memory
> hi - - - - - - - - - - - - lo

Again, the first line allows for a couple of alternatives, for example, a somewhat higher note on "soft," but a higher note on the second syllable of, say, "voices" would make no sense at all.

Once these preliminary steps are accomplished, we can start actually writing the music. The music for the vocal line should be laid out in such a way that it does not contradict the rhythm and pitch outlines of the words. The existing rhythm and contour can be enhanced—for example, a syllable that is long and high can be made longer, higher, or both—but never contradicted (unless there is a deliberate attempt at humor).

Here are two musical settings of these lines. First, let us examine a poor one. Figure 3.1 has problems with both rhythm and pitch. It is singable, but inelegant. This kind of awkward setting distracts the attentive listener from the sense and the feeling behind the words.

Figure 3.1. A poor example of text setting

Let's look at the problems here in more detail. "When" is a connective word, but here it is both longer and higher than the other words in the phrase, which gives it undeserved emphasis. "Voices" is set as a rising second, whereas no native English-speaker would ever say the word making the second syllable the higher one of the two. Similarly, "Vibrates" should not have the second syllable higher than the first, and "in" has no business being the rhythmic and melodic climax of the phrase. Set as a rising line, "memory" sounds like a question (practice saying any question out loud, and you'll notice it invariably rises in pitch).

Now compare this version with our second setting of the same text (Figure 3.2). Here the accent of the first phrase is on the first syllable of "voices," where it should be. "Vibrates" is now set going downward, and

Figure 3.2. An improved version

the chromaticism underlines the word's importance, as does the descending tritone under "memory." All the salient musical features now enhance the most pertinent ideas in the text.

## RECITATIVE VERSUS ARIA

We can understand some of the deeper aspects of text setting by looking to the world of opera. Vocal lines in classical opera generally fall into two categories: recitative and aria.

The main goal in recitative is to make the words understandable, so as to be clear about the facts of the dramatic situation. For example, the recitative will inform us who did what to whom, so we can then understand their respective emotional reactions. Recitative is therefore set in the clearest way possible, with relatively minimal accompaniment, to allow for vocal clarity.

Figure 3.3 is a short example from Puccini's *Tosca*. At this point in act 1, Angelotti has escaped from prison and is in a church, where his sister has hidden a key for him, and where, to his surprise, he discovers his friend Cavaradossi. In this short passage, Angelotti lets us know that Cavaradossi does not at first recognize him, and asks him whether prison has changed him that much. The accompaniment is a simple, sustained chord, and the vocal line has only three different pitches. The important thing is for the audience to understand who Angelotti is, what he is doing here, and the relationship between him and Cavaradossi. All this is made clear in a minimum of time, with the simplest of musical materials.

Figure 3.3. Puccini, *Tosca*, act 1, seven bars before rehearsal 22

Unlike recitative, the aria is designed for emotional emphasis, and therefore the details of the text are not as important; the music's main role is to communicate the singer's emotional state. Sometimes, in an aria, the composer will repeat whole phrases for emphasis. Once you know that John is angry with Mary, the aria will let you enter into John's emotions (or Mary's, as the case may be). The important thing is not the details of what the character is actually saying, but the emotion behind them, and of course music is very good at communicating that. So in an aria it may be less easy to follow every word, but it is also less crucial.

Figure 3.4 is an example from Wagner's *Die Meistersinger von Nürnberg*. The quoted excerpt is the first stanza of Walther's Prize Song, inspired by a dream. It will also prove to be a love song.

Notice the differences from Puccini's recitative. The harmony is much richer than in Figure 3.3. Wagner's aria is also a wonderful example of really idiomatic writing for the voice. The total span of the vocal line is from low E, in measure 7, up to the A in measure 8, more or less the full range of the tenor voice. The line starts in the middle of the range, where the voice is most at ease, moving mostly by step. There are several leaps in measure 7,

Figure 3.4. Wagner, *Die Meistersinger von Nürnberg*, Walther's Prize Song

when we have a dramatic rise into the tenor's sonorous high register, where Wagner stays for two bars before gradually descending back again into the middle of the range. The point of this kind of expansive vocal writing is not to make the words as easy as possible to understand, but to communicate to the listener the emotional exuberance of Walther's dream: the song must be good enough to win him the competition prize, which will be marriage with his beloved Eva. Here the changes of register evoke the passionate surging of Walther's love.

In practice, there are many degrees between recitative style and aria style,[3] but the basic distinction between text that makes the facts clear and text that underlines the characters' emotions remains significant. The composer needs to think clearly about what is most appropriate for each situation.

One last point about sung text: it usually takes much longer to sing than to speak. A rough rule of thumb is that lyrics often take two or three times as long to sing as to speak. The composer needs to plan the durations of the musical numbers accordingly.

## MUSICAL FORM AND THE TEXT

The form of the music should follow that of the text. The written punctuation (including line changes) should be musically audible and, as in the text, there is usually more than one level of punctuation. A comma should not be as strongly set off as the end of a strophe. If the text has higher-level subdivisions, these too must be reflected in the music, perhaps with instrumental interludes.[4]

## COMPOSING FOR CHOIR

Writing for choir places additional constraints on the composer. First, most choirs are made up of amateurs, so it is imperative to know the level for which you are writing. When in doubt, keep the vocal lines as simple as possible. With any ensemble, but especially with amateur groups, rehearsal time is at a premium, and music requiring inordinate amounts of rehearsal is hard to program.

Choral ranges are always smaller than solo ranges. Since most choristers have no vocal training, it is even more important to stay as much as possible in the comfortable middle range of the voice, saving extremes for special moments. Voice crossing, unless by very small intervals, should be used cautiously, since it may place the voices in a less comfortable range.

Occasionally there may be a reason to make one voice emerge from the others by crossing another, but this must always develop organically from the text and enhance the melodic line. The composer should generally try to keep adjacent voices within an octave of each other; when there are large gaps between voices for sustained periods of time, the choir tends to sound unbalanced and fragmented, instead of harmonious and unified.

Voice leading and ease of singing are crucial. The first rules learned by any harmony student—that conjunct movement and common tones are the norm—are based on what is easy to sing. While nobody wants to sing lines that never move, leaps in the voice are much bigger events than they are in instrumental writing. The composer needs to balance quiet, less eventful passages with more intense moments.

Always make sure there are comfortable places to breathe within the melodic lines. These places must correspond to points of natural punctuation, such as commas and periods.

Finding the pitch of the first note after a silence is always a preoccupation for performers; a composer who is sensitive to this challenge can make the choristers' experience much more agreeable. This is easily accomplished by making the note in question prominent in the preceding phrase or in the accompaniment. Similarly, leaps to notes in a different harmony can be demanding. To make finding these notes easier, include them in the preceding melodic line, or in the harmony.

Variety of texture is essential to good choral writing: in the same way one would not write for orchestra using only tutti scoring, do not write long passages for the whole choir with no respite. It can be very effective to have the women or the men sing alone for a while, or to have, say, sopranos and tenors sing high, followed by basses and altos singing in their lower registers. Contrast between homophonic and contrapuntal textures can also be used to underline important elements in the text.

Text sung in counterpoint is very difficult to understand, since the various parts are saying different things at the same time. This may be one of the original reasons for fugal imitation, where a theme is presented first alone in one voice, and then repeated in the others. This at least allows the listener to hear the text once, simply and clearly.

Composers are advised to spend some time singing in a choir; there is much to be learned from the experience.

There are several well-known composers who specialize in choral composition, including Morten Lauridsen, Eric Whitacre, and John Rutter. Their music for choir is worth examining. It is written in an easily accessible tonal style and is always comfortable to sing. Not surprisingly, choirs enjoy it. And if the choristers like the piece, there is a better chance it will be programmed more than once.

## EXERCISES

N.B. Always include all necessary performance indications in the score, especially tempi, dynamics, and articulations.

**1** Choose several short, emotional poems, of contrasting characters, to set to music as songs for one solo singer, perhaps with piano accompaniment. Poems by John Donne, by Shakespeare, and by Romantic authors like Wordsworth, Keats, and Shelley can be a good place to start. Poetry by these authors usually displays consistent rhythmic patterns as well as rhyme. This can make it easier for a beginner to set to music than modern free verse. First sketch out the rhythm and the contour of the text, as demonstrated above. Then compose a melodic line that sits comfortably within the chosen vocal range (which should be clearly indicated in the score). Use the vocal registers appropriately, according to the emotional dictates of the text.

**2** Examine a song in your own language, to see how the composer follows the text, both rhythmically and melodically. It is often useful to examine the text at first as though you had to compose music for it yourself, perhaps even sketching out a few lines. Then compare your solution with the existing version(s). Composers who set English text particularly well include Samuel Barber, Benjamin Britten, David Diamond, and Ned Rorem.

**3** Write several short passages for choir, in contrasting characters, making sure the lines are easy to sing. It is excellent practice for the composer to be able to sing each line, almost at sight. Although SATB (the standard mixed choir) is the norm, some texts may be more appropriately set for all-male or all-female groups, each of which poses a slightly different compositional challenge. Vary the texture from one passage to the next.

# 4 PLAYING

As we saw in the previous chapter, singing is at the root of a good deal of musical expression, including much of the music written for instruments. Only in the Baroque era did distinctive idiomatic patterns gradually emerge for individual instruments, exploring the things they could do that voices and other instruments could not. Looking at the repertoire of that period, we see an increasing sensitivity to the varied behavior of each instrument in different registers. The oboe, for example, gets louder as it descends, whereas the flute gets quieter. A composer wanting a rather rough passage in the oboe would be well advised to place it in the lower range of the instrument; this would not be true of the flute.

In addition to dynamic differences, the various registers also suggest distinctive musical characters. For example, asking a low flute to sound light and brilliant is unrealistic; however the high register can be very brilliant indeed. A somewhat aggressive character in the bassoon is only to be found in its low register.

As mentioned above, instruments are often required to play in a way that we associate with singing. However instruments do not literally sing, nor do they use words.[1] This leads us to an important conclusion about the relationship between voices and instruments. Since singing usually does involve words, it is exceedingly rare for a solo voice to be used as background to anything else. Words cry out for our attention. Perhaps because we associate them so strongly with human communication, there is something disturbing about vaguely hearing text in the background while instruments simultaneously demand most of our attention. This is why the voice is almost never heard acting as an accompaniment for instruments. On the rare occasions when choral voices accompany instruments, the voices are often sustained, and they usually sing neutral syllables like "ah . . ."

## WRITING FOR SOLO INSTRUMENTS

Instruments can be used in ensembles or individually. The solo instruments with by far the largest repertoires are the keyboard instruments, since they can play several lines at a time, for example, a foreground melodic line along with its accompaniment, or a polyphonic texture like that normally heard in a fugue. Keyboards also have the largest ranges, and this contributes greatly to their expressive richness. Imagine a staccato, playful melodic line in the high register combined with heavy chords in the lower part of the instrument: a composer could use this combination to suggest two contrasting musical characters simultaneously. Only keyboards and harp allow such combinations to be easily played by one person.

Most orchestral instruments, on the other hand, are basically monophonic. Even string instruments, although they can play chords, cannot comfortably sustain multiple contrapuntal lines at once for any length of time. This is the main reason why the repertoire for solo orchestral instruments is so much smaller than that for the piano.

When writing for a solo instrument, the composer has to be aware of both the musical characteristics of the instrument and the technical level of the player. A piece written for a virtuoso can include things that the average high school student instrumentalist could never play.

Solo writing tends to be more elaborate than ensemble writing, simply because one single person has to maintain the audience's attention at all times. For the same reason, in all but the shortest solo pieces, there is a need for variety of texture. This can be accomplished through contrasts of spacing, register, and articulation, and in the number of real parts.

When writing for soloists, smaller forms are common, whereas it is very unusual to write a one-minute piece for orchestra, except as part of a larger suite. It seems wasteful to bring together so many musicians for something so short, whereas solo pieces are easy to program and require less logistical organization.

Sometimes these smaller forms convey an especially intimate character, which is enhanced by the fact that they are played by just one person. Obvious examples are the Chopin Preludes, or the Brahms Intermezzi: these are often introspective pieces, as though people are quietly speaking to themselves.

We need to say a few words here about composing for solo piano, since it is so common. The piano seems at first glance to be a percussive instrument, since every note decays, and the player cannot change the sound of a note once it has been attacked. But the piano pedal can add resonance to the sound, and thus becomes a source of great richness. Not only can one write full, resonant arpeggios, but, as mentioned above, simultaneous multiple planes of tone are also possible, even sometimes including several different characters at once. In other words, the pedal adds enormously to the piano's ability to create complex, layered textures, otherwise rarely seen outside of a large ensemble.

For example, observe the three layers in the texture during the opening bars of Debussy's prelude "Les sons et les parfums tournent dans l'air du soir" (Figure 4.1). The main melodic line is on top, doubled in three octaves. The harmony is in the middle. The bass resonates throughout, alternating between a low tonic and dominant. This kind of rich, layered texture would be impossible on the piano without the pedal. If one were to orchestrate this music, it would require many instruments to render successfully.

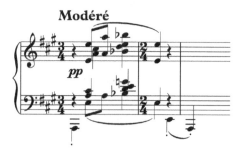

Figure 4.1. Debussy, "Les sons et les parfums tournent dans l'air du soir"

## CHAMBER MUSIC

Chamber music is a particularly intimate form of music making; it exists as much for the players as for the audience. It is a kind of group discussion, where at some point everybody has their say, where the members of the group can agree with one another (for example, playing in unison or in octaves), disagree (playing in various degrees of contrasting counterpoint), comment on each other's statements, accompany each other, or even stop completely, allowing another member of the ensemble to take center stage. Not everybody should be playing all the time. At some point in well-written chamber music, everyone should have their moment in the sun. In string chamber music, voice crossing is very common, because of the wide range of the instruments, and the fact that they can all sing with equal intensity. Voice crossing can also be a way to change the focus of the ensemble from one player to another.

As an example, let's look at the Menuetto from Mozart's String Quartet in C major, K. 465 (Figure 4.2). The first violin begins alone. In measures 2 and 3 the texture is homophonic, with the instruments in normal order. From the end of measure 4 to the beginning of measure 6 all the instruments double the top line, with the cello one octave lower. From the end of measure 6 through measure 8 we hear only the two violins, with the melody in the first violin. Measure 9 temporarily finds the second violin on top. Measure 10 repeats the previous bar in sequence, with the main line moving down into the viola; the second violin now adds a bit of filler, as if in agreement with the viola. Measure 11 again sequences the little phrase, now including the whole quartet; the main motive has now moved to the cello. In measure 12 the texture once again becomes straightforwardly homophonic. In measure 13, the first violin finds itself alone again.

Figure 4.2. Mozart, String Quartet in C major, K. 465, Menuetto

The texture changes in almost every bar, allowing each member of the quartet to play many different roles, even in such a short time. This is normal writing for string ensemble, not at all unusual.

Chamber music ensembles can be composed of homogeneous groups, like a string quartet, or heterogeneous groups, like a trio for clarinet, cello, and piano. In the first case, the instruments will easily blend, and will complement each other in register. In the latter case, the composer needs to find musical ideas that will take advantage of the differences between the instruments. This requires close attention to the distinctive characteristics of each instrument, as well as to its relative force in relation to the others in the ensemble; a clarinet in the low register has a different character from a cello playing the same notes. But whatever the instruments used in chamber music, the essential democracy of the group remains: everybody is more or less equal.

## ORCHESTRAL MUSIC

If chamber music is a democracy, orchestral music is a more or less benevolent dictatorship: there is a need for a leader (the conductor) in such a large group.[2] To begin with, there are such enormous differences in strength between the loudest brass and the quietest winds that certain combinations are simply not practical. For example, writing a low flute passage as counterpoint to a group of high trombones playing loud sustained chords makes no sense: the trombones will completely drown out the flute.

Furthermore, the sheer number of different timbres in the orchestra makes it impossible to give everybody an equal part.

There is also the fact that, as Rimsky-Korsakov points out in his classic treatise on orchestration, the ear tires of some combinations faster than others. Perhaps because their constituent timbres are quite dissimilar, the ear must work to decode a group of heterogeneous winds, to figure out who is playing what. This is why listening to a wind ensemble can feel more demanding for the listener than listening to strings for the same length of time. Of course, it is possible to write well for winds during a long section, but eventually the ear will appreciate some relief.

Certain instruments also do not lend themselves to more than one or two roles in the orchestra. For example, tuba players normally do not expect to play as often as the first violins, since their main role—providing a bass to the heavy brass—is much more specialized.

An important principle of orchestral writing is to conserve resources. Long tutti passages become tiring for the listener, who must constantly try to parse a lot of dense information. To make a solo stand out, the best thing to do is simply not to use the instrument in question for a while beforehand: this way the (relative) novelty keeps it fresh. Constantly doubled timbres make it hard to throw one instrument into relief: the music just ends up sounding gray. Sometimes just keeping one register empty for a while, before an important musical contrast, can make its arrival a striking event, whereas if all the registers are being used all the time, there is nothing special about any single register. All these techniques have in common that they hold back or limit something to make it more effective when it does fully arrive.

Here once again, what I call the primary dimensions of the music—tempo, timbre, register, dynamics—are enormously important. Refinements of harmony alone will often not suffice to make a contrast really dramatic, whereas a new tempo, a new timbre, and so forth can add immediate expressive force. Planning these nonpitch dimensions of the music is crucial when laying out the form of an orchestral piece, since it has so much influence on major contrasts and climaxes.

## ACCOMPANYING THE VOICE

While music combining instrumental soloists and an instrument capable of playing harmony, like the piano, is basically a form of chamber music, accompanying the voice is different. First, while we often exchange the foreground and background roles of different instruments in chamber music, the human voice virtually never accompanies an instrument; our minds simply seem to interpret this as though the words are not loud enough. This kind of mistake, where the listener has the impression that something is not quite right, is just an unwelcome distraction. Although voice and instrument(s) can certainly enjoy the dialogue and exchange typical of chamber music, the voice never really recedes into the background, except when it is silent.

Vocal accompaniment has to be arranged in such a way that it does not drown out the voice. Accompanying a vocal line with a harpsichord is not problematic, but some other instruments, including the piano, can easily drown out the voice if scored too heavily. An old trick from opera is useful here: if the composer wants the voice and the accompaniment to seem equally powerful within a very intense passage, give them an alternating dialogue, where each stays momentarily silent while the other speaks. This way the voice can cry out with full force before or after the accompaniment has played, without being drowned out. This creates the illusion that the voice is strong enough to overwhelm even the loudest instruments.

Saying that the accompaniment remains subsidiary to the voice does not mean that the accompanying parts should be lacking in interest. In fact, a well-written accompaniment part should still be conceived of as a kind of chamber music, since a performer will always work harder with a musically convincing part than with an indifferent one.

In the most common situation, voice accompanied by piano, the latter by nature cannot sustain a note at full intensity. There are several ways to animate the piano part and keep it alive in the background: arpeggiation, repetition, and counterpoint.

In themselves, the first two of these patterns are clichés. The secret to a richer accompaniment lies in the way the composer makes the texture more personal. Figure 4.3 offers a few examples.

In example 1a we see a basic, but undistinguished, arpeggio accompaniment pattern. The motive in the first bar is simply transposed as the harmony changes. In example 1b, just the addition of a few nonharmonic tones changes the arpeggios into something more distinctive. Note the extra eighth note in the third bar, adding momentum toward the end of the phrase.

Examples 2b and 2c show ways of enriching the simple repeated-note pattern in example 2a. Note how the introduction of a syncopated-note motive in example 2c adds interest to an otherwise rather pedestrian accompaniment.

As we can see, a bit of contrapuntal interest can make the difference between a cliché and something personal. Good piano writing often makes use of this technique. There are multiple examples in Chopin's and in Rachmaninoff's piano music of this kind of local, situational counterpoint.

To be clear, we are not talking here about counterpoint in the sense of full-fledged imitations or fugues, as too much contrapuntal density can draw attention away from the vocal line. The difficulty is to get the level of interest just right, to determine to what degree the accompaniment should capture the listener's attention. Sometimes, as is very common in Schubert, just adding a personal contour to an arpeggio is enough to give it life. At other times, depending on the character desired, the design of the accompaniment will be richer.

Another function of the accompaniment, especially when the soloist is a singer, is to supply harmonic support. As mentioned in chapter 3, the first thing the singer needs is the starting note. While there are occasional pieces

Figure 4.3. Various accompaniment patterns

where piano and singer start together (in which case the pianist will quietly play the singer's note beforehand), more often the piano accompaniment will announce the singer's entry pitch within the accompaniment. During harmonically complex music, both at the start of the piece and as it continues, all but the most experienced singers will appreciate having the accompaniment discretely help out with at least occasional notes from the vocal line, especially when the latter includes difficult leaps. However, constantly doubling the vocal line can easily become a lazy solution. Apart from the rare case where something in the text demands it, it is usually better to give the accompaniment at least some independence, reserving doubling for special moments, for instance, a powerful climax. When it does prove necessary to double the voice, if the singer has a very active part, say, with many repeated notes, it is better only to double the essential notes of the singer's line. In particular, do not double every repeated note, since synchronizing many small notes perfectly is very hard: the result often ends up just sounding sloppy.

## ORCHESTRAL ACCOMPANIMENT OF THE VOICE

Writing for the voice with orchestra poses special problems. By far the most common examples of this combination occur in opera. In opera, the orchestra normally plays in the pit, so as to keep it from interfering visually with the action on the stage. But the pit also muffles the orchestra somewhat, helping the singers to remain in the foreground. The orchestra in opera can nonetheless range from the most discreet background harmony to the most overpowering tutti climaxes, where the voice is completely drowned out. The latter, however, should only happen at moments that make dramatic sense, not as a result of poor orchestration.

The principle mentioned above, of using small doses of counterpoint to keep accompanying parts from turning into clichéd formulas, is even more applicable to the orchestra. A good part of the art of orchestration with voice lies in creating enough interest in the instrumental parts to keep them musically substantial, but not so much as to draw attention away from the voice.

Apart from opera, song cycles for voice and orchestra, like the *Four Last Songs* of Richard Strauss, use the orchestra fully, but always allow the voice its natural leadership. In such pieces, it is sometimes a good idea to reserve some sections for the orchestra alone, allowing it to play unfettered by the limits imposed by accompanying the voice. It also sometimes may happen that the orchestra doubles the voice, provided the text justifies the resulting rich sound.

## CHORAL ACCOMPANIMENT

Choral voices are as a rule less trained than solo voices, and as a result they need even more support from the accompaniment. The composer needs to make sure the choral sections can find their notes with ease, particularly at the beginnings of phrases. It is common to double important vocal lines in choral accompaniment. Accompanying choir with orchestra is less delicate than accompanying solo voices, but it still requires some discretion, since a full orchestral tutti, with loud brass and percussion, will drown out any choir.

## CONCERTI

A concerto is usually thought of as a place where the spotlight is on a virtuoso soloist. However, writing a substantial piece for an orchestra and a soloist requires a more nuanced approach if the work is to explore the full gamut of musical and dynamic expression. In particular, the composer should think through the many possible kinds of interaction between the individual (the soloist) and the group (the ensemble). Here are a few possibilities.

- The orchestra accompanies the soloist, providing a background.
- The soloist and the orchestra engage in cooperative dialogue, be it of equals or between stronger and weaker musical characters.
- The soloist and the orchestra confront one another dramatically, as opponents. Note that the orchestra is not necessarily always the more powerful character. As mentioned above, there are ways to create the illusion that the soloist overcomes the orchestra, for instance, replying alone during an interruption in a tutti passage.
- The soloist can occasionally accompany solos within the orchestra.
- The soloist can act like a much more vulnerable individual reacting to a powerful group.

When it comes to formal design, a concerto also needs to be thought through somewhat differently from a normal orchestral piece. The variant of classical sonata form seen in the concerti of Mozart, Beethoven, and others (the double exposition) has as its goal to present the soloist in a special, clearly very substantial role. The most important consideration in finding the right form for a concerto is that the soloist must appear to be an absolutely integral part of the design. This is the motivation behind Beethoven's experiments in the form in his Fourth and Fifth Piano Concerti, where he begins with the solo piano. By having the soloist enter at once, the listener is immediately aware that some kind of significant interaction or confrontation between the individual and the group is in store. It is worth studying these works in detail, and cataloging the ways Beethoven has the soloist interact with the orchestra.

For an interesting recent American example of the form, in the first movement of Tobias Picker's Cello Concerto, "Not even the rain," the cello enters soon after the beginning, following several lyrical woodwind solos. But from there on it becomes the first among equals, allowing the composer to maintain the singing style and lyrical mood throughout the movement, without ever overwhelming the soloist.

## EXERCISES

**1** Many of Debussy's Preludes are particularly rich in the kind of textural layering discussed above in the section on writing for solo piano; they are an excellent introduction to rich and refined writing for that instrument. Examine several of them and observe the variety of textures: monophonic, homophonic, polyphonic, multiple layers.

**2** Look at examples of chamber music for various ensembles and list the many possible relationships between the instruments, as we did above for the Mozart quartet. If the ensemble is heterogeneous, try to understand how the composer makes each part reflect the instrument's personality. For example, in the Brahms Clarinet Quintet, the clarinet part is conceived differently from the string parts: the clarinetist has to breathe, and the instrument's characteristic registers are also not the same as the violin's.

**3** Examine the slow movement of Beethoven's Fourth Piano Concerto, Op. 58, and observe the evolution of the interaction between soloist and orchestra.

**4** Examine the first movement of Tchaikovsky's Piano Concerto in B-flat minor. List at least three different relationships between soloist and orchestra. More advanced students can try to compose short phrases exemplifying these relationships.

# 5 PUNCTUATING

We have already mentioned that the human attention span is normally limited to just a few seconds. We cannot remember large tracts of information unless they are broken up into segments and organized hierarchically. Punctuation contributes greatly to such hierarchical organization, making the musical flow articulate, and thus easier to grasp and understand. Punctuation provides us with significant information about where we are in the piece, and about what is likely to come next.[1]

Punctuation is usually discussed in terms of harmony, but that is clearly insufficient for a composer, and even more so when working outside of traditional tonality. Even in tonal music, a cadence is never a result of harmony alone; otherwise every V-I progression would be a cadence, no matter where it occurred in the phrase. Convincing punctuation requires coordination between at least two dimensions of the music: for example, melody, rhythm, harmony, texture, and dynamics. In fact, it almost always involves some degree of rhythmic relaxation, either through slowing down, arrival on a strong beat, or a momentary pause.

The origin of the word *cadence* is the Latin word *cadere*, which means to fall, and this points to something common to many cadences: they recall speech, where, at least in western languages, the end of a sentence (unless it is a question) is normally marked by a fall in the voice. Certainly, when setting text, it would be very odd to have the music counter this tendency, say, by introducing a sharp rise in the line at the last word or two.

Of course not all phrases end with falling lines. As mentioned above, other aspects of the music also contribute significantly to punctuation. We will now look at musical punctuation as it plays out in each of these dimensions, giving us the necessary tools to control and refine it in both tonal and nontonal contexts.

As mentioned above, melodic cadences are often characterized by falling lines. A rising line, all other things being equal, implies a question, and thus is normally less conclusive than one that falls. However, the contour of a melody at a cadence also depends on the kind of line that precedes it in the phrase. For example, if the greater part of the phrase is jagged and angular, a change to more conjunct movement at the end, even if the line rises slightly, can suggest repose.

In Figure 5.1, from the first movement of Mahler's Tenth Symphony, the first violin line in measures 28–29 is quite angular. The winds take over the melody at the end of measure 29, but the intervals become much smaller in the following bar, which has a calming effect. Together with the sudden thinning out of the accompaniment and the pause at the start of measure 31, this creates a sense of breathing, of temporary repose, despite the fact that there is no cadential harmony whatsoever. (Note that the last note in the first violins, in m. 31, leads into a new phrase.)

Figure 5.1. Mahler, Symphony No. 10, first movement

It is uncommon for the final note in a phrase to move into an entirely new register, since such an unprepared shift easily sounds like a mistake. If the end of the phrase does arrive at the lowest or the highest note in the line, the register in question should be prepared: the listener should have heard several low/high notes beforehand, gradually moving in the direction of the final note.

A melodic cadence is also a function of its mode or scale. If the mode being used has varied intervals, especially if it includes semitones, the smaller intervals will sound more conclusive. Smaller intervals (especially moving toward the more stable scale degrees) have more attractive force than larger ones; we may call this the leading-tone principle.

## HARMONIC ASPECTS

The cadential formulas of tonal music should be familiar to any student of elementary harmony. They depend on a combination of smooth voice leading and a strong bass line, with a clearly directed underlying root progression.

In music where there is a clear harmonic center, the most conclusive cadence will be the one that resolves onto the tonic, which is the note with the least forward momentum. A cadence on any other degree of the scale suggests to the listener that more is to come. Dissonance is very common right before a cadence, since the ensuing consonance provides an additional release of tension. A strong root progression is also common, usually highlighting some characteristic features of the mode or scale.

Nontonal styles still share certain psychoacoustic characteristics with tonal music. For example, even the densest chromatic cluster will sound more conclusive if it is placed over a fifth or an octave in the bass. Note that distinctions between degrees of tension are relevant in any kind of harmony: there can be little refinement in any harmonic style without fine control of tension. The composer in these situations can create a sense of resolution simply by reducing harmonic tension. This can be done through the intervallic makeup of the chords (less dissonant intervals), or via more stable spacings (mainly those that are closer to the overtone series, featuring octaves and/or fifths in the bass).

The contrapuntal relationship between the bass line and the main melodic line also has a powerful influence on the cadence. A sudden change from a stepwise bass to a leap and having the outer parts converge are both common ways to create punctuation for the listener.

Figure 5.2 is a nontonal example, for strings. In this polyharmonic texture, the last chord is the only one that reduces to anything resembling a familiar triad or seventh-chord structure. It also has two of its six notes doubled: thus it is the only chord in the phrase with fewer than five different notes. This reduces the harmonic tension considerably. In addition, the outer parts come closer together than anywhere else in the phrase, moving even farther with the contrary motion of the previous bars. The rhythmic pause makes the sense of harmonic rest in measure 4 even stronger.

Figure 5.2. A nontonal cadence

Harmonic rhythm also affects the sense of cadence, as seen in Figure 5.3, from the Allemande of Bach's French Suite No. 6.[2] From measure 9 through the first half of measure 11, the harmonic rhythm remains steady, changing once per quarter note. The accelerated harmonic rhythm in the second half of measure 11 creates new, strong momentum toward the cadence in measure 12, where the harmony settles down onto one single chord for the entire bar. As we can see here, the harmonic shape of a phrase can provide the listener with important formal information. When there is a change to the previously regular harmonic rhythm, it is perceived as something special and attracts more attention. When harmonic rhythm slows or pauses momentarily at a cadence, this expectation of something unusual is confirmed.

Figure 5.3. Bach, French Suite No. 6 in E major, BWV 817, Allemande

## RHYTHMIC ASPECTS

All cadences must be laid out in time: there is no such thing as a cadence without rhythm. As we have already mentioned, it is exceedingly rare for punctuation not to involve at least some degree of rhythmic stasis. At the extreme, the music may not even have any clearly perceptible beat, but there will still be some sense of rhythmic arrival or repose from time to time: the flow can still speed up or slow down. For instance, the composer could organise a gradual loss of momentum leading to a point of relative inertia, creating a feeling of punctuation. If there is a pulse, strong beats are more conclusive points of arrival than weak beats.[3]

Sometimes punctuation consists only of a simple caesura: a pause or hiatus, without any particular harmonic punctuation. For example, the exquisitely sad, quiet ending of Shostakovich's Thirteenth Symphony uses rhythm to effect the final cadence, long after the harmony has settled onto the tonic chord.[4] A celesta solo begins at rehearsal 161, after a long passage for strings. This solo is based on a previously heard double motive, consisting of repeated quarter notes alternating with eighth-note neighbor notes. However, the mood created by this double motive is much quieter than it was earlier in the movement. Four beats of eighth notes become just two, and then, six bars before the end, the quarter notes are reduced to half notes, slowing down to complete inertia in the final two bars. The last arrival of the tonic B♭ in the melody is marked, as was the beginning of the coda, by a single bell stroke.

Another, similar example is the magical ending of the last song in Mahler's *Das Lied von der Erde*. The harmonic cadence, on C major, arrives at rehearsal 66, but the music goes on much longer, as the singer quietly sings "Ewig" (eternal, everlasting) extremely slowly. While the underlying tonic harmony is sustained—first in the brass and then, finally, in the strings—the harp and the celesta trace delicate arpeggios around the tonic chord. The celesta part at rehearsal 66 is in sixteenth notes, then, at rehearsal 67, in triplet eighths, then in plain eighths, just before rehearsal 68. Finally, after rehearsal 69, it reduces to one single chord, as the harp, which has been playing in eighth notes all through this last section, also slows down, to quarter notes. All movement ceases in the last three bars, creating a moving musical counterpart to the timeless eternity evoked in the text.

## DYNAMIC ASPECTS

To suggest cadence through dynamics requires some kind of change; simply continuing a phrase at the same dynamic level will not create punctuation. A simple example would be a loud monophonic phrase, tutti, followed by the same phrase for one quiet solo bassoon. Even lacking harmonic support, the difference in dynamics would still create punctuation.

The classical falling melodic formula, in speech and in many melodies, normally goes along with a diminuendo. Indeed, players of melodic instruments normally incorporate such a diminuendo into the end of most phrases, whether or not it is actually notated in the music.

Of course, it is also possible to end a phrase with a crescendo, although the formal implications are quite different. A crescendo creates a sense of rising energy, and therefore, used at a cadence, it is more propulsive. Normally such a crescendo will lead to the loudest point in the phrase or section, making the cadence a kind of climax.

Occasionally a cadence features a sudden, surprising dynamic change. This abrupt discontinuity usually acts like an interruption, creating suspense, and therefore it is very suitable to a nonfinal cadence. There are a few rare examples of sudden loud chords arriving after a diminuendo, making a particular kind of dramatic ending; we will have more to say about this in chapter 18.

## TEXTURAL AND TIMBRAL ASPECTS

Changes in texture and orchestration can both contribute to punctuation. Thinning texture is a kind of diminuendo, suggesting waning energy, and as such can help to create the common, fade-out cadence heard in so many pop songs. Gradually reducing the total registral span of a phrase has a similar effect.

When texture and timbre have been stable for a while, significant novelty will create punctuation, and the music will sound like it is beginning a new phrase.

In Figure 5.4, from the second movement of Tchaikovsky's Fourth Symphony, the harmonic cadence in measure 21 creates punctuation between

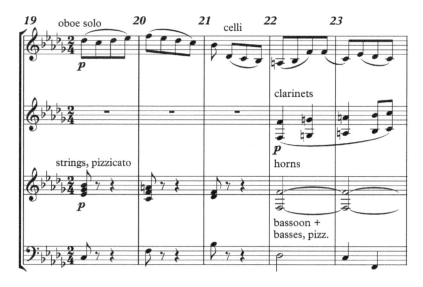

Figure 5.4. Tchaikovsky, Symphony No. 4, second movement

phrases. Had the oboe continued with the new phrase (which here arrives in the celli) transposed an octave higher, in the same register, the punctuation would have been much milder, especially since there is no rhythmic stop here at all. However, the change of texture is quite substantial. Apart from giving the melody to the celli, Tchaikovsky now has more sustained sound in the accompaniment, contrasting strongly with the pizzicati that previously provided the background for the oboe. This change of texture makes the punctuation between the two phrases much stronger.

The many possible degrees of orchestral contrast can allow for varying degrees of cadence. For example, following a flute phrase with a new one in the piccolo will create weaker punctuation than, say, having the new phrase start with the French horn. Note, however, once again that such orchestral changes cannot create cadence alone: in the absence of coordination with rhythm, line, and/or harmony, they will just sound arbitrary.[5]

ELISION

One special variety of punctuation is called elision. Here the final note of one phrase serves a dual role, also providing the start of a new phrase. Figure 5.5 is an example from the first movement of Schubert's String Quartet in A minor, D. 804. The excerpt quoted here begins in the middle of a long phrase that started earlier, in measure 23. At the end of measure 31 the music seems to be about to cadence, and in fact, if the dynamics had stayed the same, and if the viola and cello had had long notes in measure 32 like those in the violins, the resulting cadence would have been very strong,

Figure 5.5. Schubert, String Quartet in A minor, D. 804 (*Rosamunde*), first movement

especially since it arrives in the tonic key of the movement, A minor. But the sudden $f\!f$ in measure 32, plus the short notes and the new motive in the lower instruments, make what seemed like the end of a phrase into a new beginning. Thus the final A (in the lower instruments) both ends the previous phrase and starts a new one. The change of mode, from major to minor, also provides some novelty here.

## DEGREES OF PUNCTUATION

If a work is of any significant length, the composer will need more than one level of punctuation. Just as we have the comma, the semicolon, the colon, and so forth in language, music also requires many degrees of punctuation to make possible more elaborate, richer structures. These gradations allow us to differentiate the parts of a large form, making clear to the listeners where they have arrived in the piece.[6] Concretely, this means that the various musical elements that contribute to punctuation need to lend themselves to hierarchy, so that, for example, the listener can tell whether a given punctuation is just a minor, local affair or the end of a major section. The student composer should make a practice of examining punctuation with an eye to how strong an articulation is appropriate at any given point in the form, and also to exactly how it is achieved. It is good practice to attempt to quantify the various levels of punctuation, where, say, 10 would represent the end of a movement, and 1 would be an almost imperceptible breath.

Within a given work, knowing how to suggest just the right amount of qualified punctuation—a sort of "yes, but . . ."—is a critical part of the composer's craft. Even when it breathes, the music still needs to invite the listener to continue listening. If a punctuation sounds too final, the music loses, or cannot develop, forward momentum or suspense. One of the most common ways to mitigate the strength of punctuation is to have one aspect of the music contradict another. The most familiar example is the deceptive cadence (V-VI), where, although the melody may sound conclusive, the harmony suggests that there is more to come.

As mentioned above, it is useful to try to quantify punctuations within a given piece, classifying them by order of finality. While it may not always be possible to assign absolutely precise values, owing to the way many aspects of the music interact, it should be possible to say that the punctuation at measure x is weaker or stronger than those at measures y and z, and by roughly how much. This method of quantifying punctuation can be of enormous help to the composer when making fine adjustments.

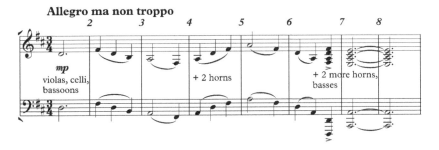

**Figure 5.6.** Brahms, Violin Concerto, first movement

Figure 5.6 is the first phrase from the opening movement of Brahms's Violin Concerto. The first theme has an arpeggio shape, moving mostly around the tonic chord, D major. The end of the phrase arrives in measures 6–7, where the harmony moves to the dominant, creating a strong, but still clearly open cadence. Notice how the monophonic texture thickens at that point, filling out the last two chords, along with the addition of two more horns, as well as of the basses in the low register. Here the textural change reinforces the harmonic cadence, creating an accent that further emphasizes the punctuation. If the phrase just arrived on the long melodic E, with no preceding accent (on the F♯) and no change of texture, the cadence would be much weaker, just a 3 or a 4 out of 10. By the same token, had Brahms made this phrase into a gradual crescendo to a huge tutti, marking the arrival with two timpani strokes, the punctuation would be extremely weighty for a single phrase at the beginning of the work, rising to around 8 out of 10. As it is, we would rate this cadence around 6 or 7 out of 10: it is not absolutely conclusive (owing to the harmony), but it is still quite strong.

Figure 5.7 shows an extremely gentle punctuation, from the Rondo in Stravinsky's *Firebird*. Since the whole phrase takes place over a static double pedal, the harmony itself cannot signal punctuation. The only elements providing a feeling of rest are the arrival on the long half note in the melody, and the descent to the line's lowest note, F♯. (Previously the F♯ only appeared once, as a quick neighbor note to the central G♯ in m. 2.) Given the music's gentle character, a stronger punctuation—say, with a change of bass or with added percussion—would be too disruptive. The extremely mild punctuation allows the music to flow on very smoothly to the next phrase. This example would merit about 2 or 3 out of 10 on our scale.

Figure 5.8 is another example, from the second movement of Ravel's *Valses nobles et sentimentales,* starting at measure 9. The first phrase here ends

**Più mosso ♩=92**

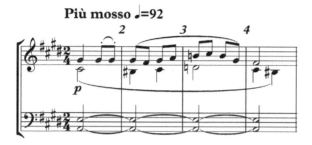

in measure 12 and is marked by the melody returning down to the opening note of the phrase. The answering phrase, in measures 13–16, ornamented with the grace note figure, finishes with much less conclusive punctuation: the melodic line rises, surging dynamically into the next phrase, which is in a higher register and has a slightly different texture. Had Ravel ended this second phrase as he did the previous one, the new texture in measure 17 would have arrived too abruptly, creating a distinct bump in the music. In effect, the punctuation in measure 16 tells the listener, "Yes, we need to breathe for a moment, but we still have to go on." This example merits a 3 or a 4 out of 10.

Figure 5.8. Ravel, *Valses nobles et sentimentales*, second movement

Finally, a somewhat longer example, the beginning of Beethoven's *Appassionata* Piano Sonata, Op. 57 (Figure 5.9), shows how many different degrees of punctuation can occur within one single passage.

There are two motives here: the first one starts on the opening upbeat, and the other arrives in measure 3 with a trill. The subtlest level of articulation, which helps to subdivide the phrase into easy-to-remember chunks, is

Figure 5.9. Beethoven, Piano Sonata in F minor, Op. 57 (*Appassionata*), first movement

simply created by the varying note values in the motives themselves. On our scale from 1 to 10, the low F in measure 1 merits no more than a 1. It is just part of the normal ebb and flow of the phrase's movement. The arrival on the C at the start of measure 3 would represent perhaps a 2 or a 3 out of 10, since in addition to a rhythmic stop there is a harmonic arrival on the dominant. The texture also thickens here for the first time. When the same chord returns at the start of measure 4, its place in the phrase's trajectory has changed, partly because it is returning to the dominant after a dissonant neighbor chord, and, more important, because it is now followed by several beats of rest: there is a clear pause in the music's momentum here. Note how the smaller melodic intervals also contribute to the sense of diminished forward movement. This moment would probably deserve a 5 on our scale. This punctuation is, however, harmonically quite weak, owing to the inversion of the dominant chord, and it leaves the listener in suspense about what is to follow.

From the end of measure 4 to the start of measure 8, Beethoven has simply transposed the first phrase up a second, so that it now comes to rest on a D♭-major sixth chord. Given that the main tonality has already been established as F minor, although this phrase is so very similar to the first one, its ending seems a bit less conclusive, since we have "left home" harmonically. Let us assign it a 4 out of 10. Also, since we've already heard the same cadence once before, and the piece didn't end, we naturally assume it won't end this time either.

Measures 9–12 alternate between the final segment of the first phrase and a new repeated-note motive, heard in the bass. The pauses after the trill motive now become much shorter. These little stops each only count for 1 or 2 out of 10.

From the explosion at the end of measure 13 until the end of this passage there is no punctuation at all. Then, in measure 16, the music comes to a very abrupt stop, including a fermata on the last chord. Notice also the very low register here, and the thicker scoring of the last chord. But there are two things that mitigate the shock of this dramatic halt: the sudden, surprising piano dynamic on the V chord in measure 16, and the fact that the chord is inverted. Both of these things serve to keep the listener in a state of excited suspense. Nonetheless, this is clearly the most important punctuation so far, so we will assign it a 6 or a 7 out of 10.

We can see once again here how useful this kind of quantification is for the composer, allowing as it does for very precise judgments about how much punctuation is needed at any given moment.[7]

## PUNCTUATION AND COUNTERPOINT

In contrapuntal textures, the various melodic lines often do not cadence simultaneously. This can be useful in attenuating the finality of a melodic line: while one part is concluding its phrase, another is already starting a new phrase.

In Figure 5.10, the melody first appears on top, accompanied by simple harmony in the left hand, in measures 1–4. The left hand becomes more melodic at the end of measure 3, and then actually becomes the main line during measures 5–6. The fact that this left-hand line overlaps the end of the right-hand phrase helps knit the passage together: the phrase structure becomes smoother, less square. (Square phrasing easily becomes overly predictable, and hence boring.)

Figure 5.10. Contrapuntal overlap

## SILENCE

To complete our look at musical punctuation, we need to discuss the use of silence. We are not talking here about the common, momentary breath between two phrases, but rather about a deliberate cessation of all activity, a sort of dramatic pause. In music not based on tonal harmony, such silences are a frequently used means of creating punctuation. The most important thing to understand is that the successful use of silence depends entirely on how it is prepared. If the silence is preceded by something that sounds conclusive, it will have no momentum: the listener will not expect any continuation. The problem with this kind of silence is that it is usually perceived as a signal that the work is over. This inept use of silence is sometimes heard in student composition concerts, where it leaves the audience awkwardly shifting in their seats, not sure whether they should applaud or not.

The more effective way to use silence is to make sure that whatever precedes it is somehow incomplete. In tonal music this can be done with the harmony. In nontonal music it can be achieved by establishing some kind of patterning, which is then clearly interrupted in midstream. Looking back at Figure 5.2, we might imagine the music suddenly stopping after the third beat of measure 3. The established pulsation and the sense that measure 3 is repeating measures 1 and 2 a step higher would lead the listener to perceive the silence as an interruption rather than an ending. As long as the music somehow manages to communicate that it will continue after the silence, the listener will fill in the silence with expectation, making it come alive.

## EXERCISES

**1** Select passages from several works of various periods and analyze how the music breathes: what aspects of the music does the composer use to create punctuation? Rate the cadences hierarchically from the most conclusive to the mildest, using our scale of punctuation, and specify what aspects of the music create the various degrees of punctuation (melodic, harmonic, textural). Experiment with modifying various dimensions in each case, and note the effect on the strength of the punctuation.

**2** Sequences, by definition, are very predictable in structure. In Figure 5.11, find a way to speed up the harmonic rhythm toward the end of the sequence, so as to better set off the cadence of the following phrase, for piano.

Figure 5.11. Exercise 2

**3** Finish the phrase for solo flute in Figure 5.12, using rhythm and smaller intervals to provide a feeling of repose.

Figure 5.12. Exercise 3

**4** Write a phrase for string quartet, ending with a sudden dynamic change, combined with a rhythmic stop. Write two more variants of the same phrase, ending in the same general way, but with different degrees of punctuation.

**5** Compose a musical phrase for a key moment of a film you know well, where there is some kind of surprising interruption in the action. How could the composer represent this in the music?

# 6 PRESENTING

As with motives, there are many degrees of similarity between phrases. Especially with successive phrases, listeners naturally compare one with the next and immediately notice how similar or how different they are. This is especially true with regard to very salient aspects of the music, like the motives in the main lines and the accompaniment, the length of the phrases, and the final punctuations. This leads us to discuss how phrases can be grouped together. Making several similar phrases into a coherent group is an important means of presenting[1] musical material: when phrases are organized into such larger units, based on the same musical idea(s), it helps the listener to become familiar with them.

These larger units are often hierarchical structures. The phrases within such structures will use more or less the same material, and in addition they often show some kind of overall progression, leading to greater intensity—a local climax—toward the end of the group. There are many possible degrees of punctuation at the end of the individual phrases within the group, but the punctuation of the last phrase will always be the strongest. As in prose, after various combinations of commas, periods, and so forth, the end of a paragraph indicates that we are ready to pass on to a new unit of thought.

Phrases may also follow one another in more surprising ways, where they do not form such coherent, hierarchical groups, but rather constantly lead the listener in new directions. We will examine these more surprising successions of phrases in chapter 16, "Exploring."[2] Here, however, we will concentrate on the former, more unified ways of combining phrases.

Hierarchical phrase groupings create a sense of formal stability, since they imply some degree of repetition and predictability. Hence the frequent appearance of these structures at the start of a large movement, where they allow the listener to "learn" the musical ideas being presented.

Phrase stability is a function of several things. In the Classical period, we often see symmetrical phrase combinations, for example, where two successive phrases are the same length. Sometimes there may be more variety in phrase length, but smooth punctuation and similar material ensure that the music flows easily and without much discontinuity within the larger unit. At the start of a piece, when the listener is not yet familiar with the musical material, too much surprise can be an obstacle to "learning" the musical ideas. Later, especially in a longer movement, once the musical ideas have become more familiar, it becomes possible to juxtapose them more dramatically.

A good analogy would be telling a story. If we introduce too many varied characters and situations too fast, the result is incoherence. Later, once the reader/listener has formed a clear idea of the main characters and of the situation, more surprising juxtapositions can occur.

In tonal music, harmonic stability—staying in or close to the home key— is a powerful cohesive force. Textural and registral stability are also significant, since too much novelty in these dimensions quickly becomes distracting.

THE PERIOD

The most common stable phrase combination is the period. A period consists of two phrases, in a question–answer relationship. The two phrases use at least some of the same material, but their cadences are different, the first being clearly less conclusive than the second. Thus, they coalesce into a larger whole, with a sense of resolution at the end.

Figure 6.1 is an example, the first half of the Ländler, Op. 171, No. 3, by Schubert. This very typical period consists of two four-bar phrases. The first ends with an imperfect cadence, with the melody arriving on the third of the tonic chord, on the weak beat. This is a clear example of the kind of "yes, but . . ." cadence mentioned in the previous chapter. The second phrase ends with a stronger perfect cadence. Both phrases end in the tonic, D major, and the two phrases are identical, except for their cadences. The literal repetition helps the listener to easily grasp the musical idea, and makes the difference

Figure 6.1. Schubert, Ländler, Op. 171, No. 3

between the two cadences stand out even more. The second phrase is not much more intense than the first, except in the sense that any repetition implies at least some degree of emphasis.

Another example of a symmetrical period, from a very well known piece of film music, can be heard in the first two phrases (mm. 1–16) of Hedwig's theme—the *Harry Potter* theme song—by John Williams. Unlike the Schubert example above, here the second phrase is definitely more intense, as a result of the higher register in the melody, and also because of the harmony, which is more chromatic.

Figure 6.2 is yet another example of a period, with a richer, more complex structure: the beginning of the Rondo from Mozart's Piano Sonata in C major, K. 309. The first phrase ends with a half cadence, in measure 8. The second phrase seems about to end with the expected perfect cadence in measure 16, but at the last minute the listener's expectations are frustrated by a detour, following the end of measure 15, leading to an impressive climactic flourish in measures 16–19. Note how, apart from introducing the higher register in these last four bars, Mozart also speeds up the harmonic rhythm, creating considerably more intensity at the cadence. This makes this period more dramatic and exciting, and creates a definite progression in the

Figure 6.2. Mozart, Piano Sonata in C major, K. 309, Rondo

music's momentum. Not coincidentally, this is from a much longer movement than the Schubert example.

Stability here comes from the texture (the accompaniment figure), the motives used in the melody, and the restriction to straightforward diatonic harmony (up until the secondary dominant in measure 16), as well as the fact that, overall, it does not modulate away from C major.

These examples show the kind of structural flexibility that is possible while still respecting the constraints of a period structure. Sometimes there is increased motivic and/or harmonic variation, which creates more novelty in the second phrase. Asymmetry between the phrases, where one of the two is longer than the other, is another powerful tool for creating intriguing structures. When grouping similar phrases together, if the phrases get successively shorter, the effect tends to be more exciting: it feels like one is breathing more and more quickly, pressing toward a goal. On the other hand, when successive phrases get progressively longer, the effect is usually one of diminishing tension, of relaxation. Of course, these effects can be mitigated or enhanced by the other dimensions of the music. (Note that this kind of variation in phrase length can apply not just to periods, but also to larger structures of more than two phrases.) Since the listener always unconsciously compares successive phrases, adjusting their phrase lengths like this is a powerful way to influence the emotional pacing of the form.

This kind of variety is commonly found within larger forms; it allows them to breathe in more flexible ways than exact symmetry would permit.


THE PARAGRAPH

It is also possible to group more than two phrases together.

In Figure 6.3, from the second movement of Beethoven's Piano Sonata in G major, Op. 49, No. 2, all five phrases are part of one larger formal unit, which we will call a paragraph. The opening two phrases seem at first to form a symmetrical period, since both are based on the same material, with an imperfect cadence in measure 4 and a perfect cadence in measure 8. The ensuing phrase uses the same motive with slight harmonic intensification (V/VI), and arrives on a half cadence in measure 12. But then the first two phrases are repeated, almost note for note, with the right hand an octave higher. What definitively ties the whole section together into one large paragraph is that the cadence in measures 19–20 is clearly a stronger version of that found in measures 7–8. The new, ornamented cadence and the higher register combine to create a sense of local climax. Furthermore, the thematic

**Tempo di Menuetto**

Figure 6.3. Beethoven, Piano Sonata in G major, Op. 49, No. 2, second movement

material is quite unified throughout the paragraph. Finally, this passage is followed by strongly contrasting material, which reinforces the listener's overall impression that measures 1–20 indeed belong together, making up one large unit.

Figure 6.4 is another example of a paragraph, from Schubert's String Quartet in G minor, D. 173. This is the beginning of the Menuetto. Here there are four phrases, built around the two motives labeled *a* and *b*. The first two phrases last four measures each, ending respectively in a half cadence in the tonic and a perfect cadence in the relative major. The eighth notes in the viola in measure 8 maintain the rhythmic momentum as we enter the third phrase, which ends once again with a half cadence in G minor, in measure 12. The last phrase in the paragraph also ends with a half cadence, in measure 16.

Note also that all four phrases have a similar rhythmic design, with the melody starting off each time in quarter notes, and then accelerating into eighth notes in the third (or third and fourth) bars. The eighth notes in the accompaniment in measures 9–10 make this phrase a bit more intense than the two preceding ones. The last phrase has less eighth-note movement overall: its character is more decisive.

**Allegro Vivace**

Figure 6.4. Schubert, String Quartet in G minor, D. 173, Menuetto

One might wonder why this is considered a paragraph, since the final punctuation is only a half cadence. What makes this last cadence markedly stronger than the previous ones is the combination of the more jagged and intense line in the first violin, the augmented sixth chord that precedes it—harmonically the most intense event in the movement so far—and the fact that Schubert has placed the repeat and the double bar here. Repeating these four phrases encourages the listener to hear them as a larger unit.

There are innumerable ways to create musical paragraphs, since the listener's perception of such groups is always a complex result of motives, punctuation, and, at times, of timbre and register, interacting in many ways. In order to be considered a paragraph, as opposed to just a simple succession of phrases, the following requirements must be met:

- There must be more than two phrases.
- Similar thematic material must be used more or less throughout.
- The articulation at the end of the last phrase must be clearly the strongest.

- What follows the last punctuation should clearly suggest something different.

As in a period, there is also usually some sense of development or progression in intensity over the whole structure. This may be a fairly linear rise from the beginning to the end, or it may form the kind of arch we often see in a literary narrative, where a problem is first presented, then developed, and finally resolved.

Note that the third requirement does not necessarily mean that the final punctuation (in a tonal piece) will always be a perfect cadence. As we have seen in the Schubert example above, it is also possible to create very strong articulation with somewhat less conclusive harmony, for example, with a pause and a marked change of register, followed by new material. Conversely, if what follows is based on similar material, but the cadence is indubitably the strongest one so far, we can also still speak of a paragraph.

Occasionally one sees a very symmetrical kind of paragraph, sometimes referred to as a double period. In a double period, there are four phrases, where the first and third phrases are almost identical, as are the second and fourth phrases. However, the cadence at the end of the fourth phrase is clearly the strongest of all, usually a perfect cadence, and ties the preceding four phrases together into a larger whole. An example of a double period can be found in measures 1–16 of the first movement of Beethoven's Piano Sonata in A-flat major, Op. 26 (Figure 6.5).

This very symmetrical structure is organized as follows. There are four phrases, ending respectively in measure 4, measure 8, measure 12, and measure 16. Both the first and second phrases end with a half cadence. The third phrase, starting at the end of measure 8, is just an ornamented version of the first phrase, with a bit more rhythmic momentum; however, it arrives at the exact same cadence. The last phrase, which starts at the end of measure 12, begins exactly like the second phrase. The only difference occurs at the end: a perfect authentic cadence that neatly closes off the whole paragraph. Notice how Beethoven uses the lowest register (in the left hand) to further set off this final cadence. This kind of very predictable, regular, hierarchical structure is typical of a double period.

The essential goal for the student here is to learn how to sensitively control both the motivic/thematic material and the gradations of punctuation, in order to create higher-level formal units when required. As we have seen, such hierarchy is a very important aspect of larger and richer forms, making them more organically integrated than simple chains of phrases would be.

**Andante con Variazioni**

**Figure 6.5.** Beethoven, Piano Sonata in A-flat major, Op. 26, first movement

## EXERCISES

N.B. Always include tempo and dynamic markings, as well as any other relevant indications necessary for performance.

**1** Add a second phrase to the given phrase in Figure 6.6 to create a symmetrical period. Maintain the same texture and style.

**Figure 6.6.** Exercise 1

**2** Continue the given melodies (in Figure 6.8, below) to the end of a second phrase, making them into period structures. Do not treat all the periods the same way: vary the lengths of the phrases, the degree of similarity between them, and the placement of the climaxes within the second phrase. These exercises are each for two instruments. Make sure to write for them in an idiomatic style.

Figure 6.7 is a model example, for solo violin, accompanied by pizzicato cello. Example 1 is the given beginning, and examples 2 and 3 propose, respectively, poor and good solutions to the problem. Both have been realized above the same bass line.

The poor solution (ex. 2) is in general too static. Measure 4 and the start of measure 5 would gain from a bit more rhythmic activity in the melody. The

Figure 6.7. Exercise 2: poor and improved versions

subsequent introduction of the quarter-eighth motive in rhythmic retrograde, in the fifth bar, leads the listener too far afield, since this is a remote motive form (remember that motives must be similar to the ear, not just to the eye). The harmony suggested on the first beat of measure 6 is a 6/4 chord, which is not properly resolved, distracting the listener. The melody in the following bars turns too much around the D, ending rather monotonously, and the added bar (m. 8) only makes an already static phrase even more so. Thus, the longer phrase length just seems gratuitous. All these details weaken the overall effect: the result is monotonous and incoherent.

In the better version (ex. 3), notice the way the top line keeps going in measure 4. The high B♭ in the next bar makes for an elegant climax, and the melodic line then follows up this higher register with a return to the high A in the penultimate bar. Also note the eighth-note activity in the violin in measures 6–7, maintaining the rhythmic momentum after the peak. The harmony also has a strong tonal direction, and the motives are a natural development of those in the first line.

Figure 6.8 presents two exercises for the student.

**Figure 6.8.** Exercise 2

**3** Complete the two phrases in Figure 6.9, and then add a second phrase to make a period. The two phrases need not be the same length. Add an extension to one of them, to intensify the cadence, as in the Mozart example examined above. Maintain the same texture and style as in the given phrases.

**4** Complete the bass (cello) line in the phrase for string trio in Figure 6.10. Then add counterpoint in the viola for measures 3–4, and continue the excerpt

Figure 6.9. Exercise 3

Figure 6.10. Exercise 4

idiomatically for at least three more phrases, to make a paragraph. The final phrase should be climactic, with all three instruments playing at the end.

**5** Compose a paragraph where all the phrases use the same accompaniment motive. Find a way to make it sound final without using a perfect cadence at the end. You may include one or two bars of the music that follows, to make the punctuation clearer. This exercise need not be in a tonal style.

# 7 ONE-PART FORMS

Instrumental miniatures can be found in all periods, starting in the Baroque era, when distinctive instrumental styles first appeared. By far the majority of them were meant for intimate situations, meaning that they usually require only one musician. Sometimes they are paired with other forms: for example, a prelude often precedes a fugue.

A common place where we often see one-part forms is the prelude.[1] Apart from the pairing just mentioned, preludes are also sometimes seen alone or in a set, along with other preludes. For example, the Chopin Preludes contain many of the best-known examples of short one-part forms. Scriabin, Rachmaninoff, Shostakovich, and others also significantly enriched the twentieth-century piano repertoire with their own sets of preludes.

The one-part prelude is normally restricted to a single musical idea, or at most perhaps two short motives in alternation. There is also usually no strong punctuation during the piece, apart from the ending: this is a form with only one main section. In contrast to a fugue, which is normally also a kind of one-part form, where the opening idea becomes the focus of dense contrapuntal development, a prelude's texture is generally simpler, without the complex pattern of overlapping entries typical of the fugue.[2]

A prelude is usually short, and, as already mentioned, without any major contrasts, which would tend to prolong the form. The beginning normally proposes a characteristic motive right away, which creates immediate interest: the listener expects an answer to the "question" posed by the motive. The motive will then reappear in a series of phrases, undergoing harmonic and melodic development. Overall these phrases need to establish some kind of progression and culmination, since there will be no significant contrast of material to renew the listener's interest. The climax is often right before the ending, or else it may constitute the ending in itself. The important point here is that the listener needs to feel that the piece presents a short but significant emotional trajectory that is complete in itself.[3]

Let us look at two contrasting examples from Chopin's Op. 28 Preludes. The first prelude in the set (Figure 7.1) is based on a simple, wavelike piano figure, presented in the first bar, on the tonic. Note the imaginative texture, with a kind of ornamental doubling of the upper motive, played in the right hand: the thumb starts earlier, the fifth finger then arrives on the same note a bit later as part of a rising arpeggio, an octave higher. They then resolve

Figure 7.1. Chopin, Prelude, Op. 28, No. 1

upward at the same time. This kind of textural richness is typical of good piano writing, making use as it does of the piano's natural resonance; Chopin's piece is unimaginable without the halo provided by the pedal.

The first phrase ends in measure 8, with a half cadence but no rhythmic stop, and then the second phrase begins the same way the first one did. Note that when the bass line in the opening phrase first rose to F in measure 5, that note underlay the phrase's melodic peak. However, when the second phrase arrives at the same bass note, in measure 13, the right hand adds chromatic appoggiaturas to the melodic line. Further, the bass, which previously only rose to G in measure 7, now keeps on moving upward. In measure 18, the right-hand rhythm becomes a quintuplet covering the whole bar, producing a rushing effect, since in the previous bars it only started on the second sixteenth note, while now it begins on the downbeat.[4]

Both the bass and the melody reach their highest points in measure 21. Note the large leap (from E down to F♯) in the bass line. This marks the climax even more strongly, as does the fact that the continuous quintuplets now gradually dissolve; they alternate with the original rhythm a couple of times before disappearing entirely. What follows is a descent to a cadence at measure 25, landing on a tonic pedal. This pedal tone lasts until the end, briefly underlying a gentle subdominant neighbor harmony. The registral descent and the harmonic relaxation give the ending a fine sense of resolution.

The second prelude is quite different, with a slow and brooding character (Figure 7.2). Again, it is the textural richness that provides the interest: in this case Chopin takes a simple neighbor-note idea, crossing it with another voice in the bass (motive *a* in the score), to create an accompaniment figure that will engender some very rich chromatic passing harmonies later on. The melodic line turns around the plain motive *b* (mm. 3–4), as well as an ornamented version of the same idea—actually, a double motive, due to the dotted notes added at the end—labeled *b1* (mm. 5–6).

The form here is quite different from the first prelude. Following a two-bar introduction, the first phrase lasts from measure 3 to measure 7, starting with motive *b*, followed by the more elaborate *b1*. At the beginning, the piece seems to be in E minor, but the first cadence, in measure 6, is in G major. The actual harmonic bass line (made up of the lowest notes in each bar, in the left hand) is very slow-moving. Measure 8 marks the start of new phrase. It seems at first to be identical to the first phrase, just transposed a fifth higher. But the harmony does not cadence as expected in measure 11. Instead the bass stays on A for four bars, from measure 9 to measure 12; after that there is still no cadence. This makes the second phrase much longer than the first.

Figure 7.2. Chopin, Prelude, Op. 28, No. 2

Given the slow tempo, this creates the sense of a heavy emotional burden, with no relief in sight.

The bass gradually descends, landing on what will prove to be the home dominant (E, that is, V of A) in measure 16. Note that up till this point there has been no clear tonal stability; the opening E minor seems forgotten. In fact, the ambiguous tonality contributes to the feeling of uncertainty and doubt. As the bass goes slowly downward, the melody in measures 14–16 recalls its opening motive, but with its first note greatly prolonged, again creating an effect of a heavy emotional weight. Together with the slowly descending chromatic harmony, this once again gives an impression of holding back, of losing energy. Motive *b1* is then heard again in measures 17–18 and in measures 20–21, but the left hand has now become intermittent, and stays poised on the dominant. Finally the accompaniment disappears entirely, leaving only a straightforward homophonic texture: the effect of the bars with no bass is rather desolate. The harmony seems to cadence on E in measures 21–22, but in the second half of the latter bar a seventh is added, making the E into the dominant of what proves to be the real tonic, A minor, that follows.

The overall shape of this prelude thus consists of a first statement (mm. 1–7), followed by a longer, higher restatement (starting in m. 8) that very gradually descends into a soft, sad ending. There is a loss of momentum during the descent, contributing to the piece's uncertain, depressed character. There is no clear climactic moment, although measures 11–15 are particularly intense harmonically. The ending stands out quite distinctly owing to the change of texture, and also because of the harmonic surprise of the final dominant seventh: as it should be, the conclusion is something special.

In addition to this kind of short prelude, there are longer and somewhat more complex examples of one-part forms, for example, many of the Chopin etudes and some of the Rachmaninoff preludes. We will examine one of the latter in detail: Rachmaninoff's Op. 32, No. 8.

While the harmony here is more chromatic than in the Chopin examples, the whole piece is still based on only two motives, both present at the beginning of the piece. A loud, opening flourish comes to a stop in measure 1, and then the same stop is reinforced in measure 3. The same material is then further developed, but quietly; the repeated-note motive in the left hand in measures 1–3 now crosses over the right hand to create a new pianistic texture out of the same idea. There is some motivic wandering, as in measure 6, but the original form of the motive reasserts itself quickly in measure 8. Until measure 10, the harmony turns mostly around the tonic chord, but in measures 11–12 we land squarely on the dominant in the bass. Starting in measure 14, the harmonic rhythm speeds up considerably and the harmony passes quickly through several neighboring tonal regions before returning solidly to the dominant and then to the tonic, in measures 24–26. On the way, we arrive at the first climax of the piece, in measure 20. Overall, this paragraph is structured like a large wave.

Measure 26 recalls measure 6. Rachmaninoff enriches the original texture with extra chords in the left hand, starting in measure 27, creating a quicker intensification than the first time around. This builds to another wavelike climax in measure 35, now in the high register, where the original oscillating neighbor-note figure from the start of the piece is transformed into a virtuoso variant, alternating between the hands. This helps create motivic richness, while still remaining recognizable in relation to the original. After a gradual descent in measures 36–41, we rise to the main climax in measure 43. The hands are far apart, creating the widest registral spread we have heard in the whole piece. The texture subsequently thins down gradually, diminuendo, in measures 44–50. The piece ends with one final, loud presentation of the main motive. This kind of structure, composed of multiple, gradually intensifying waves, is very common in Rachmaninoff's music.

As we can see, much of the interest in these pieces lies in the richness of the harmonic and textural detail. The focus on just one or two motives makes this a virtual necessity, if the music is to be rich enough to be worth hearing more than once. While the overall formal curves are often fairly straightforward, they are nonetheless not simplistic: they are nuanced enough to defy prediction and provide regular novelty for the listener.

## ELABORATIONS

Apart from the type of individual prelude discussed above, many of the preludes that are paired with the Bach fugues are also one-part forms. The ones that are not contrapuntal are usually structured similarly to the first Chopin prelude, discussed above. However, one thing that Bach often does differently from Chopin is to markedly change the figuration (or basic musical pattern) at the end, creating a strong rhetorical gesture of finality. A good example is the D-major Prelude from book 1 of the *Well-Tempered Clavier*, which has moved continuously in steady sixteenth notes through most of the piece. It finally comes to a dead stop in measure 33, on a diminished seventh chord above a dominant pedal. This is followed by a short flourish in thirty-second notes, and then a final cadential progression. This kind of dramatic moment is especially potent in these preludes, given that the next movement will be a fugue, where, by definition, the rhythmic momentum will remain more or less constant throughout. The contrast between the two kinds of musical movement enhances the effect of the fugue.

Similarly, Bach sometimes precedes a fugue with a contrapuntal "fantasia" that develops one or two main ideas. A beautiful example is BWV 562 for organ (the fugue remains incomplete). This movement develops the idea presented at the start, alternating passages grounded by long pedal points in the bass with harmonically more mobile passages, where the bass is in motion. A simple contrast, idiomatic to the organ, is the short passage without pedal in the middle of the piece. This lightens the texture temporarily, but without disrupting the overall rhythmic and motivic continuity. At the end of this movement the imitative texture dissolves into a sort of cadenza, where sixteenth notes appear for the first time in the figuration, rising to a dissonant climax before the final cadence.

## EXERCISES

**1** Examine other Chopin preludes, first analyzing first the phrase/cadence structure and then answering the following questions: How are the motivic ideas developed? How does each prelude evolve as a whole? Does it have a clear climax? How does the conclusion stand out from the rest of the piece? What makes the final cadence more conclusive than the others?

**2** Examine several Rachmaninoff preludes in the same way. Pay particular attention to the variety of the piano figuration; Rachmaninoff often adds little contrapuntal details that transform stock figuration into something much more distinctive.

**3** Compose two short piano preludes, in contrasting characters. Ensure that the details of their structures differ from one another.

Start by finding a pregnant motive, one with a strong internal contrast or an otherwise distinctive gesture that can be developed at some length. Explore its possibilities in several short sketches, referring to chapter 1 on motives as needed. Make sure to treat dissonances consistently when developing the motive; if there are to be changes in the treatment of dissonance, they should occur at significant moments, for instance, the beginning, the peak, or the cadence of a phrase. Plan the cadences: for a short prelude there will be three or four at most, and the internal cadences should be fairly light. Remember to use our quantitative scale of punctuation, indicating in some way—for instance, via the harmony or the rhythm—that the piece is not yet complete. The final cadence should stand out from the others as being clearly the most conclusive. There should be a clear, overall movement toward a moment of greatest intensity, which should happen about two-thirds to three-quarters of the way through the piece, or else at the ending itself. The climax should stand out from its surroundings, for instance, due to increased dissonance, modulation, register, or a change in figuration. Finally, work out the piece in detail.

**4** Advanced exercise: Write a virtuoso piano prelude, using the Rachmaninoff example above as a model. Follow the directives for exercise 3, but work at creating more sophisticated piano textures.

# 8 TERNARY FORM

Ternary forms[1] are the simplest forms with more than one section. Ternary forms often appear in short dance movements, like the Classical minuet and trio. In large sonata-type works, they are usually the third of four movements, and the lightest in character. The reason for this is that such simple forms do not lend themselves to great drama or emotional complexity. Positioning them after a slow movement and before the finale makes them good foils for those movements, which are usually emotionally richer, featuring more intense confrontations.

Ternary forms are also to be found in Classical opera, in the da capo aria, and in various nineteenth-century piano pieces, like some of the Chopin nocturnes.

A simple ternary form consists of a first idea, an A section, followed by a contrasting idea, the B section, followed by a return of the A section. The whole makes up a simple ABA pattern. Each section is self-contained: heard alone, neither seems to require the other.

We will start with the smallest, simplest version of ternary form. In the standard repertoire this kind of extreme simplicity is actually very rare. For pedagogical purposes, Figure 8.1 is a model example of the practice form, for piano.

Note the following:

- Each section is harmonically complete and can stand on its own, as a miniature.
- The first part in is C♯ minor, and the second part is in a closely related key, B major.
- The two parts are in the same meter, providing some basic unity.
- The contrast of tempo is not extreme.

Figure 8.1. A model ternary form

- The two sections are based on different motives, providing contrast of material.
- The register of the middle section is generally lower; registral contrast is a simple and effective way to create novelty.
- The articulation in the middle section is also smoother—legato—providing another simple and effective contrast.

Both sections are eight bars long, but the internal phrasing is different. In the first part, there is a clear subdivision into two-bar units, whereas in the second part there is punctuation only in measures 12 and 16, making the phrases four bars long. This also suits the calmer character of the middle section.

Now that we have a clear idea of the simplest ternary form, we can examine two more sophisticated examples from the repertoire. Chopin's Nocturne in C minor, Op. 48, No. 1 provides a very clear example of the form. Not coincidentally, this piece has a distinctly operatic quality; one thinks of Bellini, whom Chopin so admired for his melodic gifts.

The first section (mm. 1–24) begins with a rather vocal melody, presented first in a four-bar phrase that cadences on the tonic in measure 4. The accompaniment is of the utmost simplicity: a bass line in octaves, alternating with full chords in the middle register. The second phrase begins like the first, but the melody quickly becomes more elaborate, further developing the syncopated rhythm first heard in measure 2. This phrase modulates to G minor, where it cadences in measure 8.

This is followed by a sudden harmonic shift (V/♭II), and the melody becomes more ornate, again recalling the kind of improvised ornamentation one would find in a Bellini opera. Although the harmony returns immediately to the home key in the fourth phrase, the melodic ornamentation continues. Punctuation in this part of the piece is very light. For example, in measure 16 the melody seems to be stopping on a half cadence in E♭ major, but the underlying harmony includes the seventh of the chord, and the bass line keeps moving. This would merit perhaps 3 out of 10 on our scale of degrees of punctuation. Short melodic phrases now continue over harmony moving through the circle of fifths, reaching a climax in measure 21 on a high C. The descent from the climax into the end of the section is very ornate, eventually falling two octaves, to middle C.

What is significant about the way this first section is organized as a whole is the way the phrase structure and the harmony both get more fluid as the section develops. There is also a clear progression in the richness of the ornamentation, culminating in the long descent after the climax.

The final cadence of this section is harmonically very strong, but the rhythm never completely stops. To understand the reason for this little rhythmic "yes, but . . ." gesture, one has only to imagine the first section coming to a dead stop before starting the middle section. The effect would be too neat and square for the emotional world of this piece.

The middle section lasts from measure 25 to measure 48. Although the tonic remains the same (C), this section is in major. The texture and the thematic material are completely different from those in the first section; the contrast is immediately evident. This is typical of a ternary form, no matter how large and elaborate.

This B section starts with a very full, homophonic, declamatory texture, not at all like the vocal melody with accompaniment heard in the opening section. The piano scoring is particularly rich by contrast with the first section, providing a marked contrast in the texture.

In measure 28 the new material arrives at an imperfect cadence in G major. Then the first phrase returns, more heavily scored, now arriving at a perfect cadence in C. These two phrases together make up a period.

There follows a short sequence with more intense harmony (mm. 33–36), which overlaps with what at first seems to be a return to the phrase from measure 29, now more widely spaced in register, but still very quiet. In midphrase, however, there is now a virtuoso interjection in octaves, a concertolike response to the large, orchestral-sounding chords just heard. In fact, this whole subsection will turn out to be an elaborate variation of measures 29–36, built around this alternation between the full chords and the virtuoso octaves.

In measure 45 we finally arrive at the theme that started the middle section in measure 25. In measure 46, the piano explodes into three bars of continuous, brilliant octaves. The crescendo that began in measure 38 reaches its peak with these octaves. This passage is really both the climax and the cadence of the middle section of the nocturne.

Now, in measure 49, the opening section returns, but with a more restless accompaniment, pulsing in triplets. The melody is also thickened now, doubled more or less regularly by the pulsing chords. Formally, this section is an exact recapitulation, bar for bar, of the opening section. The only structural difference occurs in measure 72, where, instead of a clear cadence in C minor, as we had in measure 24, the harmony detours to V/♭II, allowing for a richer and more elaborate cadence, which underlines its formal role as the final, most conclusive punctuation. In measure 75, the texture dissolves and the melody wanders off alone into the high register, diminuendo, to be followed by three quiet, repeated tonic chords.

The overall symmetry of the form is unambiguous, as is the contrast between the first and the middle sections. Despite simple rhythmic links in the accompaniment, in terms of melodic and harmonic structure, each section could stand on its own.

Now let us examine another example, Don Octavio's aria "Dalla sua pace" from Mozart's *Don Giovanni*, K. 527.

Here is the text, first in the original Italian, and then in English, below.

>Dalla sua pace la mia dipende;
>Quel che a lei piace vita mi rende,
>Quel che le incresce morte mi dà.
>S'ella sospira, sospiro anch'io;
>È mia quell'ira, quel pianto è mio;
>E non ho bene, s'ella non l'ha.
>
>On her peace of mind, mine also depends,
>What pleases her gives me life,

What grieves her wounds my heart.
If she sighs, I sigh with her;
Her anger and her sorrow are both mine,
And I can't know joy unless she shares it.

Note that this short text is divided (by the periods in the punctuation) into two parts, separated by the period at the end of the third line. The music follows the text's subdivision, as follows:

- section A: measures 1–17, first part of the text
- section B: measures 17–36, second part of the text
- section A': measures 37–74, return of the first part of the text

Section A has a half cadence in measure 9 ("piace vita mi rende") and a perfect cadence in measures 16–17 ("morte mi dà"), making it a paragraph structure. There are also caesuras in measures 5 and 13. Thus the whole first part is quite symmetrically structured.

The middle section begins in G minor, with a new appoggiatura figure accompanying in the winds. The vocal line also includes several appoggiaturas, reinforcing the change of character. When the text arrives for the first time at "s'ella non l'ha," the music stands still, on a diminished seventh chord, which seems to be leading toward the dominant of G minor.

However, the resolution takes advantage of the harmonic ambiguity of the diminished seventh chord, and resolves onto a III6 of G major, twice repeating the last line of text. Note that there is virtually no punctuation of any significance within this section, apart from the pause on the diminished seventh in measure 28. The section ends in measure 36, poised on the dominant, having delicately hinted at G minor once more in the bass, with an E♭ neighbor note.

A very short vocal cadenza now leads back to the opening music, literally repeated, from measure 37 to measure 52. However, this time Mozart continues where the section previously ended, returning once again to the first two lines of text with a new melodic phrase, which repeats an appoggiatura motive four times while the accompaniment responds in kind.

At "Quel che le incresce" the original music (first heard in mm. 10–17) returns, with the orchestration somewhat enriched. The cadence, in measure 64, overlaps with a little echo in the woodwind before the voice enters for the last time in a climactic phrase full of chromatic octave leaps, repeating the third line of the text.

We can see that in this operatic example, although the ternary structure is quite clear from the text, the harmony, and the melodic material, the overall form is not really symmetrical. In fact, each section is longer than the preceding one, creating a sort of crescendo of formal complexity. Mozart has taken the framework of the simple ternary form and modified it to fit the emotional intensity of the drama at this moment. An overly symmetrical form would have been too predictable for the anguished emotion represented here.

These last two examples, like most from the standard repertoire, are somewhat more sophisticated than the practice form we will be using here.

## ELABORATIONS

More sophisticated ternary forms may have some transition between sections, especially between the B section and the return of A. This permits the overall form to accumulate greater momentum. In another, very common variant, each section is made up of a longer, more elaborate form of its own (usually binary).[2]

A wonderful example, which demonstrates an intriguing elaboration of the form, can be found in the third movement of Beethoven's Seventh Symphony. This large ternary form includes not only an arresting transition between the first and second themes, and a much more subtle transition back, but also a little joke at the end. When, after the return of the main theme nearing the movement's end, we arrive at the same jolting stop that first announced the arrival of the second theme, Beethoven actually begins the second theme again. He starts it in the same key as before (D major), only to interrupt it after just four bars with an abrupt ending in the home key (F major).

Why this novel variant of the form? First, emotional range: the ending now incorporates a touch of humor, and the varied ways of connecting the contrasting characters of the two themes enrich them both considerably, rather like characters in a novel whom we get to know better as we observe them in multiple situations. Second, the form is more subtle. Abrupt transitions tend to be effective in inverse proportion to how often they occur. If all the transitions are abrupt, after the first one or two of them the piece starts to just sound like a collection of little sections. When surrounded by other, more gradual transitions, they can provide intriguing byways within a larger, integrated whole: smooth transitions by definition make the subdivisions less obvious.

## EXERCISE

Our exercise will consist of the most elementary version of the form, that is to say, a simple, symmetrical structure with short, complete sections, including a single contrasting idea, and with no transitions between sections.

The student should write a simple ternary form for piano, based on the example analyzed at the start of this chapter (figure 8.1).

Begin by sketching out the first section in some detail. Limit the A section to one or two motives, and keep the texture consistent. Mark the cadences through changes of texture and/or dynamics, so that the phrase structure is clearly felt. The goal here is formal concision and memorability.

Once the first section is finished, choose a closely related key for the B section. Keep the meter the same. Use motives, register, texture, and/or articulation to provide contrast. Each section should each have its own distinct character, effectively setting it off from the other, but without sounding like a completely different piece. You may need to sketch out two or three possible ideas to find just the right degree of contrast. It is especially important that the beginning of the B section and the return to the A section provide an immediate, refreshing sense of novelty.

Note also that the phrase structure in the second section should be somewhat different from that in the first section.

# 9 BINARY FORM

Two-part forms, the so-called binary forms, all share several important characteristics. First, they have very strong punctuation in the middle, usually a full stop and a double bar, with a repeat sign. Second, both sections are based on one main idea.[1]

It is important to understand that binary forms are not, as their name might suggest, "AB" forms, that is, forms where a section based on one idea is followed by another section based on a different idea. While there are differences between the two sections, as we shall see, they are not to be found in the material they use.[2]

There is another important difference between the two sections, which is common to all binary forms: the second part must display some kind of increase in activity, giving the piece as a whole a distinct sense of developing intensity. In a word, the second section is notably less stable. This instability creates an important structural contrast between the two sections. It can result from more distant modulations, less regular phrase structure, changes of texture (although not too extreme), or more fragmentary melodic lines.

This is important because, like any musical form, binary form needs to evolve and deepen in intensity as the work goes on. If the level of tonal/modulatory activity, for example, were to remain the same, the second section could stagnate. There is often also an increase in the pacing of the modulations—that is, more modulatory activity in an equivalent span of time. These very salient changes serve to "raise the temperature" of the overall musical experience, making it more intense for the listener.

In this sense the second part of a binary form is a good example of what we will call the "progressing" principle, to be discussed in chapter 13.

Another common difference between the two sections in many binary forms is between the punctuation that ends the two halves: the first ending is often less final than the second. Usually the endings are motivically also very similar, which encourages the listener to compare them.[3]

Binary forms are commonly found in Baroque dances, in small nineteenth-century piano pieces, and also in the middle movements of Classical sonatas and symphonies, and as subsections of larger ternary forms.

A somewhat more sophisticated kind of binary form is the rounded binary,[4] which may in fact be the historical origin of sonata form. Looking at it in more detail, we can see why this structure lends itself to dramatic development.

In a rounded binary form, the first section often ends with a strong cadence somewhere other than on the tonic, to create a strong sense of incompleteness. Even when it does cadence on the tonic, the equivalent cadence at the end of the piece will prove to be even more conclusive in some way, as a result of rhythm, more preparation, or the textural layout of the cadence.

The beginning of the second section quickly presents some kind of harmonic surprise, creating a mild feeling of discontinuity. This sense of interruption, of a kind of harmonic digression in the form, is necessary so that when the tonic ultimately returns, the dramatic effect of "coming home" is stronger. Again, we can see the possible link to sonata form. The beginning of the second section acts a bit like the development section in a sonata, owing to its intensified harmony/modulation. The subsequent return of the tonic then feels like a resolution.

In nontonal music, a comparable increased intensity can be created by stronger and more frequent contrasts in register, orchestration, or articulation. Harmonically speaking, whatever the language, the second section will become more intense.[5]

The other characteristic feature of rounded binary form is the return, after the "development," of some, or perhaps all, of the music from the beginning of the piece: there is a definite sense of recapitulation, enhancing the feeling of returning home after a musical voyage.

We will look at three examples of binary forms. Our first example will be the Minuet II from Bach's Partita No. 1 in B-flat major, BWV 825; our second example will be the Trio from Mozart's Minuet, K. 568, No. 2, for small instrumental ensemble; and the third example, "Träumerei," is the seventh of Schumann's *Kinderszenen*, Op. 15. The latter two are rounded binaries.

In this short example by Bach (Figure 9.1), the two sections are symmetrical, equal in length, at eight bars each. The cadence in measure 8 is a half cadence in the home key, B♭ major. There is no real modulation in these first eight bars, just a passing reference to V/IV, in measure 2 and measure 6.

Figure 9.1. Bach, Partita No. 1 in B-flat major, BWV 825, Minuet II

The second half begins with the same motivic material as the first part, now starting on the dominant. It soon moves off toward the submediant, providing the only real modulation in the piece. Thus it is harmonically more intense than the first part. After a cadence in G minor in measure 12, we quickly return to B♭ major, finishing with a full cadence in that key.

Apart from the novelty added by the modulation, the second half is harmonically more intense in another way: the bass line, mostly a pedal point in the first half of the piece, is much more mobile. The eighth notes in the tenor part in measures 11–12 also add momentum.

Finally, the melody, having gradually descended from the new, high F in measure 9 (the first section never goes beyond E♭), rises even higher in measures 13–14 to G, the climax of the whole piece.

In the Mozart Minuet (Figure 9.2), the first half of the Trio consists of two phrases: measures 1–4, ending with a half cadence in F major (the home key), and measures 5–8, using the same material, but now finishing on the tonic. In other words, this is a simple, symmetrical period structure. Only the texture and the orchestration are slightly different in this phrase: in particular, the melody is doubled an octave lower in the bassoon, and now it includes a little trill in measure 7, which helps mark the coming cadence in measure 8.

The second half begins again with the main idea, but now in G minor. It also introduces the high register, using the flute for the first time, an octave above the violin. Within three bars (mm.9–11) the bass moves through three chromatic alterations, creating an unprecedented level of harmonic intensity. This phrase ends on a rather indecisive half cadence, which begins a dominant pedal that underlies most of the coming, final phrase. This fi-

Figure 9.2. Mozart, Minuet, K. 568, No.2, Trio

nal phrase is a texturally enriched variation of measures 4–8 (thus recalling mm. 1–4), so the sense of rounding off the form is very strong. For the first time here the melody is doubled in three octaves, played by flute, violin 1, and bassoon.

Notice also that the bass line at the cadence is slightly more active and vigorous in measure 15 than it was in measure 7. This is an example of how even two perfect cadences can have differing weights. Notice also the new doubling, a third below the first violin, in the second violin part in measures 12–14, which makes the texture a bit more dense this time.

Our last example of binary form, Schumann's "Träumerei" (Figure 9.3), begins with a smooth, singing four bar phrase that subdivides into two parts. The first rises up to the high F in measure 2, and the second falls gradually back down to the half cadence in measure 4. This is followed by a repeat of the same rising line as in measures 1–2, but now going higher, to A, over a V/VI harmony. The resolution, VI, proves to be the II of C major, the

Figure 9.3. Schumann, "Träumerei," from *Kinderszenen*, Op. 15

dominant key, where the first section ends, harmonically open. Note the slightly more contrapuntal texture in measures 7–8, with imitations in the inner parts, adding to the intensity of the coming cadence on C.

In measure 9, after the double bar, the piece seems to be starting over. But already by measure 10 the harmony takes a new turn, touching first on G minor, where there is a very mild punctuation in measure 12, and then moving on to B♭ major, where the main theme reappears. This is the first and only time the first half of the theme appears anywhere but in F major. The B♭ major proves to be very transient, and then seems to be preparing a cadence in D minor, in measures 15–16. At the last minute the bass line takes a surprise turn, and what seemed like a D minor 6/4 disappears, rising through a passing tone to V7 of F, the home tonic.

Now the opening phrase of the piece reappears intact, in measures 17–20. However, the second phrase takes a new turn: instead of V/VI, as in measure 6, the high A is now supported by V9/V, in measure 22. This has the effect of increasing the harmonic drive toward the following final cadence. The phrase's melodic descent returns in its original form, first seen in measures 2–4, but with one important difference: here the four rising notes before the end—G, A, B♭, D—are repeated, now harmonized as II6, V/II, II. This postpones the cadence we expect, increasing its finality, by playing with our expectations. The final point of arrival is now the tonic, instead of the dominant, as it was in measure 4.

Note how the section after the double bar is longer, and harmonically and texturally more intense, with more modulatory activity and more frequent contrapuntal writing than what we have heard previously (for instance, see mm. 11–12 and 14–16). It also contains the melodic peak of the piece, the high B♭ in measure 14.

The rounding off at the end of the form is also quite substantial. This kind of reprise, as we will see in chapter 17, "Returning," creates a certain sense of quiet resolution, suitable to the calm, dreamy character of the piece. On the other hand, the extra repetition of the melodic G, A, G♭, D adds emphasis to the final cadence, making it even more conclusive.

## ELABORATIONS

As suggested above, in practice there is a wide range of binary forms. Aspects that can vary include the degree of finality of the first section, the amount of literal reprise in the second section (sometimes there is none at all), and whether or not the second section introduces any new material, and if so, how much contrast it creates with the first section. The reprise, if there is one, may also be varied.

In examples with more elaborate development of material already presented, the result can begin to resemble the development section of a sonata form. (We will discuss techniques of development in detail in chapter 16, "Exploring.")

For an example of such a more elaborate binary form, see the third movement of Haydn's Symphony No. 104. This movement is in ternary form overall, but the individual sections are elaborate binary forms in their own right.

## EXERCISES

The binary forms discussed here offer our first chance to create a musical structure that intrinsically requires several interconnected sections.[6] These forms can help the student to develop some of the basic skills that will be needed in elaborating larger forms.

**1** Compose a sixteen-bar binary form for piano, on the model of the Bach example discussed above (Figure 9.1). Pay special attention to the beginning and the ending of the second section, so as to differentiate it from the first section, despite using the same motivic material.

**2** Compose a rounded binary form for string quartet on the model of the Mozart example discussed above. Make sure to differentiate the final cadence from the end of the first section, so that it is more conclusive.

# 10 VARIATION FORM

Exploring a musical idea through variation is in a sense the basis of all composition. Coherence requires familiarity with the material, so that the listener can follow the music with reasonable ease. Such familiarity is most easily achieved through repetition. But repetition soon requires at least some degree of variation to maintain interest.

However, variation form, the subject of this chapter, is in a special category by itself. The variation project will be our first attempt at a longer composition, since it will allow us to build up a larger form through a series of short forms, all based on a common skeleton, the theme.

The theme of a set of variations normally has a fairly straightforward structure, so as to provide a clear, easily memorable frame for the subsequent variations. A theme with a more eccentric structure, not easily grasped in one listening, will distract from the real interest of the form, which lies in the continuous fantasy and invention proposed by the variations. Also, since the same structure will be repeated in every single variation, what might be charming or interesting once or twice quickly becomes annoying.[1]

As we can see, variation form is by nature a challenge to the imagination. Within the constraints of the phrase structure, and in some cases even the melody of the theme, the composer has to find ways to create contrasting, novel surfaces that renew interest, even as the underlying skeleton is repeated multiple times. Many composers have seen this challenge as a stimulus to the imagination, writing very long and elaborate sets of variations, for instance, Bach in the *Goldberg Variations*, Beethoven in the *Diabelli Variations*, and Brahms in his two volumes of *Paganini Variations*.

Within each variation the character normally remains fairly stable. Each variation is a distinct piece, with its own character, and within each variation there is usually a high degree of motivic homogeneity. Significant mood changes normally occur only between variations.

The recurring structure of the theme creates a definite periodicity in the overall form, since even if not all the variations are in the same tempo, the proportions will always stay the same. This periodicity can become monotonous if badly handled, but it can also be used to advantage allowing the composer to organize variations into groups, thus creating formal progressions that go beyond the internal workings of a single variation. For instance, we might have three variations in a row getting gradually faster, followed by two slow variations. Other examples might include several variations with increasing density of texture, or more and more dissonant harmony. Such large formal progressions allow the form to breathe in a less predictable way, and it becomes possible to create longer sets of variations without risking formal monotony.

The one place where the form normally changes is the last variation. The reason is simple: beyond the shortest sets of variations, adding one more variation with the same structure as all the others will not sound final. Therefore the last variation often breaks away from the theme at some point, to allow for a more elaborate cadence. This last variation is typically longer and more complex than the others. Sometimes the last movement may even be cast in a completely different form, for instance, a fugue based on a melodic fragment taken from the original theme. The point is that the listener must feel the last variation as unique in its structure, and also as a sort of culmination, signaling that the piece is finally coming to an end.

Before looking at examples of the form in detail, we need to say a few words about the relationship between variation form and motivic variation, as discussed in chapter 1. As we have already mentioned, within one variation the composer is limited to exploring only one or two motives, which helps ensure unity and focus of character. The melody of the theme is not always preserved throughout a set of variations. However, there is a special kind of variation where the melody of the theme is indeed maintained, but with ornamentation. This is called ornamental variation: the composer takes the melodic outline from the theme and knits a completely new motive around it, to create a fresh melody, which nonetheless follows the contour of the original theme. Figure 10.1 is an example from Fauré's Variations in C-sharp minor, Op. 73.

On the first staff we see the first two bars of the theme. On the second we see the beginning of the second variation. The notes with "x" above them correspond to those in the theme. It is significant that, at first hearing, the

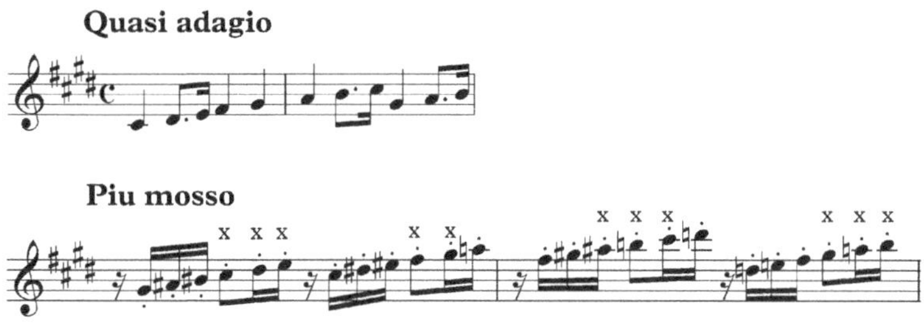

**Quasi adagio**

**Piu mosso**

Figure 10.1. Fauré, Variations in C-sharp minor, Op. 73, first bars of the theme and of variation 2

listener is more struck by the novelty of the new motive than by the similarity to the theme. The much faster tempo and the staccato articulation create an immediate freshness. But underneath the surface, Fauré is clearly following the melodic outline of the theme. Despite the contrast of character, the listener senses the same harmony, the same overall melodic shape, and the identical phrase structure.

Some Classical variations, such as the famous set from the Piano Sonata in A major by Mozart, K. 331, maintain the melodic profile of the theme quite audibly throughout; others lose it completely. The longer the set, the less likely it is to follow the original melodic contour throughout, simply because at a certain point there will be a need for more potent melodic contrast.

Our first example of a set of variations will be the slow movement from Beethoven's last string quartet, Op. 135 (Figure 10.2). This is a very short set of variations. They are continuous, rather than having a clear stop between each variation. Given the brevity of the theme (only ten bars), separating the variations would have created a rather bumpy, stop-and-go kind of structure, which would be out of place here, given the generally calm mood of this movement.

The theme is preceded by a two-bar broken chord that acts as an introduction, not quoted here. The first half of the theme (mm. 3–6) subdivides into two two-bar segments, alternating between tonic and dominant. The next four bars have a more intense harmonic trajectory. They seem to reach a cadence in measure 10. However, Beethoven attenuates the punctuation here by keeping the cello moving, and then, at the start of measure 11, imitating its material, now heard in the first violin. This contrapuntal overlap allows the melody to go on for two more bars, reaching a peak in measure 12. The upper parts in the second half of measure 12 act as a kind of

Figure 10.2. Beethoven, String Quartet in F major, Op. 135, third movement

appoggiatura, gracefully delaying the actual arrival of the tonic until the start of measure 13, where the second variation begins.

This theme is exceptionally sober in its harmony: only the V/VI and the V/II in measures 7–8 venture momentarily outside the diatonic scale of D♭ major.

The first variation (mm. 13–22) has the same general texture as the theme, but gradually rises in register. The form also follows that of the theme, but the harmony becomes more adventurous, reaching a new level of intensity with several chromatic appoggiaturas, underlined by sudden accents. In contrast to the theme, the last two bars descend from the climax. This kind of variety, in the overall melodic curve between variations, is a nice way to subtly temper the inherent periodicity of the form, making it subtler and less obvious.

The second variation is in C♯ minor. Classical variations often contain a "minore" like this; the change of mood immediately gives a new color to the material. The texture is now completely homophonic and is based on a new, halting rhythmic motive. The tempo is slower, although sixteenth notes do appear here for the first time, in effect moving the music into a different gear. Like the preceding variation, this one reaches its climax in its eighth measure (m. 30), before descending in the final two bars.

Just as the halting motive is heard for the last time in measure 32, it returns to major. In the following measure, we also return to the original eighth-note rhythm for several bars.

The third variation presents the theme in the cello, with free imitations in the first violin, which have the effect of making the phrase subdivisions less square. In measure 37 the accompaniment again accelerates into sixteenth notes, creating a new level of energy. Because of the delay created by the imitation in violin 1, the true climax of the variation arrives a measure later than the cello climax, in the penultimate bar, measure 41. The bass then in turn echoes the first violin, further spinning out the contrapuntal web.

The last variation (mm. 43–52) introduces a drastic change of texture: the accompanying middle parts now consist of arpeggio figuration, slightly ornamented so as not to sound overly formulaic. The main melodic line is again on top, in the first violin, reaching its peak in measure 52. The accented B♭ is the highest point of the entire movement. This variation has flowed along in continuous sixteenth notes, now accented with a *fz* dynamic, creating a rhythmic climax to accompany the melodic one.

Finally, Beethoven adds two bars of coda at the end, over a tonic pedal. This little coda brings the two-note thirty-second-note motives closer together, so that, despite the dying away in the dynamics, there is a rhythmic sense of culmination, of completion.

Within this short structure there are many subtleties; we have only mentioned the main ones. The student is encouraged to compare each variation in detail with the theme, taking note of every discrepancy, and trying to see what effect it has on the form. Experiment, by changing these moments to more closely resemble the original theme, to better understand why Beethoven introduces these little enhancements.

Our next example of variation form will be Brahms's much more elaborate Variations and Fugue on a Theme by Handel. Handel's theme, in B♭ major, consists of two phrases, the first ending with a half cadence in measure 4, and the second ending with an authentic cadence, in measure 8 (Figure 10.3). Both phrases are four bars long, and the harmonic rhythm is very regular, apart from a slight deceleration at the cadence in measure 4. The motivic structure is also quite simple, with much repetition. As already mentioned, such a simple structure in the theme allows for much repetition

Figure 10.3. Brahms, Variations and Fugue on a Theme by Handel, theme

without attracting too much attention to itself. There is a gentle melodic climax rather early on, in measure 3. Placing the climax before the midpoint of the music is unusual, and in fact Brahms will reposition the climax much closer to the end in many of the variations.

There are twenty-five variations in all; we will examine each one to see how Brahms creates continuous novelty while always remaining faithful to Handel's theme.

The start of the first variation (Figure 10.4) immediately presents a vigorous contrast to the theme. While it follows the melodic contour of the latter, the staccato articulation, the more active, widely jumping accompaniment figure, and the wider registration suggest increased energy. Note the little syncopation at the end of the third beat in the right hand, in the first bar: a small detail that adds greatly to the interest of the motivic idea behind this variation. (The first two beats also contain offbeat accents, but the third beat adds a dotted note in the melody, making the attack on the fourth beat particularly weak.) Note also how Brahms now moves the climax,

Figure 10.4. Brahms, Variations and Fugue on a Theme by Handel, variation 1

originally in measure 3 of the theme, to measure 6, with a brilliant thirty-second-note run.

The next variation is also quite distinctive. Both hands are in the medium-high register, it is legato throughout, and the smooth melodic figuration is now in triplets, against plain eighth notes in the left hand. The gentle climax is placed right at the end. Although the phrase structure and the main harmonic punctuations faithfully follow the theme, the harmony within the phrases is now much more chromatic.

The third variation is lighter, with a kind of free stretto imitation between the hands, using a new appoggiatura motive. The climax arrives in the penultimate measure.

Another strong contrast follows: the fourth variation is very fully scored —a sort of pianistic tutti—and covers the widest register yet heard. It is quick, staccato, and characterized by offbeat accents. (Although the preceding variation, in eighth notes, also had a mildly syncopated feel, here the accent is on the weakest sixteenth note, creating greater rhythmic intensity.) The harmony in measures 2–3 now lightly touches on VI, whereas the original theme remained on I. Although the melodic sequence (mm. 5–6) in the original theme was barely noticeable, here, in the same bars, Brahms makes it more explicit, and dramatizes it further by moving momentarily into B♭ minor. The rising sequence reaches its culmination in measure 7, the climax of this variation. Both the sequence and this climactic moment are intensified by repeating the offbeat accents on several successive beats.

The contrast moving into variation 5, in B♭ minor, is quite dramatic. Apart from the change of mode, this variation is much smoother, all legato, with no offbeat accents. The register returns to the middle of the keyboard. The theme's melodic rise in measure 3 from scale degree 3 (D) now becomes the pretext for a new harmony: here the mediant replaces the theme's original tonic. The second half now begins by momentarily touching on F minor, and then the rise to the climax in measure 6 is underlined by the more intense Neapolitan harmony. The last two bars recede into a kind of echo of the opening. Although this is also true of the theme, the much greater range of the melodic line here makes the return, with its sudden fall from the climax register, much more salient.

The following variation is again in B♭ minor, based on what seems like the same motive, but now it is in the form of an austere two-part canon in octaves. In the second half, after the double bar, the left hand leads the canon, now by inversion.[2] The climax arrives once again in measure 6, after which the canon reverts to simple imitation (that is, not inverted).

Thus variations 5 and 6 form a little group, linked by their common minor mode and their smooth, legato character.

Variations 7 and 8 form another group. Their respective beginnings are shown in Figure 10.5. Note how they share a light staccato texture and a prominent repeated-note motive: an eighth note followed by two sixteenth notes. In the seventh variation, there is a crescendo to the cadence, in measure 4, and then a much bigger crescendo, scored much more thickly and covering a greater range, leading to the final cadence. In the eighth variation, Brahms uses invertible counterpoint to derive measures 3–4 from measures 1–2; only the cadence is different.[3] He also writes out the repeat of the second half, again using invertible counterpoint to give the music a new surface despite using the same material.

Figure 10.5. Brahms, Variations and Fugue on a Theme by Handel, variations 7 and 8

Variation 9 stands on its own. It is heavily scored, another tutti for the piano. The sixteenth-note momentum of the last few variations here disappears completely; in fact, the two-against-three rhythm has a distinct braking effect. To emphasize the more dramatic character, Brahms now moves to more remote keys: D major in measures 3–4, and then F♯ major in measures 9–10, each with a pedal point. These symmetrical, chromatic third relations are the most striking tonal shifts heard in the work so far. Here again the repeat of the second half of the theme is written out and varied.

Variation 10 returns to simpler harmony; the only new tonal color here, compared to the theme's original harmony, is some borrowing from B♭ minor. This variation is more playful, owing to the staccato articulation and the climbing up and down between registers: one easily imagines different orchestral families in dialogue with one another. The triplet rhythm on its own has not been heard since variation 2, and thus it is quite refreshing here.

Variations 11 and 12 are quiet and lyrical. The wide registral span of the preceding two variations has disappeared. Notice how the theme's final perfect cadence becomes a less energetic plagal progression in variation 11. After the energy of variations 7 through 10, the combined calm of these two is an effective contrast.

Variation 13, in B♭ minor, is slow and suddenly drops into the low register, with very thick arpeggiated chords in the left hand. The melody is doubled in sixths throughout. The repeats in both halves of the theme are written out: each one takes the melody of the preceding four bars and transposes it an octave higher. This simple contrast between registers adds new, refreshing color, giving the repeats an extra richness.

Variation 14, like the preceding variation, follows the theme's melodic contour quite faithfully, albeit using motives very different from those heard in the theme. Variation 14 is energetic, with continual leaping octaves in the left hand. Syncopated accents in the last two bars underline the final cadence.

Variations 15 and 16 form yet another small group, owing to the fact that they use the same motives, but with a vivid difference of character, created entirely by the dynamics and the musical texture. In variation 15 there is a dialogue between widely spaced, loud, full chords and tight figuration in the middle of the keyboard, whereas in variation 16 the chords become humorous, staccato dots of color. In effect, variation 16 is a variation on another variation (variation 15). The dynamic is quiet throughout variation 16.

Similarly, variations 17 and 18 share a common motive: the left-hand motive of the former comes back, syncopated, in variation 18, alternating between the hands. However, the remaining motives used in the two variations are different, as is the general texture. Variation 17 is made up of only eighth notes, and is rather calm after the two preceding, lively variations. Variation 18 adds flowing arpeggio figuration around the syncopated motive mentioned above. Although this variation is not explicitly contrapuntal, the alternation between the hands seems to be inspired by invertible counterpoint, and it creates a sense of dialogue, even in a texture consisting of just simple arpeggios.

Variation 19 (Figure 10.6) is for the first time a gentle dance movement in 12/8 time, inspired by a siciliano or a jig rhythm. After the wandering figuration of the preceding variation, it is stable and dignified. Both repeats are written out: in the first half, the repeat is simply played an octave higher, whereas the second half alternates two low bars with two high bars within each phrase. Another interesting textural detail in this variation is how, in each half, the first four bars feature the melody in the middle part (the lower voice in the right hand), and the second group of four bars places it on top. This is an excellent example of Brahms's well-known penchant for counterpoint. What is fascinating here is how Brahms moves around what we perceive as the foreground melody. For all intents and purposes, the shapes of the upper and lower lines don't change between measures 1–4 and measures 5–8. But he uses ornamentation of various kinds to draw our attention to one line over the other three (since the overall texture remains constant, in four parts). This also exemplifies Brahms's attention to details of orchestration, even when writing for solo piano: good orchestration requires that the main line not always stay in the same place.

### Var. XIX

Figure 10.6. Brahms, Variations and Fugue on a Theme by Handel, variation 19

Having ended the previous variation with both hands in the high register, variation 20 begins low, in what is essentially two-part counterpoint, thickened with homophonic inner parts. The harmony is very chromatic, a nice contrast to the relative simplicity of the preceding variation. Notice how the second half wanders more between registers, reaching its peak, once again, in the third bar before the end.

The twenty-first variation is an arabesque of two-against-three arpeggios, for the first time on another tonic, here G minor. After twenty variations centering around B♭, the tonal contrast is quite dramatic, despite the quiet character of the variation itself.

Variation 22 returns to the home key and takes place all in the high register. It is built entirely over a bell-like B♭ pedal. Given the harmonic variety in the theme and in the preceding variations, this pedal creates a very effective contrast of harmony.

Variations 23–25 form a final group, gradually rising and gaining energy. Variation 23 is low and staccato, except for its last two bars, which suddenly rise into the higher register. Variation 24 alternates rushing sixteenth notes between the hands, and explodes even more dramatically in its final bar into an extravagant flourish in the high register. The effect is quite stunning because, for the first time in this variation, both hands have sixteenth notes.

The last variation, vigorous and affirmative, provides the climax to the set. There is only one accidental to be seen in the whole variation: the E♮ that appears as a fleeting neighbor note to F in the thirty-second-note upbeat at the end of measure 4. This extreme tonal simplicity contributes to the variation's sense of finality and directness.

The set ends with a fugue (Figure 10.7), whose subject is inspired by the first two bars of the theme. After the repeated start-and-stop nature of

Figure 10.7. Brahms, Variations and Fugue on a Theme by Handel, fugue theme

the variations, the continual drive of the fugue reaches a huge climax over a dominant pedal, a fitting culmination to this major work.

Although the student project described below will be less ambitious than the Brahms, the Handel Variations are a valuable source of ideas for variation treatment. While rigorously respecting the theme's phrasing, and at times its melody as well, Brahms plays with the following elements, at various times and in various degrees:

- details of harmony; contrast between diatonic and chromatic harmony
- motives
- tempo, rhythm, and articulation

- register
- texture, ranging from completely homophonic to quite elaborate counter-point
- placement of the climax within the individual variations

We have already noted how Brahms groups the variations into units of two or three variations, which helps to mitigate the squareness inherent in the necessary periodicity of the form. By definition, the variations within such groups are not as strongly contrasting. In fact, the degree of contrast between variations is itself subject to variation, since the same amount of contrast between many successive pairs of variations would in itself become monotonous. Most of the contrasts from one variation to another are moderate, but with occasional more surprising juxtapositions.

Note also the overall progression in the pacing of the more energetic variations, ranging over the whole set. The first example, variation 4, is simply a local contrast to the preceding variations. Variation 9 follows two quick but lighter variations. Variations 23 and 24 provide a clear build-up toward variation 25, making it the climactic variation of the set. The culmination of the fugue, at the end of the entire work, is the most emphatic peak of all. This hierarchy of climaxes gives the overall form a well-directed shape.

ELABORATIONS

Both sets of variations we have examined here are very rigorous about respecting the formal outline of the theme.

It is also possible to play with the proportions of the theme in at least some of the variations. For example, in the theme from Fauré's Op. 73 mentioned above, several phrases are repeated. Some variations do not include these repetitions, while others do. The effect is to make the individual phrases quite recognizable in the variations, but the overall form is not entirely predictable from one to the next.

Occasionally the composer may feel the need to add a little transition between variations, as in Schubert's Impromptu, D. 935, No. 3.

Haydn (Piano Sonata in F minor, Hob. XVII: 6) experimented with double variations, alternating variations between two contrasting themes.

Franck's *Variations symphoniques* is in effect a piano concerto in one long movement, and combines variation form and sonata form. This allows for a more dramatic structure than a simple variation form would permit. The variation sections are also continuous, not separated by full stops, and material from the theme reappears in the sonata sections.

Finally, we need to mention the passacaglia and the chaconne, two contrapuntal versions of the variation form. They are always continuous: there is no stop between one variation and the next. Indeed, part of the art in composing a passacaglia or a chaconne lies in the details of how the individual variations are joined together. Often the texture of a new variation will begin slightly before the actual first note of the theme, or the old texture will continue a bit after the final note. There may also be some contrapuntal overlapping of material.

As in the Classical variation form, grouping is used to create momentum across variations, and the last variation is almost always set off in some way, so that it breaks the regularity of the overall form and creates a stronger sense of finality. The most famous example is the Bach Passacaglia and Fugue in C minor, BWV 582, for organ.

For a more recent example, the last movement of Shostakovich's Fifteenth Symphony is an elaborate passacaglia for orchestra, which plays with the proportions of the theme itself as the movement intensifies toward its climax. Unusually for a passacaglia, it also has an introduction, which recalls thematic material from other movements in the symphony.


## THE VARIATION PROJECT

**1** Analyze variations 1–4 in the first movement of Beethoven's Piano Sonata in A-flat major, Op. 26, comparing them with the theme. Look at the cadences, the details of the harmony, the motives, the placement of melodic peaks, and Beethoven's use of changes of texture and register. Compare the varying degrees of contrast between each variation and the next. Try to quantify them on a scale from 1 to 5.

**2** Using the theme in Figure 10.8, write a set of between five and ten variations.

First, analyze the theme's phrase and harmonic structure: where are the main punctuations, and what is their relative strength? This will provide the frame for the variations.

Next, using the Brahms variations as a source of ideas, sketch out the first few bars of several possible variations on the theme. Sketch more than the number of variations that will be needed. This will allow for more choice as to the final arrangement.

Figure 10.8. The theme for the variation project

Examining these sketches for variation beginnings, try out various orders for them. The beginning will be sufficiently representative, since within each variation there will be a high degree of consistency. Aim for a few strong contrasts in the series, but also for groupings of two or three variations that are relatively similar. There should be a climactic variation, usually the last one, or the penultimate one if the last movement is in a different form, as in the Brahms.

Now work out each variation in detail. Check the overall order to see if the determined contrasts and groupings are as effective as planned, when listened to in context. Is there a palpable progression to a climax within the set? Make changes to the order as needed to fulfill these requirements.

Last, decide how to end. Will the last variation be in a completely different form? Students who have studied sufficient counterpoint may wish to try composing a fugue as an ending. Another alternative would be a simple cadential extension to the last variation, as in the Beethoven example (from his Op. 135) discussed above.

# 11 CONTRASTING

In any but the shortest musical forms, occasional significant contrasts are essential, in order to renew the listener's interest and to throw important ideas into relief. But not all contrasts are created equal. As a rule, the larger the form, the stronger and the more varied the contrasts it will require. Once a given idea has been presented, finding the appropriate degree of contrast can be a challenge. The solution will depend on where in the piece it will occur, and also on the amount and the kind of transition connecting the respective ideas. (We will discuss transitions in detail in chapter 12.)

It is important to note that over a whole piece there will always be more continuity than contrast. Too much novelty, arriving too often, just breaks up the music into small, unconnected fragments. This makes it harder for the listener to hold the various ideas in memory, and the music quickly becomes incoherent. The exact proportions of continuity and contrast will vary, depending on the mood and the form, but as a rule, too many strong contrasts in close proximity tend to destroy musical continuity and unity.[1]

As a working method, the student is advised be alert to moments when the listener's interest needs renewal, and then to roughly quantify the amount of novelty required. This will make it easier to adjust details as necessary, adding to or subtracting from the amount of contrast. Given the many possible degrees of contrast, in this situation a scale of 1 to 10 will be useful, where 1 is almost imperceptible and 10 is the musical equivalent of an earthquake.

Musical character results from the way the various elements making up the music—the melodic line, the harmony, the rhythm, the articulation, the tempo, the register, the timbre, and so forth—interact. The level of contrast is a function of how many of these dimensions change at the same time, by how much, and how fast they evolve.[2] Note that in some cases various aspects of the music may temper each other as well, making a given contrast more subtle.

Thus, contrast is usually best thought of not as just one single change, but rather as the result of several changes at once. To take a simple example, transposing a motive down an octave does not in itself create a strong contrast. We also need to consider other aspects of the two presentations: tempo, rhythm, dynamics, articulation, harmony, and so forth. If we transpose the motive and also change the timbre, the contrast will be somewhat more marked than with the transposition alone. The more elements change, the greater the degree of contrast: the quantified number (out of 10) will increase. If many elements stay the same, the contrast will be mild; if most of them change, the contrast will be strong. Also, within each musical dimension, there is a range of possible change; for example, one could transpose the original phrase by one octave or by two octaves. Again, finding the right amount is critical. It is not enough just to know that "it feels wrong"; the composer needs to know, at least roughly, by how much.

It is worth noting that contrasts in different dimensions are not all equal in impact. For example, changes in harmony, unless they are very crude, are usually less potent than changes in timbre and register. This has to do with the way we process sound information. Evolution has made us use information like register and timbre as a way of distinguishing the sources of sounds in the environment, in order to quickly notice danger. Perception of harmony is much more subtle.[3]

Here are a few examples of quantifying musical contrast. If, for example, the timbre changes from flute to piccolo, that is a mild change, say 1 or 2 out of 10. Changing from flute to tuba is a lot more striking, say, 5. If the change from flute to tuba is accompanied by a significant change in tempo, the contrast will be even more dramatic, perhaps 7 out of 10. When assigning a number, the student should list the musical elements that stay the same and the elements that change, then attempt to roughly measure by how much each element changes.

In the first two bars of Figure 11.1, Beethoven presents the main idea of the movement. Measures 3–4 then repeat it, changing only the last note. This would merit only a 1 out of 10 on our scale of contrasts. Measure 5 begins with the same motive once again, an octave higher, in violin 1. The accompaniment however is now sustained harmony instead of just doubling of the main line. Tonality, meter, the scoring, orchestration, and the tempo all stay the same. This would receive perhaps a 3 on our scale: the first four bars still have more elements in common than elements that change. Such

**Allegro**

Figure 11.1. Beethoven, String Quartet in F major, Op. 18, No. 1, first movement

minor changes are of course appropriate here, considering that they all take place within the same phrase.

The next two excerpts are from Mendelssohn's *Rondo capriccioso*: the introduction and the beginning of the rondo. Since the introduction (Figure 11.2) is meant to evoke a mood quite different from that in the following quick section (Figure 11.3), there is considerably more contrast between these two ideas than in the Beethoven example above. When the quick section arrives, in measure 27, the slow introduction makes its character much more vivid, throwing it into relief through contrast.[4]

In this case, apart from the much faster tempo, the mode is also different (E major becomes E minor), the meter has changed, and the motives, articulation, and general register of the passage are all new as well. The only elements that have not changed are the timbre (solo piano) and the overall harmonic style. This contrast would deserve 7 or 8 on our ten-point scale.

Figure 11.2. Mendelssohn, *Rondo capriccioso*, Op. 14, introduction

Figure 11.3. Mendelssohn, *Rondo capriccioso*, Op. 14, mm. 27–31

For a more current example, such stronger levels of contrast are very often seen in role-playing video games. These games normally have an exploration mode and a fighting mode. The music for the former is usually continuous, noncontrasting, texturally static, often even looped. Once the confrontation begins, there is a sudden, drastic contrast, suggesting combat. These abrupt contrasts should be in the upper numbers of our scale, otherwise the mood suggested by the music will not adequately support the action.

Now let us work out a practical example, from a short, lyrical piece for solo piano, showing concretely how to adjust degrees of contrast. Version 1 of the phrase shown in Figure 11.4 changes very abruptly when the legato, singing line in measures 1–3 becomes the jerky rhythm of measures 4–5. Such a sudden contrast in midphrase is inappropriate in a short, quiet piece. It presents the listener with too much novelty to process all at once, thus creating a distinct formal bump. Although timbre and tempo remain constant, this contrast would merit perhaps a 7 or an 8 out of 10 on our scale of contrasts, owing to the simultaneous new register, new motive, new articulation, modulating harmony, and suddenly loud dynamics. What we need here is something much milder, perhaps a 2 or a 3 out of 10.

To fix the problem, we can start with the above list of what has changed. The list is too long, and as a result the degree of change is too strong here, producing an overly dramatic new character. Knowing this, we can adjust the phrase to a more appropriate level of contrast.

Versions 2 and 3 each propose such subtler levels of contrast. In version 2 we keep the melodic contour and the somewhat distant modulation of the original. However, register, rhythm, dynamics, articulation, and texture now stay closer to those in the first part of the phrase. This reduces the contrast to around 2 or 3 out of 10.

Figure 11.4. A very abrupt contrast, followed by smoother versions of the same phrase

In version 3, we maintain the contrasting rhythm and articulation of the original, but we avoid changing register, and we keep the dynamics soft and the modulation closer to the home key. The resulting contrast is thus around a 3 or a 4.

In each case, by changing fewer aspects of the music at once, and by more modest amounts, we arrive at a more convincing continuation for the given phrase. There are other possible solutions here, but the point is that having a specific and detailed idea of what is wrong, and by how much, makes the problem easy to fix. Listing the elements that create the abrupt contrast gives us a very precise tool for adjusting the details by just the right amount.

Note that we could also have made the change somewhat more forceful than in versions 2 and 3, if that were desired, using the same method; this approach is very flexible.

Of course, we could also have fixed these problems by creating a smooth transition between the two ideas, as discussed in the next chapter, but for the moment we are assuming that we want to preserve the length and overall contour of the phrase.

Here is another example, for a different kind of musical situation. Let us suppose that our apprentice composer needs two successive themes for a movie, each to be associated with a specific character. The first, as shown in

Figure 11.5, is quiet and mysterious. For another character, who is somehow in conflict with the first, the first idea to suggest itself is shown in Figure 11.6.

Figure 11.5. A quiet, mysterious theme

Figure 11.6. First sketch for a possible contrasting theme

The problem here is that the second theme, while it might be satisfactory in another context on its own, is not sufficiently different from the first. It is shorter and the timbre and register have changed, but both ideas are in similar their tonal/modal regions, both are in the same tempo and dynamic, both are legato, and they also show some rhythmic/motivic similarity: the motive of four eighth notes followed by a longer note. On our scale of contrasts, this first attempt merits 3 or 4 out of 10.

How can it be made more distinctive? Figure 11.7 is a better version. In this revision, the theme has been transposed to a different key for a stronger, immediate tonal contrast, the articulation has been changed to staccato, and the rhythmic motives are more obviously different from the first theme, owing to the added offbeat accents. This raises the contrast level to around 7 or 8 out of 10.

Figure 11.7. An improved version of the contrasting theme

If the narrative situation requires more obvious tonal continuity between the two, Figure 11.8 provides an alternative solution. As in the previ-

**Allegro**

Figure 11.8. Another improved version of the contrasting theme

ous example, the articulation changes to staccato, but now the dynamic is loud. The result, again, is more novelty, but within the same tonal region as the original idea.

Again, there are of course many other possibilities. The method presented here is simply a way to explore musical contrasts in a controlled way.

When composing a larger work, the composer faces two tasks with regard to important contrasts: inventing the new material, and getting the degree of novelty just right for the musical context. While there is no simple rule for knowing the exact amount of contrast required in a given situation, usually the composer will have a sense of whether the music produces a disturbing bump. If so, it means the contrast is too marked, or that it needs a more gradual transition.

Once having invented the contrasting ideas, the composer can use the method described above, and/or the techniques of transition described in the next chapter, to fit them precisely into place. Since both of these approaches function in essentially the same way—by listing and measuring the amount of change in each aspect of the music—they are easily compatible.

Another principle applies to contrasts within a large work: do not repeatedly follow the same idea with the same contrast. The same material followed by the same contrast will not actually provide the same level of contrast, since the listener, having already heard the given succession of ideas, is no longer as surprised by it. Thus, the effect of the contrast will actually go down by a point or two.

Figure 11.9 is an example from Aaron Copland's *Appalachian Spring* Suite. Before rehearsal 6, the character is quiet: the clarinet plays a slow, lyrical phrase. Then a new, much more vigorous motive enters. Although the timbre of this new motive still consists of strings plus piano, the articulation changes drastically. The register is also much higher, and the low register disappears completely. The key remains the same (A major), but the tempo is significantly faster. On our scale of contrasts, this ranks quite high, perhaps 7 or 8 out of 10.

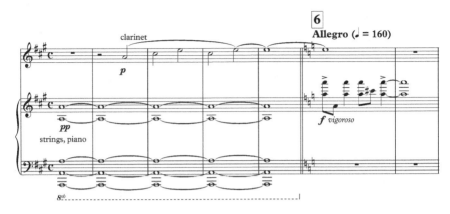

Figure 11.9. Aaron Copland, *Appalachian Spring*, Ballet Suite for 13 Instruments. © Copyright 1945 The Aaron Copland Fund for Music, Inc. Copyright Renewed. Boosey & Hawkes, Inc., Sole Licensee. Reprinted by permission.

Much later in the piece, before rehearsal 55, another contrast arrives, preceded by the same music, although now in A♭ major and with the lyrical theme played by the flute (Figure 11.10). This time, however, the tempo change is less drastic, and although the change of register resembles that heard in Figure 11.9, the character remains lyrical and the articulation legato. As a result, the contrast is perhaps 4 out of 10.

The point here is that the same music precedes these two contrasts, but it does not lead to the same destination. The contrast at rehearsal 55 contributes to the overall unity of the form, owing to the familiarity evoked by

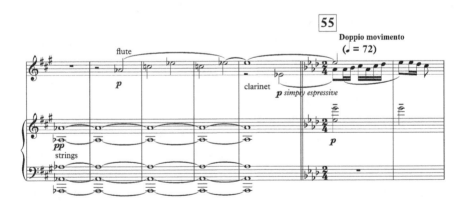

Figure 11.10. Aaron Copland, *Appalachian Spring*, Ballet Suite for 13 Instruments. © Copyright 1945 The Aaron Copland Fund for Music, Inc. Copyright Renewed. Boosey & Hawkes, Inc., Sole Licensee. Reprinted by permission.

the lyrical phrase, but also to its richness, since it takes the listener to a new, unexpected destination.

## EXERCISES

**1** Compare the listed phrases in the following works. Which elements change, and by how much? Which elements do they have in common? Assign each one a value on a scale of contrasts from 1 to 10. Note that all the comparisons are either between phrases that immediately succeed each other, or between important themes in the same movement.

- Haydn, Symphony No. 94, first movement: compare measures 18–22 with measures 22–32.
- Franck, Prelude, Chorale, and Fugue for piano: compare measures 1–7 in the Prelude with measures 8–11.
- Brahms, Symphony No. 2, third movement: compare measures 1–4 with measures 33–36, and also with measures 126–31.
- Mozart, Piano Sonata in F major, K. 332, first movement: compare measures 1–4 with measures 5–12.
- Mozart, Piano Sonata in C minor, K. 457, third movement: compare measures 1–8 with measures 26–30.
- Beethoven, Symphony No. 7, second movement: compare measures 3–6 with measures 101–09.
- Prokofiev, Piano Sonata No. 2, first movement: compare measures 1–8 with measures 8–11.

**2** Figure 11.11 shows two successive ideas within the same phrase. The contrast introduced in measure 5 by the brass is quite extreme. Without changing the length of the existing music, make the effect more subtle by adjusting motives, dynamics, timbre, register, and so forth as needed. It is not necessary to change

Figure 11.11. Exercise 2

all these things; just make sufficient changes to bring the contrast down from, say, 8 out of 10 to about 4. Propose two different solutions.

**3** Figure 11.12—a longer version of the example used above to illustrate composing contrasting themes for a film—has the opposite problem: it becomes monotonous toward the end. Make alterations to the last four or five bars to add more contrast, moving it from about 1 or 2 out of 10 to 5 or 6. The new version should not only create more interest, but also suggest that we are gradually moving away from the original idea. Again, do not modify the overall length of the phrase.

Figure 11.12. Exercise 3

**4** Sketch three different ideas, for string quartet, wind quintet, and solo piano, respectively. Then generate variants of each idea with various degrees of novelty, to be used as contrasting material later in the same movements. Of the three variants, one should be a mild contrast (say, 2 or 3 out of 10), another moderate (5 or 6), and one very powerful (8 or 9).

# 12 CONNECTING

In a sense all music requires connecting musical ideas. The listener hears one thing, which then evolves into something else in a coherent way, so as to constantly maintain interest in a way that makes sense.

Here is Richard Wagner, discussing transitions in his own music:

I recognize now that the characteristic fabric of my music (always of course in the closest association with the poetic design), that my friends now regard as so new and so significant, owes its construction above all to the extreme sensitivity that guides me in the direction of mediating and providing an intimate bond between all the different moments of transition that separate the extremes of mood. I should now like to call my most delicate and profound art the art of transition, for the whole fabric of my art is made up of such transitions: all that is abrupt and sudden is now repugnant to me; it is often unavoidable and necessary, but even then it may not occur unless the mood has been clearly prepared in advance so that the suddenness of the transition appears to come as a matter of course. My greatest masterpiece in the art of the most delicate and gradual transition is without doubt the great scene in the second act of *Tristan and Isolde* [i.e., scene 2]. The opening of this scene presents a life overflowing with all the most violent emotions—its ending the most solemn and heartfelt longing for death. These are the pillars: and now you see, child, how I have joined these pillars together, and how the one of them leads over into the other. This, after all, is the secret of my musical form, that, in its unity and clarity over an expanse that encompasses every detail, I may be bold enough to claim has never before been dreamt of. If only you knew how that guiding emotion has inspired me to invent musical devices that would never have occurred to me previously (devices in terms of rhythm, as well as harmonic and melodic development), you would realize that even in the most specialized branches of art no truth is ever invented that does not derive from such grand primary motives. That, then, is art![1]

Although Wagner is discussing his operas in this quote, it really applies to all music. The way musical ideas are connected is at the core of music as a temporal art. One thing must lead to the next, and for the composer to do this convincingly means to constantly create satisfying transitions between motives, phrases, contrasting ideas, and entire sections.

All music, at any given moment, includes both elements that stay the same and others that change. The art of transition involves using common elements as a kind of structural glue when joining ideas. Thus, while introducing something new, the composer must at the same time stimulate the listener's memory, thereby associating the new with the familiar, to make its arrival feel consequent and coherent.

Transitions in program music and in opera are normally dictated by the narrative. For example, at the beginning of Verdi's *Otello*, as the ship carrying Otello and his men finally leaves the storm behind and comes safely into port, the music gradually evolves from the harsh waves of wind and rain, which begin the act, to the quieter atmosphere that prevails as they finally arrive safely on land. By the time the Cypriots cry "Vittoria!" and "Evviva!" for the last time (at rehearsal R in the Ricordi orchestral score), Verdi has already begun this transition, now to be completed by an instrumental interlude, after which the choir sings, "Si calma la bufera" (The storm is subsiding). This last phrase occurs right after an ominous cluster in the organ pedals, heard continuously since the beginning of the act, finally disappears.

If we examine the interlude at rehearsal R more closely, we see the same motives being repeated in gradually descending sequence, until the bass lands on a sustained pedal E. The rushing sixteenth-note rhythm heard underneath the agitated staccato eighth notes begins to alternate with chromatic scales in legato eighth notes. The quicker sixteenth notes gradually disappear entirely, and after a few last flurries of dissipating energy, the music settles down to the calm evoked by the text.

The rhythmic slowing down, the registral descent, the change from staccato to legato, and the arrival of the sustained low E all combine here to effect the smooth transition.

Transitions are also everywhere to be seen in instrumental music, since as soon as any music includes major contrasts, the composer must have varied ways to make them arrive convincingly, with differing degrees of surprise.

In this chapter we will first focus on how to effect gradual transitions, where the listener does not feel any bump during the change. Later we will have a few words to say about several other kinds of more sudden and dramatic transitions. In any case, even when a certain amount of surprise is needed, once the student has mastered the art of making smooth transitions successfully, it is easy to make them less gradual. The method proposed here gives the student complete control over the degree of continuity/surprise required.

Recall that for music to have any character at all, it has to limit its focus: that implies choosing all aspects of the music with a definite character in mind. A piece with random notes, random rhythms and tempi, and randomly changing timbres and register is not likely to interest the listener for any length of time. If the composer combines the various dimensions of the music in a less arbitrary, more coherent way, there will be a clearer focus on a specific character. This focus allows us to remember the various musical gestures more easily and to develop clear associations and expectations about them, which the composer can then manipulate to shape the form of the piece.

A transition between two musical ideas/characters thus always has to address all the dimensions of the music, at least to some degree. Again, it is important to remember that, apart from the pitches and rhythms we see in the score, all music takes place at a specific tempo, in a specific register, with specific articulations, and in a specific timbre and texture. These things are not visually as salient in the score as pitches and rhythms, but they remain very obvious to the listener.

The fundamental principle governing smooth transitions is that multiple dimensions of the music should never change simultaneously. Some aspects of the music will always remain constant, and others will change in varying degrees and at different rates. If we quantify contrasts between ideas from 1 (imperceptible) to 10 (earth-shattering), no matter how big the contrast between the two ideas, each step along the way should never feel like more than a 1 or a 2. A corollary of this principle is that the more contrast between the ideas in question, the longer it will take to move smoothly between them.

The composer needs to be constantly aware of how each aspect of the music contributes to its character. The things that contribute most strongly to the musical character are the things that will create the most disruption when altered. If I listen to a piece for solo cello, the cello timbre itself is a large part of the expressive character, and also a powerful unifying element of the piece. I normally will take for granted that the only instrumental timbre I will hear will be the cello. If I suddenly hear two notes on the trumpet, it raises a red flag. Pizzicato cello, while not as surprising as the trumpet, still represents an important change. Even within the closed world of a cello, played only arco, the composer still can vary pitch, rhythm, articulation, tempo, and register. The bowed cello timbre creates a basic level of unity, and the changing elements provide variety. Note again that unity rarely involves just one dimension: most of the time, fewer things change than remain constant. A constant, high rate of change in many dimensions at the same time is extremely demanding for the listener, and easily creates incoherence, since the listener begins to have difficulty keeping track of consistent elements in the music.

Things that stay the same tend to fade into the perceptual background, like the cello timbre above. For evolutionary reasons, our attention is drawn to what is new in the environment.[2] In music, if only the pitches are changing, that is what we will notice. If the piece uses a motive built around repeated notes, their rhythmic grouping, and perhaps changes of timbre, register, and so forth will come to the foreground as they evolve during the passage in question.[3]

The key to composing a successful transition lies in deciding what remains constant and what changes at every moment. The composer needs to find common ground to hold together every stage of a transition, so that there is never too much novelty all at once.

In the example from Verdi's *Otello* discussed above, the harmony stays fairly stable, moving around E during the registral descent and the general slowing down. The timbre also does not change much through the whole passage: the running sixteenth notes all stay in the strings and the eighth notes remain in the winds. Verdi is very careful to balance the changing aspects of the music with the more stable ones.

Now we will apply this method to a concrete example. As an experiment, we are going to recompose the beginning of the first movement of Haydn's Piano Sonata in F major, Hob. XVI: 23. Figure 12.1 shows its original form. The piece begins with the idea in measures 1–4. By measures 13–14, Haydn is presenting a new theme. How does he get there?

First, from the end of measure 4 to measure 6, we hear an ornamented version of measures 1–2. While the second part of the phrase, which starts at the end of measure 6, takes a different turn from measures 3–4, it does maintain the little arpeggio motive of four thirty-second notes. When the cadence arrives (mm. 11–12) we hear a four-note scale motive in sixteenth notes (in m. 11), while measure 12 has an appoggiatura motive, which recalls the ones in measures 4, 7, and 8. When the new idea begins, at the end

Figure 12.1. Haydn, Piano Sonata in F major, Hob. XVI: 23, opening

of measure 12, we hear the now familiar thirty-second-note pattern that began the second phrase (at the end of m. 4), now followed by a descending scale, echoing measure 11. This scale ends with an ornamented appoggiatura, recalling measure 12. The articulation in measure 13 is now staccato, but this and the alternating accompaniment figure are all that is really new, along with the gentle tonal shift into D minor.

Thus, whenever Haydn introduces novelty, he also takes pains to stimulate the listener's memory at the same time with something familiar, creating an easy-to-follow chain of associations that leads toward the destination. This helps to make the musical flow more coherent and convincing. Also, let us not forget how many things we take for granted about this passage, which help unify it: the timbre (solo piano), the tempo, the overall key (F major), the general register of the top line, and the light articulation. Although we tend not to notice these things, because they are constant, changing any one of them would increase the degree of contrast.

Now let us compare Haydn's original music with the modified version shown in Figure 12.2, where the new idea arrives with a distinct bump. By removing the appoggiatura at the cadence in measure 12, as well as the four thirty-second notes that originally began the new theme, and by changing the scale contour in measure 13 to zigzag leaps, we have removed three important elements that held this transition together. Thus this alternative version is much less convincing.

Figure 12.2. Haydn, Piano Sonata in F major, Hob. XVI: 23, opening modified

## PROCEDURE FOR COMPOSING A TRANSITION

It is impossible to compose a transition without knowing both the departure and arrival points; this would be like leaving on a trip without knowing one's destination.

Once the composer knows both the starting and ending points of the transition, the next step is to list the differences between the two. The list can be in any order, but it is critical to include changes in register, timbre, tempo, texture, and articulation, in addition to pitch, harmony, and rhythm. Once the list is established, never change more than one item at a time while composing the transition.

Again, we can see that very gradual transitions will take time, and that the more things need to change, the more time will be required: the duration of a smooth transition is generally proportional to the number of elements that need to change, as well as to how much each of them changes.

Note that this procedure for effecting a smooth transition makes it easy to introduce more drama or intensity if desired: simply changing two elements at a time, or making a larger change in one dimension, will have considerable effect. Keeping precise track of the number of things that have changed, and how fast they are evolving, allows the composer to exercise fine control of transitional sections.

For a more recent example of a smooth transition, let us look at how Henri Dutilleux joins the first and second movements of his cello concerto

*Tout un monde lointain.* At the end of the first movement, the cello rises, with a very fast scale, from the low register to some of the very highest notes it can play. Timpani and basses punctuate the rise, with attacks on three pitches: G♯, B, and D. At the top of the scale, the chord shown in Figure 12.3 appears, bouncing in quickly repeated notes, in the strings. Notice that this chord contains the G♯–D tritone just heard in the timpani and basses, and that its outer notes are G♯ and A. The cello now moves, tremolo, between G, G♯, and A, still in its highest register, finally slowing to pause on the top A. By this point all that is left of the orchestra is a mysterious, extremely soft roll in the suspended cymbal.

Figure 12.3. Henri Dutilleux, *Tout un monde lointain*, harmony from the end of the first movement

Then the cello leaps down an octave, and this new, lower A becomes the first note in a calm, descending melodic phrase, which begins the second movement. This new phrase contains all the notes in the chord above, adding E and D♯ exactly in the middle, which changes the color of the harmonic world at this key point. The G♮ also disappears, for the moment. After only one bar, this phrase is quietly interrupted by harp and basses (pizzicato and arco together), sounding the G♯–D tritone once again.

What Dutilleux has done here is to unify quite strongly contrasting musical characters by creating salient melodic and harmonic associations between the end of the first movement and the start of the second. To bridge this transition the composer has used common tones in the harmony, the timpani gesture, and a simple, overall rising-and-falling contour to unify the music's evolution into something new. On the other hand, the rhythm and the tempo change quite a lot, as do various aspects of the orchestration.

## TURNING POINTS: CADENCES, CLIMAXES

Apart from smooth transitions, there are also a few situations that lend themselves to more abrupt transformations.

For example, cadences and climaxes, since they are significant moments, can become turning points in the music, where the composer can overlap one idea into another, contrasting character in a convincing way.

Figure 12.4 is an example from the introduction to the first movement of Beethoven's *Harp* Quartet, Op. 74. Here a cadence, which is also a small, local climax, acts as a turning point.

Figure 12.4. Beethoven, String Quartet in E-flat major, Op. 74 (*Harp*), introduction

In measures 18–24, Beethoven is building up to the arrival of the main theme of the Allegro. The long, rising sequence in the first violin, combined with the denser texture in measures 21–24 and the crescendo added in measure 24, reaches a peak with the final tonic, on the first beat of measure 25. But the first beat of measure 25 is also the beginning of the coming theme.[4] This overlapping[5] creates tremendous momentum into the new section. Perhaps a lesser composer would have stopped at the cadence, ending the phrase in measure 25, and then begun the Allegro in the next bar. But this would have resulted in a distinct loss of energy. Beethoven's overlapping technique creates an effective musical turning point at a strategic moment, where it will attract a lot of attention and maintain musical momentum.

A turning point can sometimes be much shorter, a sort of interruption, as in Figure 12.5. Imagine that we have reached a point in a video game where we are resting in a peaceful place. The music is looping measures 2 and 3 continuously for a while, perhaps transposing them occasionally with mild random variations of tempo to avoid monotony. Suddenly, danger appears: this is signaled by the chord in measure 4. (Note that this chord does not necessarily arrive after the end of measure 3; it could arrive at any moment during the loop.) The mood dramatically changes with the arrival of the xylophone/marimba chord. Note, however, the grace notes that precede the chord. They go by very quickly, but they still provide a tiny rush into the interruption, a kind of preparation. These grace notes help make the sudden chord sound less random.

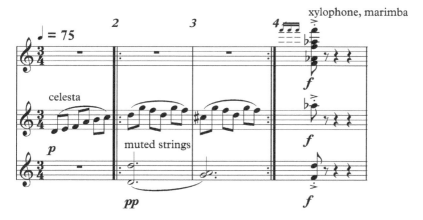

Figure 12.5. A video-game transition

The reason this kind of interruption is very useful in video-game music arises from the games' nonlinear structure. Since the player's choices are never entirely predictable, determining the timing of important events is sometimes impossible, making long-range transitions impossible to plan.

## CROSS-CUTTING

There is a distinctive way of moving between ideas that is a major feature of Stravinsky's style, and is occasionally seen elsewhere: cross-cutting. It can be a very useful technique in certain contexts.

The opening of Stravinsky's *Symphony of Psalms* (Figure 12.6) is a good example of how cross-cutting works. This passage presents two distinct ideas, juxtaposed very abruptly: a sharp, staccato chord, played by most of the orchestra, and smooth arpeggios in the oboe and the bassoon. This kind of strong contrast, in itself, is not unusual at the start of a large-scale work. But what follows is eleven more bars of alternation between these two gestures. After a final interruption by the staccato chord, in measure 14, Stravinsky leads into a more stable section in measure 15. The new section is based on the arpeggio idea, which has gotten longer at each presentation (mm. 2, 5, and 9) during the introduction, gradually pointing us toward the new section. This more stable section in turn prepares the entry of the choir.

The important point here is that despite the frequent alternation between the two ideas in measures 1–14, the listener nonetheless senses a formal progression, increasingly emphasizing the arpeggio idea over the staccato chords. It is as if, in cross-cutting, there is always a sort of confrontation

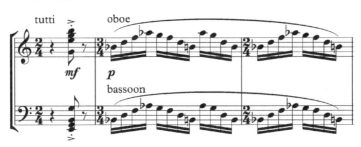

Figure 12.6. Stravinsky, *Symphony of Psalms*, opening. © Copyright 1931 by Hawkes & Son (London) Ltd. Revised version: © Copyright 1948 by Hawkes & Son (London) Ltd. U.S. copyright renewed. Reprinted by Permission of Boosey & Hawkes, Inc.

between two ideas, one of which eventually has to "win." Note that cross-cutting loses interest if the timing of the cuttings becomes overly predictable.

One last general point, before we look at transitions as separate sections: in the course of a whole movement, not all transitions should be constructed in exactly the same way. Varying the elements that remain constant and those that change, as well as altering the overall pacing of the transitions, will ensure sufficient variety of construction. Or, for example, several smooth transitions might be followed by another, more abrupt one, using a climax as a turning point.

## THE TRANSITION AS A LARGER SECTION

In a movement in sonata form, there is usually a section that serves to connect the two main thematic areas. We will examine the way Brahms makes the transition between the first and second themes (which start in mm. 1 and 82, respectively) in the first movement of his Second Symphony, to see how the above techniques are applied over a larger span of music.

Note that while some analysts consider the beginning of a transition section as the material following a clear, cadential ending of the first theme, in practice matters are not always quite so neat. As we will see, the first main theme in the Brahms movement does not end on a conclusive cadence, but rather on a dominant pedal. Instead of a clear stop and restart, the music just seems to gradually open up and become more exploratory. Given the fact that both main themes are quite lyrical in character, a more definitive stop would have disrupted the gentle flow of the music. For our purposes, the goal is not to pinpoint one specific bar as the start of the transition, but rather to see how Brahms gradually makes the music evolve from one idea to another.

Figure 12.7 is a catalog of the main thematic material of this movement, up to the arrival of the second group of themes (*f*).

Figure 12.7. Thematic material in the first movement of Brahms, Symphony No. 2

Theme *a* begins the symphony. In D major, it has two components: the neighbor-note figure in the low strings, and then the four-bar phrase, appearing first in the horns and then in the winds.

The music arrives at a dominant pedal in measure 14, modulating to A major, in which key idea *b* arrives at measure 19. This idea picks up the neighbor-note figure that started theme *a*, extending it and giving it a new rhythmic profile, suggesting a kind of hemiola: despite the triple meter, this motive is grouped in twos. This is a beautiful example of counterpoint knitting together two ideas, as the strings and winds overlap with different rhythmic profiles. A held E (dominant of the coming key, A major) in the strings starts in measure 17. As the winds reach a peak on a high E in measure 19, the strings take up the same note, now in the same register as the winds, and begin to sing idea *b*. The overlapping winds slow down to end their phrase several bars later. This arrangement has the effect of shifting the listener's focus at a key moment—a high point of the phrase —to something new, while the overlap smoothes over any possible discontinuity.

Then motive *b* descends gradually in the strings, reaching a stop in measure 31, but without a harmonic cadence. In measures 32–43, Brahms alternates between neutral low brass chords and the high winds, who return to the neighbor-note motive already heard in the fourth bar of theme *a* and in the second measure of *b*.

In measure 44 theme *c* arrives, in the violins. It also begins with a neighbor-note motive, but in a new rhythm. The last statement of the winds before this new idea (mm. 42–43) prepares the exact same pitches that begin it: A, G♯, A. The accompaniment to theme *c* in measure 44 is new: a gentle eighth-note tremolo figure in the lower strings.

Starting in measure 54, the new idea (*c*) takes on a more agitated character, allowing the gentle accompaniment figure to become more vigorous. It becomes staccato in measure 59, producing figure *d*. The orchestra now presents motive *d* in counterpoint with the original quarter-note neighbor figure from theme *a*.

In measure 66, the neighbor-note idea adopts the staccato eighth-note rhythm from *d*, giving us motive *e*. This in turn proposes a dialogue with a legato version of theme *d*. The activity calms down in measures 78–81, which harmonically prepare the new key, F♯ minor, while bringing back the hemiola idea mentioned above. Then, in measure 82, the new theme *f* arrives in the new key, accompanied by the legato version of motive *d*.

Once again, we can see how, whenever Brahms adds novelty, he also recalls something familiar. Before the two most important new ideas arrive (in mm. 44 and 82), he also creates harmonic tension, so that the new idea provides a sense of resolution. Thus, he reframes the new material in a way that makes it seem natural, even inevitable.

There are of course other ways to organize a transitional section, but this one clearly demonstrates how Brahms connects the ideas in a convincing way. Again we see our fundamental principle at work: change is always associated with at least one element that stays the same or that recalls something already in the listener's memory.

This example also illustrates another aspect of successful transitions, which our method makes easy to apply: there is no precise rule about what to change at any given moment. The method described here does not entail a simple linear succession of gradations; rather, it provides a way to develop sensitivity to the degree of novelty being introduced at any given moment. This allows for a certain degree of fantasy and imagination overall, such that two composers could start with the same pair of ideas and compose two different but equally successful transitions between them.

## EXERCISES

Our transition exercises will propose pairs of ideas that need to be joined. For each one, the student should make a list of the differences between the two contrasting ideas, then change one element at a time to create a seamless transition. All these exercises are written for piano, but they can be realized for other instruments if desired.

1 We need to connect the lyrical theme in the first two bars of Figure 12.8 with the more vigorous second idea that follows. Here is a list of the differences between them. Note that not all are equally important, e.g. the modulation from A♭ major to F minor is not very distant, whereas the difference in texture is much more marked. As we have already noted, stronger contrasts require more time to make gradually.

- tonality (A♭ major, F minor)
- dynamics (piano, forte)
- articulation (legato, staccato)
- texture (homophonic, contrapuntal)

Figure 12.8. Exercise 1: two ideas to connect

- register (high, middle, low)
- motives (all quarter notes, mainly eighth notes)

Finally, note that the two ideas have different lengths: the lyrical idea takes two measures, while the second idea (without its imitation) is only a measure long.

Figure 12.9 shows a proposed solution. We begin by simply sequencing the original phrase down a third, in F minor. We add one repeated eighth note, on the last beat of the left hand in measure 3. Then we sequence just the first bar of the right hand up a fourth in measure 5, while the left hand fills out the remainder of the coming eighth-note motive, as a counterpoint. Having been anticipated in measure 3, the repeated notes are no surprise here. Another step in the sequence lands on the dominant of F minor, and then by imitation puts the eighth-note figure, now inverted, in octaves, played by the right hand. The last two bars widen the spacing between the hands to achieve the final, desired layout.

Specific techniques to notice here include: sequence, counterpoint, and always associating something new with something familiar.

Figure 12.9. A possible solution

Figure 12.10. Exercise 2: pairs of ideas for transitions

**2** Following the model above, the student should compose transitions between the pairs of ideas shown in Figure 12.10. It is a good idea to compose more than one version of each, to compare different solutions. Note that the time between the pairs of ideas is not necessarily a single bar.

**3** Take one of the solutions to exercise 2 and make two slightly different, less gradual versions (shorter transitions).

**4** Take one of the beginnings in exercise 2, build it up to a climax, and use the climax as a turning point to bring in the new idea.

**5** Return to the ternary-form project composed in chapter 8 and add a transition between the middle section and the return of the first section.

**6** Create an interruption (a turning point) for a video-game scene, as follows. Create three short musical excerpts:

- one minute of ambient music: a fairly calm, stable background, which must be looped: the beginning and the ending must hook up smoothly together;
- one minute of combat music: fast, energetic music, which also must be looped; and
- a ten-second transition cue, starting with a big punch (not looped).

The situation: the ambient music starts playing, looped, when the player enters the forest. When the player meets the monster, the transition cue interrupts the ambient music. The combat music starts playing as soon as the transition cue is over, and loops until the combat is over. This means the transition cue must be able to interrupt the ambient music at any time. Thus, the transition cue will work best if it is quite a strong contrast to the ambient music. On the other hand, the combat music will necessarily be preceded by the transition cue, so it is important to create smoother continuity between the two musical ideas.

# 13 PROGRESSING

Unlike the music of some eastern cultures, western music usually has a strong sense of direction. Although the twentieth century saw some experimentation with more static forms of music in the west (in part influenced by music from other cultures),[1] making music directional has some important advantages, especially for large works.

First, direction makes the music more dynamic, as it creates a feeling of expectation and suspense. Each moment pushes forward into the next, making the music more intriguing and captivating for the listener.

Second, in substantial works that incorporate major contrasts, an overall feeling of direction helps draw together the various sections of the work into a larger whole: the listener notices certain salient relationships over stretches of time longer than one section. For example, it is extremely common for the climaxes in a large work to be graduated in such a way that the last one, usually at or near the end, is clearly the most intense. A basic principle in psychology tells us that repeated stimuli have less and less effect. If all the climaxes in a larger work were equal, they would actually seem to be getting less intense.[2]

This kind of incremental gradation of intensity contributes to perceived unity. It creates a perspective where even the most intense moments are gauged relative to each other, which helps the listener to perceive the overall form as one large gesture, rather than just as a series of unrelated, local events.

Note that the word *progression* here does not refer just to a harmonic progression in the conventional sense, but to any clearly incremental pattern, either locally—a crescendo within one phrase would be the simplest example—or stretching over long spans of time, like the progression of climaxes described above.

Such structural progressions can be rising or falling, getting more or less intense. Normally the former tend to outweigh the latter. Imagine a movement consisting of a series of long diminuendi: after a while, the music would lose all momentum. This is because a large-scale reduction of tension, unless it occurs at the end of a work, is rather like resolving all the conflicts in a novel by the third chapter: there is no more curiosity about the continuation. This is why falling progressions are often not as long as rising ones, and when they do occur, apart from endings, they often end with some sort of minor discontinuity or surprise, as a way of keeping the listener involved and intrigued about what is to follow. Such little surprises renew the listener's interest precisely because they break away from the existing progression rather than just fulfilling it.

Progressions can occur in many different aspects of the music. There are a few very common examples of rising progressions. Pitch can gradually rise, as seen in the succession of melodic peaks during several successive phrases. Rhythm and tempo can accelerate. The music's registral spread can widen. Timbre can get more intense: think of a melody heard first in the low register of the flute, then in the oboe, then in the trumpet. Successive contrasts can become more dramatic, and/or they can occur closer and closer together.

Progressions can occur on a local scale or over a whole piece. A familiar example of a local progression is a simple rising sequence. We need to mention one particularity of such short-term formal progressions here. A local and uninflected progression, like a literal sequence, easily becomes overly predictable, even trite. Since there is no distraction at all from the regularity of the pattern, the listener quickly gets bored. For example, a melody in equal note values, just going up a chromatic scale, with no dynamic or timbral changes, will lose the listener's interest very quickly, since the progression is simply too obvious: there is no suspense. Once we have discerned the overall pattern, we are ready to move on.

A simple example will illustrate this point. Notice how version 1 in Figure 13.1 is already totally predictable by the fourth step of the sequence.[3] The

Figure 13.1. Two versions of a rising sequence

rising direction is obvious, and the rhythmic pattern never changes, so by the time we arrive at the fifth repetition, the listener's attention is flagging.

Version 2, on the other hand, introduces a mild motivic variant on the fourth step of the sequence, and catches the listener's interest once again, making the culmination of the phrase more satisfying. Lengthening the last note also contributes to the sense of arrival. Despite these minor changes, the overall rise in the line remains very clear.

So we may formulate a general principle for such small, local progressions: the overall design and direction need to be simple and clearly perceptible, but the details also need to include some mild unpredictability, so as not to become too obvious. This is the reason behind the old rule that requires introducing some variation after the third step in a sequence.

In the case of progressions over longer spans of time, the intervening other activity between the moments that make up the overall formal progression can lower the risk of monotony. On the largest scale, this "other activity" can even include major contrasts and detours in the form. Of course, progressions of events that are not immediately adjacent in time must attract enough attention to stay in the listener's memory, otherwise their effect will go unnoticed. So by definition we are talking here about progressions of very salient features, such as climaxes, and not about subtle details, for example, the voice leading of the harmony within the accompaniment over several strophes of an art song.

Progressions in more than one dimension, even when going on at the same time, are not necessarily always coordinated. For example, successive melodic peaks can gradually rise during a diminuendo, or the music can get quieter while accelerating. Coordination, or the lack of it, between simultaneous structural progressions gives the composer a tool of great power and refinement for controlling the overall drive and intensity of the music.

On the other hand, when multiple simultaneous progressions do move in the same direction, the music gains in simplicity and clarity, since there are no conflicting indications to resolve.[4] The main climax of a major work is typically prepared by simultaneous intensification in several dimensions at once.

## CLIMAX

As we have seen, the high point of a rising progression creates a climax, whose force can range from quite mild to overwhelming. Finally reaching the climax gives the listener the satisfaction of having correctly understood and anticipated the main lines of the piece. As mentioned above, often in a larger work there will be a hierarchy of climaxes, with the last one being the most intense of all. This will be obvious from the uniqueness of the goal it will attain, for instance, the highest note, the most dissonant harmony, or the most extreme register. Such culminating climaxes also stand out in their degree of preparation.

This is because a high point alone is not enough to make a climax; the feeling of culmination actually results mainly from the gradual accumulation of tension preceding it. Simply inserting a random high note into a melody will just sound like a mistake. To be effective as a peak, the note must be prepared: the listener must be led to expect it, and must feel a need for it. For a major climax, a long build-up is a necessity. In a long symphony or an opera, such preparation can take many minutes.

For most climaxes in a work, a straightforward progression is enough to create the needed intensity. For a final climax, there are a few things the composer can do that in effect notify the listener of its impending arrival: simplification and acceleration.[5]

Simplification implies making the pattern of the progression simpler and more obvious. If, after a period of building up, perhaps including some mild unpredictability as mentioned above, the last few steps of the rise become easier to predict, any doubt the listener has is finally dissipated. The pattern is finally completely clear; this suggests that climax is imminent.

Also, speeding up the progression just before the main climax can create a feeling that we are almost at the goal. For example, if a sequence has been repeating every four beats, and then it is compressed, accelerating to repeat every two beats, the listener will feel that the goal is closer. This is like shifting into a higher gear, at a point when the listener feels that the music is already at maximum intensity. The effect is exhilarating.

Let us examine some examples of progressions and climaxes. Since these examples are quite long, the student should have the scores handy and should listen to each example several times before reading the discussion.

One of the simplest but most effective formal progressions is a crescendo, especially if it is orchestrated by gradually adding instruments. Starting softly and ending loudly is a common strategy for organizing a large section or even a large piece. If it takes place over a long time, the cumulative effect can be very potent indeed.[6]

The second act of Wagner's *Meistersinger*, making up about one hour of continuous music, culminates with an immense crescendo. The first five scenes in the act are relatively short, starting with a light-hearted ensemble featuring the young apprentices. This is followed by various more serious solos and dialogues between important characters in the drama. But the sixth scene, which is by far the longest, moves gradually from the simplest of beginnings, where Beckmesser just strums the open strings on his lute, toward progressively richer textures, finally climaxing in an astonishing riot scene, with various characters and groups singing, at a very brisk tempo, in no less than eleven-part counterpoint. At the most intense moment, the night watchman's horn sounds, the riot finally breaks up, and the act ends shortly thereafter.

This build-up is not a simple straight line. But, as in the narrative, where several dramatic conflicts come to a riotous head, here in the music, despite many detours and local contrasts, the crescendo clearly dominates the structure because of its sheer length and intensity. It pulls together this enormous stretch of music into one unified musical gesture, which nonetheless breathes in a very organic way.

Apart from dynamics, register is another aspect of the music that easily lends itself to formal progressions. The middle register is our norm, where the human ear is most comfortable, while extremes of register are rarer. Thus a work can gradually spread out to cover wider registers at key points, occasionally returning to the middle register to allow the form to breathe. Successive peaks and low points create a sort of frame for the listener, so that when the music finally does reach the extremes of register, there is a sense of culmination and climax.

A powerful example of this process occurs in the first section, "Lever du jour," of Ravel's *Daphnis et Chloé* Suite No. 2, which suggests the emerging daybreak by starting in the low/middle register and then gradually expanding, in two large waves, up to a climax at rehearsal 168 (the score begins at rehearsal 155). At the top of the first ascent, at rehearsal 163, the piccolo, which has been doubling the melody, suddenly changes roles and momentarily participates in the accompaniment, adding a distinct shimmer at the peak. After a receding wave downward (but not all the way down), there is a new rise leading to rehearsal 168, at which time all the brightest percussion instruments in the orchestra finally appear: celesta, glockenspiel, cymbals, and triangle. Most of the exhilarating effect of this movement up to here comes from the widening range of the orchestra; the high, shining percussion crowns the crescendo.

Note that there are constant mild variations in the details of the orchestration, so that the progression is not overly simplistic.

This is also a wonderful example of an important corollary of the progression principle. Often the most effective moment in a build-up is a result of holding back something special until the peak; at that point, its addition creates a sudden climax of sensation—in this case a new, gleaming timbre.

As is often the case, following this long rise, the descent is much quicker: by rehearsal 170, the texture has completely changed, the high register has vanished, and a rather distant variant of the preceding theme begins in the oboe. This local novelty keeps the release of tension somewhat incomplete, and thus prevents the form from losing too much momentum.

Another example of crowning an already strong climax with a new timbre occurs in the last movement of Mahler's Third Symphony, which ends with a tutti passage turning around the tonic D-major chord. The combination of high trumpets and timpani gives great power and force to this last section. However, the trombones are still playing quietly throughout this passage, and Mahler instructs them to play loudly only at the final chord. The effect is stunning: we think we have already reached the most intense moment of the work, and the sudden blaze from the trombones at the end proves us wrong. The filling out of the middle range with their last held chord adds greatly to the impact of this magnificent conclusion.

Harmony also lends itself very well to large formal progressions, since there is such a clear hierarchy of harmonic tension available, both through dissonance and through subtle play with harmonic direction.

It is not an accident that in many symphonic sonata forms, the development section often features the liveliest modulatory activity, as new harmonic information arrives much faster than in the exposition. Similarly, the harmonic distance from the tonic often gets wider. These forms of harmonic intensification contribute to the greater intensity required in this part of the form, and serve to lead naturally to the climax that normally arrives near the end of the development section.

An archetypal example illustrating these kinds of harmonic intensification can be seen in the first movement of Beethoven's *Eroica* Symphony in E-flat major, where the dissonant chord that arrives in measures 276–79 is the sharpest in the whole movement. Likewise, the speed and the range of modulation in the development section are much increased, going as far afield as E minor in measure 281. All these elements contribute to the overall harmonic intensity of the development section, so that when the tonic finally does return, at the beginning of the recapitulation in measure 380, the feeling of "coming home" is correspondingly potent.

Apart from these formal progressions in the harmony, this movement also illustrates several other kinds of progression. For example, the first passage in which we hear the aggressive syncopated rhythmic motive lasts for ten bars, measures 25–35. Although this motive returns momentarily in measures 128–29, its real fulfillment occurs in measures 248–79, where, over very distant harmonies, it creates a sustained and very dramatic climax in the development section, which then leads to the E-minor passage mentioned above. The fact that this passage is three times as long as the earlier presentation of this idea marks it as a very significant moment in the form. The listener will unconsciously compare the final presentation that starts in measure 248 with the previous ones. The fact that it is so much longer once again contributes to the generally greater tension in the development section.

In measure 366 there is also an unusual formal progression here in the dynamics. At the end of the development section there is a sudden, dramatic reduction of texture and rhythm. As the harmony moves back toward the home dominant over a rising bass, there is a long diminuendo, broken only in measure 396 by a sudden, loud tutti. This idea of finishing a progression with the opposite dynamic from the one we expect is often seen in Beethoven, and it creates a novel kind of dramatic surprise. This unexpected turn at the end of a progression also adds enormously to the drama.

Still another striking aspect of this movement is the fact that Beethoven feels the need to add such an enormous coda (mm. 551–691). Perhaps this is because without the coda, the development section would have been by far the most intense part of the movement. With a conventional recapitulation, coming home to the tonic for such a long stretch could have seemed anticlimactic. But this movement, as is often the case in Beethoven, is characterized overall by an extremely high level of energy, which a straightforward recapitulation could not have adequately sustained. Hence the need for an elaborate coda, filled with still more harmonic surprises, and ultimately a large crescendo leading to the end of the movement. In effect, the coda moves the climax of the formal progression from the development section to the end of the movement.

For an example of a formal progression in a nontonal context, we will look at the beginning of the third movement of Peter Maxwell Davies's First Symphony.

The first section of this movement, up to rehearsal 78, is built around an expressive cello line. This line is quite angular, but there is a very clear progression in its melodic peaks, rising first to middle E♯ in the fourth bar, then to a higher D in the bar following rehearsal 76, and then finally to a climax, with the A♯ above the treble staff in the bar following rehearsal 77. After that the cello descends toward the end of the section.

During the cello's rise, the piccolo and the flutes gently comment from above. Their three phrases, up to the cello's peak, get progressively longer: two bars, four bars, and then five bars. Increasing (or decreasing) the length of repeated ideas is often an effective way to create a sense of natural evolution in the music. Then Maxwell Davies sets off the cello's climax with a much shorter phrase in the winds.

There are many famous examples of salient progressions in film music. One classic instance is the build-up during "Meld," from Jerry Goldsmith's music for *Star Trek: The Motion Picture*. This is an archetypal example of how to organize successive waves of sound, gradually rising to a climax, after more than two minutes of preparation. The growing intensity here is quite richly detailed, not just simple and linear. Starting low and relatively slowly, the music goes through many successive waves, each one making a little crescendo in its own right. Overall, there are multiple progressions working together here, for example, the gradual arrival of the higher registers in the brass, the increasingly energetic orchestral movement that occasionally emerges from the background in the homophonic texture, and the occasional surprising harmonic shifts in this generally diatonic context, which contribute sudden moments of intensity.

The dynamics in this passage also produce a significant part of the overall effect. Goldsmith starts with short, more or less symmetrical waves of crescendi and diminuendi, but as the music develops, he begins to use more and more crescendi that are followed by a sudden return to softer dynamics, each of which in turn triggers a new rise. This kind of frustration of the listener's dynamic expectations creates great tension, and the successive unresolved crescendi contribute importantly to the music's momentum.

Note that while these different progressions work together during this large build-up, they are not coordinated in any simplistic way: although the listener has a clear sense of the overall rising shape, the details are never entirely predictable.

In a work of absolute music, a really long and significant local progression (that is, a progression that is not interspersed with significant contrasts) can be used to signal a major formal event to come. In such cases, the sheer scale and richness of the build-up suggest to the listener that something very important is on the horizon, creating so much tension that the only possible resolution seems to be a major change of some sort.

The best-known example of such an impressive formal progression, announcing a landmark structural change, is the long transition between the Scherzo and the finale in Beethoven's Fifth Symphony. Following the spooky, pizzicato return of the theme that begins in measure 244 of the Scherzo, the music arrives at a deceptive cadence in measure 324. The harmonic surprise is reinforced by a vivid textural contrast, as sustained sound, absent for a long time in the preceding passage, returns in the strings. This strong punctuation sets off a new formal process, the progression toward the next movement. Very soon the timpani recall the famous four-note motive first heard in the opening movement. Then we hear the first phrase of the Scherzo theme once, now legato again, in the violins. Beethoven then focuses exclusively on the last three notes of the phrase, repeating them four times while the bass circles around the dominant. The harmony then settles onto a dominant pedal in measure 350, while the timpani mysteriously continue on C; this harmonic conflict adds to the suspense. The violin theme then begins a slow rise that culminates in measure 367, more than an octave higher. Only at this moment do the dynamics finally open out into a crescendo, as these last few bars of the movement rush to their culmination, which proves to be the C-major theme of the finale. The fact that the rising pitch progression at last triggers a crescendo gives a sense that the climax is finally imminent, as does the fact that the violin motive finally dissolves into simple repeated notes, over the omnipresent dominant pedal.

The arrival of the finale like this is much more dramatic than it would have been if Beethoven had resolved all the tensions of the Scherzo with a conventional ending, and then simply begun the new movement, unprepared. The rich build-up has the effect of making the arrival of the new theme feel inevitable, like the long-sought solution to a problem,[7] greatly reinforcing its victorious, affirmative character. It is worth trying to imagine the last movement beginning as a separate piece to realize how much more potent Beethoven has made its arrival through this long, rising progression.


## EXERCISES

The real-world application of these principles, especially on a large scale, will be in the rondo and sonata projects in the coming chapters.

**1** Seek out climaxes in works in the standard repertoire, and determine what elements in the music create their intensity.

**2** Quantify successive climaxes over whole movements of pieces from the repertoire, where a rating of 1 is, say, the highest note in a single phrase and 10 is an earth-shattering explosion.

**3** Take the climaxes in the previous exercises and experiment with them, strengthening and weakening their effects by playing with specific elements of the music. (It may be useful to find scores that are already available in notation software formats online, and experiment with cutting/copying/pasting.) Make a small climax larger, or a large climax more modest, to better understand how they work. For example, if the formal progression is based on rising high notes in the line, add or subtract a note or two at the culmination, or else make the progression shorter by starting later. This kind of recomposition of existing works takes effort to do convincingly, but it is an invaluable tool in developing a sense of form.

**4** Film-music students should plan the music to a large battle scene, with increasingly violent excitement, using different sorts of progressions. Try to create at least three waves of progressions, making sure to avoid too much predictability in all but the last wave, and using different aspects of the music as material for the progressions. In the final wave, ensure that several aspects of the music build up simultaneously.

# 14 RONDO FORM

The rondo form derives from one variant of the old French rondeau, which consisted of a refrain alternating with contrasting episodes.

The rondo will be our first larger form. It requires contrasting themes, varied returns of previously heard material, and several different ways of connecting the individual sections. It will also serve as a bridge between the shorter, simpler forms studied in the first semester and our final project, a sonata form.

Unlike the ternary-form project, where one main contrast was set off all by itself within a stand-alone section, here there will be two contrasting sections. However, they will be somewhat less independent than the middle section in our ternary form, being more closely joined with the refrains that precede and follow. As in most rondos by major composers, we will attenuate the squareness of the basic rondo form (ABACA) with varying degrees of transition.

We will examine two model examples here, in different styles. The first will be the opening movement of Haydn's Piano Sonata in G major, Hob. XVI: 39.

Measures 1–16 present the main theme. Figure 14.1 shows the opening bars.[1]

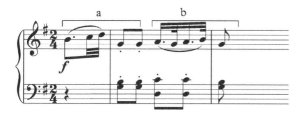

Figure 14.1. Haydn, Piano Sonata in G major, Hob. XVI: 39, opening motives

The theme contains several different motives, but motives *a* and *b* are the most prominent, occurring at important moments during the theme, including the final, cadential phrase in measures 12–16. They will also serve as prominent landmarks at the start of several of the contrasting sections in the movement.

Both halves of the theme subdivide symmetrically into phrases of 2 + 2 + 4 measures. The first half (mm. 1–8) has a light punctuation on the tonic in measure 2, a half cadence in measure 4, and a somewhat stronger perfect cadence on the dominant in measure 8. The second part tonicizes A minor momentarily, where there is again a very gentle punctuation in measure 10. Then it returns to G major, with a half cadence in measure 12. The last four bars begin with an imitation of the main motive, then reach the climax of the main theme with a long descent (mm. 14–15), based on motive *b*. Finally we arrive at a strong cadence in measure 16, on the tonic. Notice why this perfect cadence in measures 15–16 is so much more decisive than the same chord progression in measure 2: the bass line is more angular, with descending octave leaps on the dominant and the tonic. This is important, because if these cadences were equal in finality, the end of the section would not be as well defined.

Another aspect that makes this formal division very powerful is that it is followed by a strong contrast: measures 16–32 constitute the first contrasting episode in the rondo form. It begins with the same motive (*a*) as the first theme (Figure 14.2). However, the tonality is now G minor, and the line progresses quite differently from that in the refrain. Motive *a* is now followed by a new, syncopated motive, which recurs several times in the first half of this section. These first eight bars are divided into two phrases of four bars each, ending respectively on a half cadence in G minor and a perfect cadence in B♭ major.

Figure 14.2. Haydn, Piano Sonata in G major, Hob. XVI: 39, first contrasting episode

The second half of this episode starts with a sequence of 2 + 2 bars, first on V/IV, then on V/V. Although the opening once again refers to motive *a*, the appoggiatura motive at the end of Figure 14.2 recurs several times, attenuating the possible association with the main theme by adding some novelty. Then in measure 28 another two-bar phrase rises to a half cadence, in G minor. At this cadence, as in the one in measure 23, we hear a reminder of motive *b*. Now, given the overall symmetry of the piece so far, we expect another two bars, leading to stronger punctuation. But Haydn plays with our expectations by simply echoing the same half cadence, transposed down an octave: there is no really conclusive cadence to this second theme at all. This avoids an overly simplistic form, making it more intriguing. After the echo, a neutral chromatic scale leads to a clear reprise of the first four measures of the first theme, starting in measure 32.

At this point, everything points to a straightforward recapitulation of the main theme. But Haydn has another musical joke in store: in measures 36–52, we have a complete presentation of the main theme that restates the beginning, chord for chord, bar for bar—but now built around a new motivic variant (Figure 14.3).

Figure 14.3. Haydn, Piano Sonata in G major, Hob. XVI: 39, first reprise

The symmetry of the design has been upset by those extra four bars (mm. 32–35), which turn out to have been a sort of false reprise. In other words, Haydn is playing with the boundaries of the formal divisions. Note that the final cadence of this section, which arrives in measures 51–52, is a direct quote of measures 15–16, including the return to motive *b*.

In measure 52 we arrive at the second episode, which is based on the material shown in Figure 14.4. While this dotted-note motive is reminiscent

Figure 14.4. Haydn, Piano Sonata in G major, Hob. XVI: 39, second contrasting episode

of motive *b* from the first theme, there it was not a constant presence. Here the entire episode is based exclusively on this motive.[2]

This new episode has a first section, ten bars long, that starts in E minor and reaches a half cadence in measure 56. It then modulates to B minor, where it arrives at a perfect cadence in measure 62. The second section, beginning in the second half of measure 62, begins once again with a four-bar phrase in E minor, again ending with a half cadence. The following phrase, however, is much longer: it goes all the way to measure 75, where there is another half cadence in E minor, which replaces the expected perfect cadence. This phrase is quite impressive, with its long tonic pedal (mm. 67–72) moving down onto an augmented sixth chord in measure 73, right before the final dominant. This augmented sixth chord is the most dramatic moment in the whole movement thus far, and, combined with the longer phrase length, makes this punctuation very salient. The fermata provides further emphasis.

As in measure 32, in measures 75–79 we hear a false reprise of the first four bars of the main theme. This time it has an added charm, because the final melodic B of the cadence in measures 74–75 changes its meaning, in a sort of musical pun, becoming the third of the G-major tonic triad. This is a novel and effective way of joining the two sections.

This literal reprise of the first four bars of the main theme, as before, leads to the "real" reprise of the main theme in measures 79–95. However, it is now varied, with flowing sixteenth notes, so as to completely remove any reference to motive *a*.

As we can see, the word *reprise* can cover many degrees of similarity. Each time the refrain returns, it gives us a clear reminder of the first presentation, but it is always changed in some subtle way(s), to make it worth the listener's while to listen again in detail. This kind of generosity—never just taking the easy way out—is typical of the great composers.

At this point, measure 95, we have reached the same strong cadence on the tonic as in measure 16. But given all that has preceded, more is needed for a really convincing conclusion, so Haydn adds a coda, enhancing the overall accumulation of intensity. Now we hear a brief, imitative reference to the triplet motive of the first main reprise (see m. 36) over dominant harmony. This is followed by a literal quotation of the first two bars of the main theme in measures 98–100. There follows a slightly ornamented version of the same, again with the triplet figuration from the first reprise. A quiet little echo of the second motive alone is followed by a second repetition, but now loudly. A simple, full-textured V-I cadence concludes the movement.

As we can see, despite the apparent simplicity of the rondo form, there are many possible refinements.

In a usually symmetrical style like the one here, small irregularities are very noticeable. So the two false returns and the pedal point at the end of the second episode stand out prominently. Similarly, the added coda, with its fermata in measure 98 and its final fragmentation of the theme, makes the ending much more conclusive than if Haydn had just stopped at the end of the last reprise in measure 95.

The fact that the two interior episodes both end inconclusively, with half cadences, also mitigates the squareness in the divisions of the theoretical formal scheme. Using open cadences at these moments leaves the listener in suspense, rather than simply closing off the music, which would require a fresh start each time.

Note also that the contrasts between the refrains and the contrasting episodes are not entirely clear-cut, given the false returns and also the way the motives sometimes overlap. In our scale of contrasts, these episodes would each deserve something like 5 or 6 out of 10, certainly enough to refresh the listener's interest, but not so dramatic as to threaten the generally fairly light-hearted ambiance. All this contributes to the success of this movement as a large design, while keeping it from sounding overly simplistic.

Our second example will be Ravel's *Pavane pour une infante défunte*. The musical examples are taken from the piano version for ease of reading, but we will nonetheless refer to the orchestration at times, since it serves to enhance the form.[3]

The first theme, heard in the horn in measures 1–12, starts in G major and ends with a modal cadence on E (m. 11), followed by a little extension that shifts to B. Figure 14.5 is the beginning of the main theme, with its characteristically vocal phrase in the upper part. The accompaniment motive provides a good deal of the unity within the section.

## Assez doux, mais d'une sonorité large

Figure 14.5. Ravel, Pavane *pour une infante défunte*, opening

The first phrase is six bars long, followed by an echo of its last four notes (A, F♯, E, F♯) in the flute. The melody then moves up to B, in the horn, where there is a momentary pause. This B anticipates the first note of the second phrase, which lasts from measure 8 to measure 12 and is played by the horn again, but now doubled by the violins, an octave lower. This new phrase lasts three bars and is followed by a short response, rather similar in character to the echo in measure 6, and then by the final cadence. This cadence, in measures 11–12, introduces G♯, which is the first accidental so far in the piece; this reinforces the distinctly modal color. This harmonic novelty, and the somewhat heavier texture, make this cadence quite forceful, even though its tonal placement on B tells us that it is clearly not the end of the piece.

The second section (mm. 13–27) immediately presents a contrast in register and in the accompaniment motive, which is now based on repeated notes. Notice that this new theme is not very far removed from the first section's material: the long note at the start of the latter is now replaced by two notes; the G is preceded by an appoggiatura (Figure 14.6).

**très lointain**

Figure 14.6. Ravel, Pavane *pour une infante défunte*, first contrasting episode

The first four bars of the new section appear in a contrasting timbre, the oboe, accompanied by a high bassoon, which moves in contrary motion. They take place over a B pedal; note that this is the same note we heard in the bass of the first theme's last chord. The cadence of this phrase, which arrives in measures 18–19, stands out because the repeated-note accompaniment disappears, and because of its very angular bass line. Note how the harmonic rhythm becomes much faster here, more emphatic, which also serves to mark the cadence. The cadence itself is a modal cadence on D. The melody and accompaniment in measures 20–26 are identical to those in measures 13–19, but now take place in the strings. The bass line, however, is no longer a pedal point, but now is mobile. From the second half of measure 26 through measure 27, we hear a repetition of what we just heard from measure 25 to the middle of measure 26. However, the dynamic is louder, and the bass now moves in parallel with the melody. The last two chords in measure 27 include chromatic passing notes. This repetition adds a sort of rhetorical emphasis to this cadence, which ends this episode. Note once again how strongly Ravel underlines the final cadence of a section, be it via the harmony, the texture, the rhythm, or with other aspects of the music.

The refrain returns in measures 28–39 (Figure 14.7). The texture is richer here, but the phrase and harmonic structure are almost identical to the first presentation. Only when the final cadence arrives is there a significant harmonic change: the bass note is now G, the tonic. However, the G underlies a seventh chord. The seventh then moves down two steps, to the fifth, in the middle parts, making this cadence impressive, but far from final.

**Reprenez le mouvement**

Figure 14.7. Ravel, Pavane *pour une infante défunte*, first reprise

The second episode starts with the upbeat to measure 40 and extends to measure 59. There is an immediate sense of novelty, owing to the higher register and the offbeat accompaniment figure (Figure 14.8). This episode

**1er mouvement**

Figure 14.8. Ravel, Pavane *pour une infante défunte*, second contrasting episode

is divided into two symmetrical subsections, measures 40–49 and measures 50–59. Apart from an added flourish in measure 55, the two subsections are identical. Each subdivides into a four-bar phrase (for example, mm. 40–43), followed by a longer second phrase (mm. 43–49). This second phrase is more heavily scored and in a lower register.

This episode ends with a strongly tonal perfect cadence, clearly in G minor. Although the harmony within the episode has been more modal, it always centered on G.

The final presentation of the refrain, in measures 60–72, is structurally identical to the first presentation of the theme up until measure 70. Note that the accompaniment figure here is in sixteenth notes during measures 60–65, which provides a gentle sense of rhythmic culmination to the entire work (Figure 14.9).

Figure 14.9. Ravel, Pavane *pour une infante défunte*, final reprise

Instead of ending on B, the bass now goes down to G, as it did at the end of the first reprise, in measure 39. Unlike measure 39, however, here the middle parts resolve conclusively onto the low G, underlining the finality of this cadence.

As in the Haydn example, we note that the contrasts here, although quite distinct, are not extremely dramatic. Again, the melancholy mood would not be well served by exaggerated contrasts.

## ELABORATIONS

Rondo forms in the repertoire are extremely varied, although always built around the basic idea of alternating refrains and episodes. Here we have focused on using various types and degrees of punctuation and contrast, as well as (in the Haydn) occasional added phrases, in the form of false reprises, to mitigate the squareness of the basic design. Another way to achieve the same goal would be to add various kinds and degrees of more elaborate transitions between sections. The composer may also sometimes make one episode into a true development of previous material, after the manner of a sonata, to make the form more tense and dramatic. Longer examples of rondo form exist as well, in more than five sections, which sometimes display surprising fantasy in their larger organization. For example, in Beethoven's Violin Sonata in A minor, Op. 23, the last movement seems to be a rondo with four different episodes. But then at the end all the episodes return, one after the other, in reverse order, culminating in a final refrain, texturally enriched, which then dissolves into repeated cadences for a more decisive ending.

## THE RONDO PROJECT

Having examined these models in detail, the next step is to actually compose a rondo, for a solo instrument or a small ensemble. Follow this procedure.

First sketch out three thematic ideas, for the main theme and the two episodes, respectively. Each section should focus on one or two well-defined motives. The sketches should be not only melodic, but should also include ideas for the harmony and the texture. Keep in mind that, apart from motives, a simple contrast between registers, or a new accompaniment figure, can be an effective source of novelty in a new section.

There should be sufficient contrast between the three ideas so that the listener's first impression at the start of each episode is one of novelty rather than familiarity, say, above 5 on our ten-point scale of contrasts. On the other hand, there should not be so much contrast between them that the listener loses all sense of coherence. Judging how much contrast is appropriate is one of the most important steps in planning a large form: too much contrast will weaken the unity of the whole, while too little will bore the listener. Again, try to quantify the degrees of contrast between the ideas. The two episodes should not rate exactly the same on the scale.

It is worth trying more than one idea for each section, as well as trying different orders for the ideas. In particular, the refrain must be amenable to being repeated, while being varied in some interesting way.

Next, plan the tonal structure: the episodes should start and take place in keys other than the tonic. The end of each section, apart from the cadence of the last reprise, must communicate in some way that the piece is not really over: once again, "yes, but . . ." This can be achieved through the melody and the harmony, by avoiding overly conclusive melodic lines and cadences, as well as through the rhythm, for example, by avoiding major pauses, or perhaps eliding the final melodic note with the first note of the new section. The texture can also contribute to smoothing out the joints, say, by anticipating a coming accompaniment figuration. Overall, what is important is to vary the degree and the kind of punctuation. Quantifying the strength of the various cadences will once again be very useful here.

Finally, work out each section in detail. Ensure that the phrase structure in the episodes is different from that in the refrain, so as to avoid excessive squareness. The joints between sections may also need refining, and they should not all be handled in the same way. Some should be more leisurely than others, taking more time; this will help the form as a whole to breathe.

Once the piece is complete, let it go for a few days without looking at it, and then listen to it as a whole. Pay special attention to problems you notice on the first listening, before habituation sets in. Sometimes formal problems only become obvious with a bit of psychological distance. The form as a whole should move to a climax, a special moment that sticks out above all others. In the Haydn example, it is the little cadenzalike passage in the coda; in the Ravel, it is the final reprise, with the sixteenth-note accompaniment and (in the piano version) the loud ending on the tonic. This climax should be the natural result of a preparatory progression and should arrive relatively late in the form, as discussed in the previous chapter. Such culminating moments are very significant to the final result: they give clearer focus to the movement as a whole.

# 15 BEGINNING

What are the structural requirements for beginning a substantial musical movement?

Any music meant to be listened to with full attention needs to quickly stimulate interest in the listener. Background music, some kinds of film music, and music for video games may also sometimes have this requirement, but it is not always present, since their primary role is support. However, when the music itself is the main focus, the opening must attract the listener's attention, suggesting a clear musical character and creating curiosity about what is to follow.

This first appeal to the listener also has to be made very quickly. Imagine a piece with a boring beginning, for example, a single completely static note, held for one minute, on the organ. In a matter of seconds, the listener will conclude that there is nothing of interest to come.

The beginning is also one of the most memorable moments in any piece, since we often remember the parts of a piece exhibiting the most significant contrasts. As the beginning is generally preceded by silence, everything about it is likely to contrast with what preceded it.[1] Thus we can see why the composer has every reason to put a lot of effort into creating a provocative beginning.

We have already noted that music has multiple dimensions: melody, harmony, rhythm, timbre, and register, among others. Not all of these dimensions always need to point in the same direction. In fact, if one aspect of the music seems to contradict the others, the listener will wonder why. We can use this principle to compose a provocative beginning. For example, even with our monotonous example above of the long organ note, just punctuating the held note several times with a pizzicato chord in the strings would create a sense that something more interesting is to come. It is as though the pizzicato gesture calls the long note into question, and that is excellent for a beginning. We would wonder about those interruptions, which seem to point in a different direction from the long held note. What do they signify? Where do they come from, and where are they leading?

In the smaller forms discussed so far, a simple motive usually suffices to attract the listener's attention and to set the music in motion. A motive, by definition, is not neutral: it normally includes some internal contrast of rhythm, register, or melodic direction. Starting with a provocative motive is like proposing an interesting topic for discussion: it invites elaboration, qualification, and possibly even contradiction.

But in larger movements the beginnings are usually richer, often suggesting variety of character and emotional depth to come.

We will explore various possibilities for beginning larger works in the following examples. Following our discussion of each example, the student should experiment with it by slightly changing the notes, the rhythm, the register, or other relevant aspects of the music. This is a good way to discover why these examples work as well as they do as beginnings: observe how various changes make them less effective. All of these examples are taken from the start of the movement in question.

Figure 15.1 is the beginning of the fugue from Beethoven's Piano Sonata in B-flat major, Op. 106. Although preceded by an introduction, this is the point where the fugue subject is presented for the first time. It starts with two short bursts of energy, each coming to a stop, before settling into the headlong momentum that will characterize the main body of the movement. This "1-2-3-go" kind of beginning is often found in movements that are rhythmically very homogeneous and characterized by nonstop activity.[2]

Figure 15.1. Beethoven, Piano Sonata in B-flat major, Op. 106, fugue

The opening of Mozart's *Jupiter* Symphony (Figure 15.2) consists of an alternation between tutti and strings. Motive, timbre, dynamics, and register are among the easiest elements for any listener to perceive, and Mozart incorporates contrasts in all of them during this beginning. Abrupt changes in these dimensions tend to suggest interruption, and therefore imply later resumption. Here the immediate, sharp contrast between the opening widely

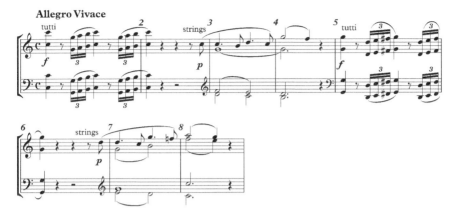

Figure 15.2. Mozart, Symphony No. 41 in C major, K. 551 (*Jupiter*), beginning of the
first movement

spaced tutti motive and the quieter sighing motive in the strings' middle
register (mm. 2–4) leaves the listener curious to hear more. What are these
two dissimilar gestures doing together in the same piece?

In the opening of the third movement of Prokofiev's First Violin Concerto (Figure 15.3), the five bars before the arrival of the soloist introduce a
rather mechanical, clocklike figure in the clarinet and the upper strings that
proves to be the accompaniment for the thematic material in the bassoons,
and then for the following idea, which arrives in the solo violin in measure
6. The rather simplistic character of the opening figure suggests that it is not
in itself a major theme, but rather is designed to become a background for
something more interesting. Note the increasing momentum in the bassoon
part: more and more eighth notes.

The continuous, rocking sixteenth notes that open Bach's *St. John Passion*
(Figure 15.4) create an immediate sense of restless movement. The mood is
uneasy, since the sixteenth-note movement stays more or less in place, as if
constrained, rather than clearly rising or falling. Meanwhile, the suspensions
in the winds create surging waves of harmonic tension: by delaying some
notes of the harmony while others change, suspensions create momentary
doubt about the harmonic context. Starting a work with a long tonic pedal
in the continuo like this suggests the scale of the movement to follow, since
the harmony above it seems to be trying to change while the bass stays stubbornly in place. The longer this goes on, the greater the tension to be resolved.

Once again, Bach's opening is greatly enriched by the immediate use
of contrasting material. However, the contrast in this case is not between

Figure 15.3. Prokofiev, Violin Concerto No. 1 in D, Op. 19, beginning of the third movement. © Copyright 1921 by Hawkes & Son (London) Ltd. Reprinted by permission of Boosey & Hawkes, Inc.

successive motives, but rather between simultaneous planes of tone: the suspensions in the winds versus the undulating strings. Note how the combination is much more intriguing than either gesture is alone: in music, multiple dimensions working together can sometimes create a powerful synergy.

At the start of Wagner's *Tristan und Isolde*, an appoggiatura motive, over very unstable harmony, suggests tension and inner conflict (Figure 15.5).

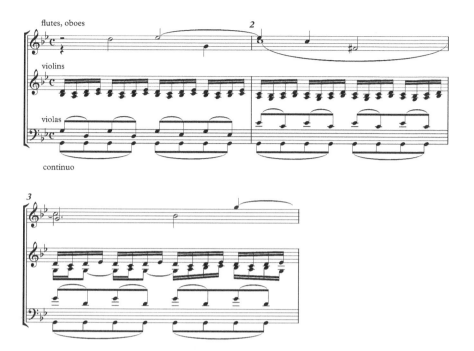

Figure 15.4. Bach, *St. John Passion*, BWV 245, beginning of the first movement

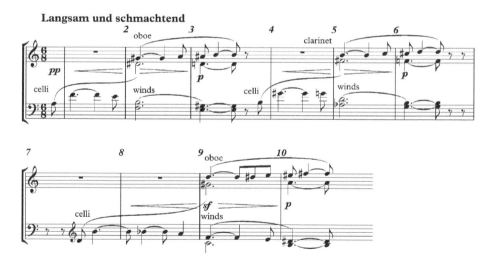

Figure 15.5. Wagner, *Tristan und Isolde*, opening

Note also that the appoggiaturas are much longer than their resolutions, emphasizing the instability and immediately suggesting the passionate longing for love that will be the central theme of the whole opera. The appoggiatura motive is twice repeated, in sequence, and the third presentation, which starts in measure 7, is somewhat prolonged. These repetitions help the listener to "learn" the motive, but they also intensify the sense of questioning, with increasing urgency, inasmuch as the harmony never completely resolves. Note the varied, slightly more intense version of the motive at the third repetition. The extremely slow tempo also creates suspense: the long silences between the members of the sequence create uncertainty, as they are too slow to suggest pulsation. The listener has no framework for specific rhythmic expectations, and is left uneasy, wondering about what will follow, and when.

Our next two examples arrive at the start of slow introductory sections. Here we will first consider them as beginnings in their own right, and then we will discuss an introduction's place in the larger form.

From his earliest compositions Beethoven experimented with musical form, always seeking to widen his expressive range.[3] The beginning shown in Figure 15.6 is a sort of musical joke. The piece starts with what sounds like a cadence in F major: the half-note V7 chord of F goes directly to what seems to be the tonic. But this tonic is surprisingly short: it lasts only an eighth note, which makes it sound almost perfunctory, somehow not quite satisfactory. Furthermore, the first, dominant chord is accented, but immediately reduces to a soft dynamic, a telling example of something Beethoven develops all through his career: the use of dynamics as formal signals.

Figure 15.6. Beethoven, Symphony No. 1, opening of the first movement

Following this odd, frustrated cadence, it turns out that F major is only a temporary resting point, on the tonic of the wrong key. The same pattern is immediately repeated, now in C major, but with a deceptive cadence, which again leaves the listener slightly perplexed, since it provides neither finality nor arrival. Once again, the short duration of the second chord in measure 2 suggests that something has been interrupted. A third version of the motive seems to take us into G major, at which point Beethoven begins a longer phrase. Note that now the *fp* dynamic is gone. There is also a crescendo, which is again an excellent way to create energy.

Only when the G-major chord finally transforms itself into the dominant seventh of C major, with the arrival of the seventh in the bassoon line in measure 5, does the tonality stabilize.

This passage eventually will arrive, at the end of the whole introduction (not quoted here), at what seems to be a cadence in C major, but where the final tonic is actually the arrival of the fast section, which proves to be the start of the main body of the movement.

Figure 15.7, by Bartók, quickly brings together several contrasting musical ideas. First we hear the slow melodic line, moving in fourths in the lower

Figure 15.7. Bartók, Concerto for Orchestra, Sz. 116, first movement. © Copyright 1946 by Hawkes & Son (London) Ltd. International Copyright Secured. All Rights Reserved. Reprinted by Permission of Boosey & Hawkes, Inc.

strings, ending with the C♯ pedal. Over that, a quiet chromatic blur emerges in measures 6–7, in the upper strings, but now as a tremolo, which expands a bit and then closes back in. The juxtaposition of the singing line with the chromatic tremolos suggests mystery: what is behind these vague, rustling sounds?[4] Then the flutes close off the phrase in a surprisingly casual way, in measure 11. Indeed, this little interruption by the flutes almost seems to mock the previous character. Note the delicate way the flute part starts, flutter-tongued, creating a subtle link to the tremolo sound.

Combining these three very different musical characters in such a short time leaves the listener curious about what will follow, and how they will eventually relate to each other.

In its larger context, the passage just discussed is repeated, and then followed by some new material, which eventually creates a climax, and then accelerates, building up great energy and momentum as it moves into the main body of the movement.

All these openings have several things in common. They immediately suggest a clear musical character (or characters), and at the same time they leave something open-ended.[5] All of them employ salient contrasts of material and/or harmony, timbre, register, and so forth to suggest emotional richness and depth.

Here are some things that normally do not qualify as beginning gestures: fade-outs, cadential harmony (when presented in gestures that evoke finality), thinning out of the texture. All these things suggest loss of momentum, or completion. Note that they may nevertheless occasionally appear in a beginning, provided that some other dimension of the music remains clearly provocative and incomplete.

## THE INTRODUCTION AS A SEPARATE SECTION

The Bartók example discussed above is actually just the beginning of a substantial introductory section in its own right. When a major work is introduced in this way, by a large, distinct section, set off from the ensuing music, it normally implies a substantial form, since the rest of the movement will be the main section and will presumably last much longer. As with any beginning, the function of an introduction is to provoke interest. A separate introduction accomplishes this in an especially impressive way. The introduction to a fast movement is often in a slower tempo.[6] The work thus immediately presents the listener with a strong contrast, between the slow introduction and the faster body of the movement. The slow tempo of the introduction makes the faster movement that follows more vivid, by contrast.

Although one might expect an introduction to announce at least some of the material to come, this is not always the case. In fact, sometimes the introduction may not be thematically related to the succeeding section at all. But it must nonetheless create suspense, and it needs to demonstrate very clearly that it is incomplete, for example, by ending on a tensile harmony, an upbeat, and/or with a rising progression of some kind, for example, a crescendo.

Now we will examine two very substantial introductions from the point of view of their role in the whole movement. The first is the introduction to the first movement of Beethoven's Piano Sonata in C minor, Op. 13 (*Pathétique*).

This slow introduction proposes a strongly defined, very memorable first motive (a dotted rhythm including heavy appoggiatura chords), which is then repeated several times, with dramatic pauses. The loudness and heaviness of the piano texture and the dissonant harmony are very striking, coming together to create a beginning of great intensity. The introduction finishes with a fast scalar flourish that stops on a fermata on the dominant chord, which creates suspense, partly through its harmonic instability, and partly through the relatively thinned-out texture. This introduction has its own theme, which in fact returns, reverting to the slow tempo, later in the movement. This return of this slow introduction later in the piece was a very bold stroke at the time, once again engendering a great expansion in the music's emotional range. Its return is such a vivid contrast, and in such an unexpected place, that it dominates the musical landscape, presenting the listener with a kind of anomaly that attracts even more attention.

The second introduction we will examine is the beginning of the first movement of Brahms's First Symphony.

This massive beginning could not be more impressive. It begins loudly, tutti, over a tonic pedal, reinforced by the pulsing timpani, immediately presenting a rising chromatic progression in the upper voices. After a dramatic change of texture in measure 9, Brahms explores various distant harmonic regions over a rising bass line, leading eventually to a Neapolitan sixth chord, which is followed by another long pedal point, this time on the dominant. This pedal underlies several marked changes of character. The introduction ends, rather surprisingly, under a quiet suspension, whose sudden, unexpected, loud resolution sets off the main body of the movement. The sheer harmonic richness and the wide textural variety of this introduction promise the listener a very substantial movement. Unlike that in Beethoven's Op. 13, this introduction presents motivic material and distant harmonic regions that will be important in the rest of the movement. However, the context (the slow tempo especially, and the mood) is so different that, once again, the contrast makes the arrival of the fast main body of the movement much more vivid. It is worth trying to imagine this movement had it begun directly with the Allegro: the effect would be much too abrupt, generally less convincing. Once again, this kind of hypothetical experimentation is an excellent way to develop the student's sense of form.

## EXERCISES

**1** Compose three beginning gestures/phrases, intended for larger movements, for various instruments or voices. Model each on one of the approaches described above. Specify what makes each a convincing beginning.

**2** Compose a short introduction for piano and violin meant to precede a lively staccato movement in 3/4 time, but which is unsuccessful. Explain why.

**3** Examine the openings of the following three major works from the standard repertoire: Bach, *St. Matthew Passion*; Beethoven, Piano Concerto No. 5 in E-flat major, Op. 73 (*Emperor*); and Sibelius, Second Symphony. Explain how these beginnings work. Experiment, changing various aspects of the music, to make them less convincing. For example, in Beethoven's First Symphony, discussed above, simply changing the second chord to another half note makes it sound more final.

# 16 EXPLORING

Every piece of music needs to explore and develop its material, in order to create interest in a coherent way; otherwise, it would just be a random assortment of unrelated events. In a short piece, as we have seen, simply keeping to the closer variants of a previously presented motive over several evolving phrases is enough to maintain coherence. However, in a longer work, the music needs to go farther afield, exploring more striking contexts for the work's ideas. That is the subject of this chapter.[1]

Well-chosen contrasts can make a musical idea more vivid, throwing it into relief. Psychologists have long known that contrast highlights perception. Seeing one color beside a strongly contrasting color makes both of them stand out. Our sense of taste works via contrast effects all the time: something mildly sweet will seem sweeter after a bitter taste. Similarly, hearing something we know in a novel situation, and, over time, exploring how it fits into an unfamiliar context, give us an opportunity to re-evaluate its meaning, and thus can enrich the original idea. Done well, this can greatly deepen the music's effect, in the same way that seeing a familiar character in a novel relating to somebody new, in an unforeseen situation, can show us unexpected sides of the original character's personality. It lets us get to know them better.

When first encountering musical material, we inevitably get to know it in one guise, and then later, as we explore other ideas, we see more of its potential: various confrontations shed different sorts of light upon it. This way of enriching the web of associations around a musical idea is one key to giving the listener a more potent and memorable musical experience over the whole work.

In other words, the key to development lies in exploring the material via various kinds of surprises, since they create novel and intriguing contexts for ideas already encountered. Of course, the surprise must be appropriate to the size and character of the piece. As we have already mentioned in chapter 11, the longer the piece, the more numerous and the more dramatic the contrasts normally will be. This makes sense: repeating the same thing becomes more and more monotonous as time goes on, and therefore ever more novelty is required to keep the listener's interest.

This is, once again, an area where the aspiring composer should roughly quantify the degree of surprise required. A key principle in large forms is that the degree of surprise should not always be the same during the various musical confrontations showing different aspects of the original ideas. At times two contrasting ideas will be linked fairly gradually; at others, they should be more dramatically opposed. The technique of gradual transition, discussed in chapter 12, provides us with a systematic way to control the amount of surprise during these juxtapositions of musical ideas.

The developmental surprises we are talking about can take many different forms. A melodic idea previously heard with a simple harmonization could be presented with new, wandering harmony. Motives can evolve into more remote variants. Harmony, tempo, timbre, register, and dynamics can change more or less drastically, giving a completely new character to a familiar musical idea. Now let us look at a few ways to prepare and undertake such development.

## UNSTABLE PHRASE STRUCTURE

A very important and common practice when developing and exploring musical material is to let the listener hear it again, but with a less stable phrase structure. In chapter 6, on combining phrases, we saw the kind of predictable phrase structures that often occur early on in a piece as a way of delimiting the material and allowing the listener to get to know it. Once the listener is familiar with the material, other possibilities open up, and the pacing of novel events can increase, raising the emotional temperature.

Phrase structures that are less predictable, with regard to their length or the details of their motivic organization, create instability and tension. When known ideas appear in such less predictable contexts, we experience a combination of recognition and intrigue, since we wonder what will happen to them now. This contributes to the general sense that, as a piece goes on, it gets more intense. This gets the listener more involved, creating deeper and richer associations with the original material.

Counterpoint is another useful way to show the listener a new side to a familiar idea. Counterpoint, by its very nature, is incompatible with square phrasing, since voices often overlap. Because one phrase rarely ends before another begins, it tends to feel more driven than the predictable structures often seen earlier in a large work. This is why many development sections from otherwise mostly homophonic works include fugato passages: they are a way of cutting through the neat phrasing heard in earlier presentations of thematic material. Furthermore, combining one idea contrapuntally with another idea, formerly perceived as a contrast, helps to confirm for the listener that they really do belong together.[2]

As a first, simple example of developmental exploration, the reader is referred again to the Minuet II from Bach's Partita No. 1 in B-flat major, BWV 825, discussed in chapter 9, on binary form. The increased intensity of the second half, after the double bar, is a perfect example of a developmental process in miniature. While based on familiar material, the quicker harmonic rhythm and the faster pacing of modulations add a new level of intensity, before we eventually return to the tonic. As already mentioned, this is typical of many binary forms: the contrast provided by the second half is not so much in its thematic material as in its harmonic construction, as we move to more distant tonal regions, and as the timing of the cadences becomes less predictable. Such harmonic exploration can easily create asymmetrical phrases.

For a larger and more impressive example, let us examine the introduction to the first movement of Beethoven's Seventh Symphony. Although an introduction's first function is to create expectation for the coming main part of the movement, in this case, its structure also behaves very much like an exploratory section, acting as a sort of giant, unstable anacrusis to the rest of the movement.[3] This sense of the introduction as a kind of formal upbeat is even more striking because this particular introduction does not even refer to the main themes of the movement proper; it works exclusively with its own material. This gives the arrival of the theme of the following Allegro special emphasis, owing to its novelty.

Figure 16.1 shows the three main motives heard in this introduction. As soon as these ideas have been presented, Beethoven begins to explore combining them, in quite startling ways.

The soft, lyrical phrase, labeled motive *a*, that appears at the start of the work in the oboe already includes a surprise, since it is triggered by a brusque, loud tutti chord, which will recur two bars later. In fact, this "trigger" eventually is heard as part of the thematic material itself. Here again,

Figure 16.1. Beethoven, Symphony No. 7, Op. 91, ideas from the introduction

Beethoven is using dynamics to enhance the larger structure: the sudden shift from the tutti explosion to the quiet oboe solo is very striking, and indeed, this kind of sudden *fp* recurs several times.

Already by measures 5–9, the chromatic bass line is creating notable harmonic instability. As it reaches its goal, the dominant in measure 10, motive *b* arrives. This is a striking rhythmic contrast. The rising scale creates tension.[4] From measure 10 through measure 16, motive *b* alternates with a fragment of motive *a*, before both are contrapuntally combined in a tutti (mm. 17–22). After all these rising lines, which include many strong accents, this last bar arrives at a rather surprising diminuendo, which then makes space for motive *c*. This new theme seems at first to be slightly more stable, but by measure 27 it becomes clear that the phrase symmetry of measures 23–26 is being disrupted by a sequence. In measure 28 it seems once again like a cadence is imminent, but instead the V7 of C major again triggers motive *c*, now accompanied by pulsing sixteenth notes. This turns out to be a preparation for a return of motives *a* and *b*, again in the full orchestra, starting in measure 34.

Much of this is repeated until we arrive at sustained dominant harmony in measure 53, which underlies a rhythmic transition into the main theme of the movement, in 6/8 time. The numerous dynamic, harmonic, and motivic surprises described above give a very dramatic character to this introduction.

Another example of such an unstable, exploratory structure, but with quite a different character, can be found at the beginning of the third movement of Sibelius's Fourth Symphony. This movement, and indeed the symphony as a whole, are formally very unusual. The slow movement begins with a motive in the flute, over unstable harmony (Figure 16.2).

Figure 16.2. Sibelius, Symphony No. 4, third movement, m. 1

It is immediately imitated twice, still in the flute. Tellingly, the third statement of the motive stops on the upbeat, creating a caesura, which feels distinctly incomplete. In measure 3 the clarinet picks up the same motive, in a slightly varied, syncopated form. Starting in measure 4, before the end of the clarinet phrase, the accompaniment suddenly changes drastically, from sustained chords to a tremolo in the low strings. This makes the mood rather nervous and calls the phrasing into question, since a notable change of timbre like this would normally occur between phrases or else at the peak of a phrase. This tremolo seems to galvanize the flute response into a faster rhythm as the line continues, rising to a peak on a high F, over a harmony that is quite remote from the tonic of this movement, C♯ minor. Motivically, the flute is now adventuring into more remote variants. Indeed, the connection with the original is far from obvious, apart from the end of measure 4, where the original motive-form reappears momentarily in midphrase. The lower strings in measure 5 stop the tremolo immediately following the flute's peak, playing another rather remote variant of the motive: it is now augmented, with two notes added at the start and one at the end.

The flute line then simply halts in midstream at the end of measure 6, overlapping contrapuntally with the bass, which is echoing its entry in measure 5. The celli recall the original unadulterated motive in measure 7, which is now imitated in the woodwinds three times, ending in measure 8 once again on an upbeat, followed this time by a fermata.

Nothing proposed so far has led to anything resembling a normal cadence: each statement has finished with unstable harmonies and on an upbeat, repeatedly leaving the listener in a state of unresolved tension. This uncertainty about the punctuation, and consequently the phrasing, persists in the following phrases.

In measure 9, a new, very remote variant of the motive appears in the horns: the stepwise intervals are now transformed into leaps (Figure 16.3).

Figure 16.3. Sibelius, Symphony No. 4, third movement, m. 9

This is followed by several phrases in the strings, the one in measures 12–14 being based loosely on a diminished inversion of the above variant. The string line is rhythmically syncopated, again taking us quite far afield from the original motive-forms. Various imitations of these new variants, which again make for very supple phrase lengths, carry us up to measure 20, finally overlapping with the original form of the motive, which is presented three times in bassoons and clarinet. As before, they end on the upbeat, reinforcing the generally restless character of this movement. Harmonically, we remain far away from the opening tonic, and we never stay for long in any single tonal area.

Starting in measure 22, the strings pick up a motive that resembles the leaps from measure 9, once again ending their phrase on an unstable harmony, a D-minor 6/4 chord with a fermata. Variants of the original motive finally return in measure 28, proffered first by the violas and then by various woodwinds. This time, however, the texture is filled out and more intense, including imitations within the woodwinds over a timpani roll.

Yet again, this all fades away with no sense of completion, to be followed by an inverted variant of the leaping motive–form first heard in measure 9, now in the woodwinds alone.

A further development of the remote variant itself now appears as a tremolo accompaniment figure in the upper strings, in measure 38. Below this, the celli finally present a longer, more stable melodic phrase in sustained notes, based on the same leaping figure. This is the first time in this movement where we have any sense that the music has settled down into stability. It acts, finally, like a formal downbeat, following a long series of structural upbeats.

Presenting this material in such a restless and uncertain way, where the motives and the punctuation often arrive at surprising moments, gives the music a feeling of constantly searching for something, but never finding it. The musical character that results is very extraordinary indeed.

### INTERRUPTING

Surprise implies having our expectations at least somewhat thwarted.[5] Here we will discuss a kind of surprise that is particularly useful in developing musical ideas: interruption. By this we mean a kind of formal jolt, the sense that something expected has suddenly been curtailed, and that something else has taken its place. The sensation thus created is a combination of frustration, as a result of expectations not being fulfilled, and curiosity about what will follow the surprising interruption. This of course creates suspense for the listener.

An interruption is a kind of structural shock, something that disturbs the established momentum of the piece, either bringing it to an abrupt stop, or else suddenly pushing it in a new direction. This kind of discontinuity is a powerful tool for a composer, especially in longer forms, where it helps to avoid what I call the "alphabet form." In an alphabet form, which can be represented as a-b-c-d-e, one completed section simply succeeds another, and eventually the music stops. The overall form becomes disjointed and very square.

Interruptions can be of local importance or, more rarely, they can have long-range implications.

Let us consider two examples, from Beethoven's Ninth Symphony. The first comes from the first movement (Figure 16.4).

This example demonstrates a simple kind of interruption, which then becomes an alternation between two contrasting ideas. Repeating an interruption has the paradoxical effect of making it somewhat predictable, and

Figure 16.4. Beethoven, Symphony No. 9, Op. 125, first movement

thus less disruptive. The alternation then seems to be simply working out the interaction between the two ideas.

In measure 96, the orchestra begins a phrase consisting of scales in contrary motion, in the winds and strings. The phrase is organized as a rising sequence of three two-bar units.

At the peak of the phrase, in measure 102, the scales are interrupted by a forceful, declamatory motive, played by the whole orchestra. Note that, despite the brusque new rhythm, the previous rising scale has led to the high F. For an interruption not to sound arbitrary, it needs to be somehow prepared, even if, when it arrives, one is more struck by its novelty than by the underlying continuity.

This new motive is followed in measure 104 by a soft, lyrical idea in the woodwinds. Again, note that the woodwind phrase starts on the same chord that ended the tutti, providing some continuity.

The rising flute line in measure 105 reaches its peak on the F in measure 106, but the character underneath that note suddenly changes: the declamatory idea is back. Now its second bar turns around E♭ minor, instead of E♭ major. This in turn leads back to the lyrical idea, in measure 108, now in B major, which is harmonically much more distant. Finally, the forceful motive emerges in a new guise, as a quiet murmuring in the strings, in measure 110.

This passage can be seen as an exploration of the interactions between two ideas: the brusque dotted-note motive, and the lyrical woodwind phrase. It is particularly interesting to note how the final, quiet version of the declamatory motive, in measure 110, seems somehow to be the result of their interaction.

We have already discussed gradual transitions, in chapter 12. An interruption can act as a more abrupt transition. Figure 16.5 comes, once more,

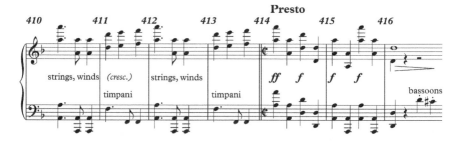

Figure 16.5. Beethoven, Symphony No. 9, Op. 125, second movement

from Beethoven's Ninth Symphony, in this case from the gigantic second-movement Scherzo.

The main idea of the Scherzo has already been worked out for over 400 bars by this point, and is by now reduced to a kind of obsessive repetition, which culminates in measures 410–13. The timpani have now joined in, punctuating the quick repeating motive in every second bar.

When measure 414 arrives, the tempo suddenly gets even faster, the meter changes to duple time, and the octave leap, which was part of the previous motive, suddenly cascades through several repetitions into a cadence, in measure 416. But this cadence itself is quite brusque, and the bassoons immediately enter with new, contrasting material, which will form part of the Trio section. The whole-note D also turns out to be the start of a new theme.

Measure 414 acts here like a musical gear change, interfering enough with the already established momentum to finally bring it to an end.

At the end of the movement, the same process takes place once more, starting in measure 547. The Trio seems to be starting again, but after only a few bars it stops uncertainly, and in the next bar, measure 557, the cascading octave leaps once again jump in and abruptly end the movement.

Here we see an example of the formal potential of a major interruption: not only can it expand the emotional range of a given passage, but it can also be a striking means of transition, suddenly taking the listener somewhere else, surprising and new. Indeed, in music that develops unusually powerful momentum, it can sometimes seem like an interruption is the only way to change direction.

## FORMAL ANOMALIES

Interruption is really one special kind of anomaly, where a sudden event changes the direction of the music. But there are other kinds of formal anomalies, which can add greatly to the form's richness. The main distinguishing feature of the kind of anomaly we will discuss now is that, at least at first presentation, there is no short-term follow-up at all. Normally a major contrast leads to immediate changes in the subsequent music. In this kind of anomaly, the follow-up comes only much later.[6]

Such moments attract quite a lot of attention. They create doubt and leave the listener with a strong need to explore further, in order to resolve the tension engendered by something left hanging. They can also open the door to long-range formal possibilities, in a longer work, where the ultimate "answer" to the formal "question" is not made clear for a long time. If the anomaly is striking enough, as it must be to function properly in this situation, the composer can return to it even after a great deal of intervening material. This helps to tie together large sections and to give a sense of high-level structural resolution.

One way of creating this kind of anomaly is to dramatically interrupt a phrase early in the piece, simply leaving the listener hanging, and then to interrupt the same phrase later in the piece, but now with the interruption leading to a more elaborate continuation of the new character.

The best-known example of this process can be found in the first movement of Beethoven's Fifth Symphony, at measure 21. Not only does the orchestra come to an abrupt stop, but the violins, instead of falling to silence like the rest of the orchestra, sustain their note for a significant amount of time under a fermata. For fresh ears, this can actually sound as though the performers have made a mistake, since this gesture resembles nothing heard before, and it also seems to simply ignore the way the sudden chords seem to be trying to interrupt the musical flow.[7] The music then goes on its way, returning to the headlong energy that will be typical of this movement. But now the listener has a nagging question: what did that single sustained note—the anomaly—mean?

The real reason for this interruption only becomes clear when we arrive at the corresponding spot in the recapitulation, where the same stop leads to the same note being sustained, but this time in the oboe rather than in the violins. Arriving at this powerful, striking event for the second time, Beethoven follows up in a way only a great master could imagine: the oboe now embarks on a melancholy solo in a free, improvisatory tempo, before returning to the main, driving character of the movement. In the midst of all this tempestuous energy, this oboe solo is a moment of respite, a momentary glimpse of another emotional world. Being so very salient, it enlarges the emotional range of the work considerably. Such wide emotional range is characteristic of the best composers, and this is a wonderful way to achieve it. It is very hard to convincingly change character in midstream. Beethoven has found a way, through this powerful anomaly, to prepare us, far in advance, for an extreme contrast later in the movement, which ultimately makes the oboe solo sound completely convincing.

Of course, for such a prominent formal interruption to be successful, as it is here, it must ultimately lead to something really special, if it is not to disappoint. In other words, the more dramatic the interruption, the more impressive must be its ultimate resolution.

This level of discontinuity cannot happen very often in a musical form, especially not with the prominence we see in the Beethoven example. It would be like a novel where many chapters begin "And then something really strange happened." The effect would soon lose its force, and the overall form would simply fall apart.

## EXERCISES

**1** Compose a period, and then, using nothing but the material already presented, repeat it, making it more intense by varying the phrase length.

**2** In Figure 16.6 we have a six-bar period. The two phrases are lyrical in character, and the second phrase ends on an E♭-major half cadence. Transform this cadence into an interruption, leading to a new phrase with a contrasting character, which follows out of the interruption. Complete this new phrase.

Figure 16.6. Exercise 2

**3** Figure 16.7 is a phrase containing a striking, sudden contrast. (The instruments can be chosen by the student.) Compose two different continuations for this phrase, adding one or two more phrases in each case. Also, describe how this contrasting idea could eventually be worked out later in the piece in a way that would make it structurally and emotionally powerful.

Figure 16.7. Exercise 3

**Lento**

*pp*

Figure 16.8. Exercise 4

**4** Extend the phrase for solo cello in Figure 16.8 for at least ten bars in a surprising way. Alternate between the new idea (the surprise) and the old one.

**5** Compose three consecutive phrases, each ending with some sort of interruption. In the first two, the interruption goes nowhere (as if it were just punctuation), but in the third, the interruption develops into something different.

# 17 RETURNING

Musical form is the map for an adventure, where the composer takes the listener on an emotional voyage to experience an imaginary world that should be fascinating, absorbing, and satisfying. As in any adventure, there is an element of risk. In this case of course the risk is not physical; rather it takes the form of the excitement in the face of something unknown. Then, as we explore the new terrain, the new experiences create ever-richer associations in our memory, gradually becoming more familiar.

The overall trajectory of a musical work starts from some kind of problem, doubt, or question, moves through deeper exploration of the material, and then eventually turns toward a final resolution that usually involves some substantial reprise of previous material. This chapter focuses on this returning stage of musical form.

We have seen how stable and repetitive structures serve to present material in ways that make it easy to learn, and also how, in the course of development, the pace of novelty generally increases, moving toward one or more peaks. Sometimes the largest climax constitutes the end of the piece; sometimes it occurs earlier. But in both cases, in a work of any substantial duration, at some point along the way the music needs to relax, to breathe. As mentioned in chapter 13, on progressions, a straightforward linear crescendo, with no inflections on the way, is not of much interest. The overall shape quickly comes to seem too obvious and predictable, and therefore disappointing.

The most important resources the composer has to make the music breathe are familiarity and predictability. Of course, these are relative terms: total familiarity and complete predictability are boring; there must always be some degree of novelty. But over the course of a piece, there will be moments where the listener is more caught up in the tension of exploration, and other moments where the listener is in a state of relative relaxation. This organic feeling of breathing is one hallmark of a well-balanced musical form.

Just as the degree of tension and suspense can be very finely controlled by the composer, so too can degrees of relaxation. They can range from the reassurance of a solid cadence after some wandering harmony in a simple sixteen-bar minuet to a gigantic recapitulation, with its concomitant feeling of tremendous release, in a Mahler symphony. In such cases, after a long time building suspense, a correspondingly sustained feeling of finally "coming home" serves to balance the form.

Since art differs from life in that it takes place within a well-organized and controlled "frame" (in the case of music, the silence preceding the beginning and following the ending of the piece), art at its best can offer a kind of enclosed perfection not often to be found in our lives. This sense of resolution and balance is an important formal requirement in most artistic structures: it contributes greatly to the satisfaction we experience after a long and dramatic musical voyage.

The first standard form we have seen where this is a built-in feature was the simplest ternary design, where after the "adventure" of the contrasting middle section, the opening section returns note for note, evoking a strong sense of familiarity and resolution. In the simplest cases, the clear-cut sectioning of the form provides no hint that this return is imminent. But in more sophisticated examples, there can be a link or a transition between the contrasting section and the reprise of the first section, giving the listener advance notice that relief is coming, and thus making the overall experience subtler and more nuanced.

The rounded binary form demonstrates a more organic way of achieving this, since the return is not a separate section, but rather grows out of the exploring/developing process that normally begins after the first double bar. This return can range from the most concise, subtle reminder, consisting of a mere fragment from the first section, to a virtually complete recapitulation of the opening. The latter case, in fact, is not so far from a ternary form.

In the case of a rondo, because by its very nature the form includes multiple returns of the original material, the composer can play with the sensation of familiarity in intriguing and delightful ways, as we saw in the Haydn example in chapter 14, with its teasing false returns. Sometimes the refrain may also be varied, so that the sense of returning home is accompanied by a certain amount of surprise: home is not quite as we remembered it. Such variation can be ornamental, as when a theme returns with new motives built over the original harmonic/cadential design, or it can be structural, as when the composer adds transitions or changes important formal reference points, like cadences and contrasting motives.

In the full-fledged sonata form, the recapitulation, although normally very substantial and not substantially varied, nonetheless contains at least one critical structural difference from the exposition, as we will see in chapter 19.

At a minimum, an important return of previously heard material always combines familiarity with at least a change of context, since the first time we encountered the material in question it was new, and in subsequent presentations it has become at least somewhat familiar. If there is more than one substantial return of old material, by extension, each time the context will be—should be—slightly different. Even if the music is unchanged, we as listeners do not approach or leave the return in exactly the same way, given its new position in the overall form.

Now let us examine a few examples to see how returning works in practice.

Our first example will be the Courante movement from Bach's Partita No. 4 in D major, BWV 828. This is a rounded binary form, with a very substantial portion of the first section returning, with no alterations at all, apart from now taking place in the tonic. Specifically, after the modulatory section that follows the double bar in measure 16, measures 32–40 are identical to measures 8–16, just transposed back to the tonic. (Note also that m. 8 is itself just an ornamented version of m. 1.) The effect of such a large and obvious return is to give the listener a strong sense of coming home, which elegantly rounds off the form before the final cadence.

Our second example will be the third movement of Mozart's String Quartet in D major, K. 499. The Menuetto is in the home key. Overall, it presents a fairly straightforward binary form. What is somewhat unusual is that its first section ends on the tonic, rather than in a related key. As one would expect, the final cadence in the minuet is of course also on the tonic. The Trio is in the tonic minor, so again there is no change of tonal center. Even more surprisingly, however, the first section of the Trio also ends on the tonic. Since the second section of the Trio (itself a rounded binary form) will of course end up in the same place, this makes four major punctuations in a row, all arriving at the same place, the same tonic.

But finally, after the expected repeat of the Trio, Mozart adds a new transition to lead back to the minuet. This transition is approached as was the cadence the first time through the Trio, but now it becomes a deceptive cadence instead, leading to a short four-bar transition, which remains poised on the dominant. The effect is extremely potent, because by this time we have heard all those previous cadences and their repeats, always stubbornly remaining in the home key. This little transition makes the return to the minuet much more special, since the constant clinging to the original tonic has created quite definite expectations by this point. When, for the first time in the movement, Mozart finally does something unexpected, the contrast is very prominent. And indeed it shows the difference between a clumsy composer just bumping along, and a wonderful composer, who makes what could have been a formal problem into something special.

Our final example will be a recapitulation within a sonata form. Normally there is a clear correspondence between the way the exposition ends and the way the recapitulation ends. But here we will briefly discuss a movement that actually ends differently from the first presentation of the material: the first movement of Beethoven's Eighth Symphony. When the recapitulation seems to have finished, in measure 302, it goes on for a moment just as it did at the start of the development (m. 105), but now in the more remote key of D♭ major. However, the harmony soon takes a different turn, returning to the tonic. Beethoven is playing with our expectations about the way the recapitulation ends, since we normally would hear something similar to the end of the exposition at this point, although now in the tonic. Since this passage also evokes the start of the development, one might also assume that it was simply an old-fashioned, full-scale repeat of everything after the double bar. However, Beethoven avoids both of these conventions, striking out on a new path for the coda.

What these last two examples have in common is the way they depend on thwarting the listener's expectations. A familiar pattern leaves the listener expecting a specific continuation, but the composer then goes off in a new direction, giving the returning music a surprising twist. The result is to make the experience of recognition richer, and also to tie the work into a larger whole, challenging the notion of a black-and-white separation between the familiar and the novel.

## EXERCISES

1 Using the ternary form composed in chapter 8, write a different ending for the middle section (the trio), to effect a smooth transition back to the first section, making the form less square. Possible ways to make this change include a deceptive cadence, a change of key, or perhaps some irregular phrase lengths.

**2** Advanced exercise: Compose a rounded binary form that brings back at least half of the first section before the end. This return may be somewhat varied, but the sense of recapitulation should be clear and sustained.

**3** Write a short theme, to be associated with the beginning of one segment in a video game or a film. Compose another short passage of music, for later in the game, imagining how this could subtly lead back into the opening material, making a very smooth transition into the return.

# 18 ENDING

An important theme that has come up from time to time in this book is that our experience during a significant musical work should not be entirely smooth and even-textured. Some moments should be more potent and more salient than others; they should stay longer in the memory. These special moments are important, since almost nobody can remember everything after one hearing, so the composer needs to pay special attention to those parts that are important to remember. Psychologists now know that we store experiences in memory in summary fashion. The summary includes primarily what seems important: the things that strike us most forcefully. In music, such moments are the beginning, major climaxes and contrasts, and the ending.

We have seen how the main function of a beginning is to create interest, to somehow ask a question, to which the rest of the piece will be a kind of response. We have also pointed out that internal punctuation often includes an element of "yes, but . . . ," to avoid the impression that a large form is just a succession of small unrelated statements. This kind of qualified punctuation—one that lets us breathe, but without really stopping in a definitive, conclusive way—is in fact one prerequisite for a satisfactory large form, if the music is to build up any real momentum and intensity. One of the commonest faults in student composition is having too much strong punctuation in midstream, and thus unnecessarily losing formal energy. While this kind of sectional structure can sometimes have a certain charm in shorter, simpler forms, like the basic ternary, developing the kind of momentum and intensity that characterize a fully integrated large form requires more subtle kinds of punctuation. It is not a coincidence that the smaller, more rigidly sectional forms are not as well suited to the more dramatic forms of expression:

their very predictability makes them unable to build up significant, sustained tension.

The difference between small and large forms is a lot like that between a short story and a novel. In the latter, there is usually more than one plot line, and, apart from at the ending, they do not all move in sync with each other. One question may be answered, but another will be left in suspense.

Only at the end of a novel, or of a musical work, will everything be resolved. If this were not the case, the listener would be left hanging and the ending would not seem final.[1] Thus, a really convincing ending provides a sense of resolution, the feeling that all the outstanding questions have been answered.

All this is to say that the ending, especially of a substantial piece, must be a very special moment, if it is not just to sound like an arbitrary stop sign. The temporal arts normally have some kind of underlying narrative structure with, at a minimum, a beginning, a developing middle section, and a conclusive ending.[2] In more down-to-earth terms, if the audience has no idea if the piece is over, they will not know when to applaud!

Another very important aspect of the process of ending is the question of momentum. Music can be seen as a special kind of structured movement in sound, and direction and momentum are important formal processes in most musical structures. When listening to a major work, the composer hopes that the audience will enter deeply into the experience. That means getting taken up in the work's momentum, feeling the need to continue, and being curious about the consequences of previously presented material. A composer who does not succeed in getting the listener involved will not attract an audience for repeated listenings.

Ending is the ultimate goal of all these processes. There are various kinds of endings, which provide different ways to achieve this sense of satisfying resolution. Two of the most common kinds of ending, the climactic ending and the fade-out ending, share the fact that they both reach extremes, giving the sense that one cannot go any farther. The extreme might be one of register (the lowest or the highest moment of the whole piece), of dynamics (the loudest or the softest point), of tempo (the fastest or the slowest in the movement), or, at times, a simple extreme of consonance or dissonance. Whatever the details, the extreme suggests to the listener that no further progression is possible, which contributes to a strong feeling of finality.

Unlike internal punctuations, the final moments of a piece require that all the dimensions of the music work in harmony with each other. Often, an unsatisfactory ending in a student's work is the result of reaching an extreme in one dimension while other dimensions still seem to be in need of resolution. An example would be arriving at a strong cadential harmony, but without any sense of progression and culmination in the dynamics or the texture.

Such extreme endings require a good deal of advance preparation: the sense of release is proportional to the degree of tension built up beforehand. Since the final punctuation must by definition seem more conclusive than all the others, the composer must find a way to make the listener feel it coming well in advance, by setting up progressions in multiple dimensions of the music, thus creating strong momentum and direction toward the ending, where they will all resolve once and for all. Generally, the larger the work, the more preparation is required.

A loud ending will usually be the most potent climax of the entire work; having a secondary climax as an ending is a recipe for disappointment in the listener. Again, a climax depends not only on the high point reached, but also on the amount and the intensity of the preparation that precedes it.

Similarly, an ending that fades away needs to do so in a more extreme fashion than, say, the ending of a subsidiary section. Here too, both the endpoint and the preparation will be longer than the occasional internal moments of relaxation that allow the form to breathe.

A third kind of ending, more common in smaller works, might be called a rounding-off. In this case, rather than reaching an extreme, the work will recall a substantial amount of material, enough to give the listener the sense that the music has come home after various adventures. Familiarity lowers tension, and this kind of ending is, in a sense, a kind of relaxation. It is not necessarily quiet, but it does depend on the listener feeling a strong sense of resolution, by virtue of returning to known terrain. The difficulty with this kind of ending lies in creating enough familiarity to provide a sense of resolution, but not so much as to end up boring the listener.

Let us look at a few examples of endings. First, a short piece in binary form by Bach, the Allemande from his French Suite No. 6 in E major, BWV 817. We have already referred to this piece in chapter 1, on motives, as well as in chapter 5, on punctuation. Here we will compare the end of the second section to the end of the first (already discussed in chapter 1).

Figure 18.1 gives the last seven bars of the piece. Comparing them with the end of the first section (see Figure 1.4), we can see that the music from the second half of measure 22 to the end of measure 24 is nearly identical to that in measures 9–11. And indeed, apart from perhaps adding a flourish

Figure 18.1. Bach, French Suite No. 6 in E major, BWV 817, Allemande

similar to that in measure 12, Bach could conceivably have ended the piece at measure 25.

However, the passage quoted here ends not just the second section, but also the whole piece. Further, it follows a section with various modulations, which have intensified the music's harmonic trajectory. So while simply transposing the first section's ending to the tonic would have been possible, to make the final section more conclusive, Bach feels the need for something more forceful. Although measure 27 echoes music first heard in measure 7, near the end of the first part of the piece, the real thrust of these added few bars is to make the final cadence now seem stronger. First, there is a rising sequence in measures 25–26, including V/IV and V/V, which lands on the home dominant in measure 27. This is intensified by the bass movement down to the seventh of the V7 chord. This is followed in turn by the faster harmonic rhythm in measure 28, which comes right after the melodic climax in measure 27. All these things give this last point of arrival a stronger sense of resolution than anything heard before.[3] This ending combines a sense of rounding off the form—returning to music heard earlier in the movement— with several other processes, making the final punctuation the most intense and conclusive.

A dramatic example of an elaborate fade-out ending occurs in Elliott Carter's Symphony for Three Orchestras. The climactic section of the movement has arrived in measure 318. This climax is characterized by slashing tutti chords, dramatically halting the music's momentum, which has up to this point never once completely stopped. This is especially striking because Carter's style in general is characterized by a more or less constant polyphony of entire textures, so that while one idea is ending, another is usually starting or already in progress. So when these energetic, slicing chords arrive, they easily become the most striking moment in the piece. The chords alternate several times with what seem to be vain efforts to restart the music's momentum, first twice, timidly, in the strings, and then eventually twice, loudly, in the whole orchestra (mm. 329 and 333), but these attempts do not succeed. Each fragment ends up losing energy or being interrupted by another loud chord. After several more such incomplete gestures, the piano explodes one last time in measure 384, with dissonant chords alternating between the hands, and then quickly falls into the depths of its lowest register, while short fragments in other low instruments provide a bit of support. Then all movement dies away, to end in silence. This example shows what can be done even with a fairly common kind of ending (the fade-out), when it is imaginatively elaborated. One has the impression that a teeming, lively world has finally lost all its energy and faded away.

## THE CODA AS A SEPARATE SECTION

In a large-scale work, the ending sometimes requires an entire section, a separate coda. The first movement of Beethoven's Seventh Symphony provides an impressive example. Here the coda, which starts in measure 389, starts just like a second development section, interrupting the same rising scale that had finished the exposition in measure 174. But whereas the latter finished on the leading tone of the dominant, this one calls into question the home tonic (A), which has arrived in measure 386. This time the G♯ turns out to be really an A♭, which then leads in a new and surprising harmonic direction starting in measure 391.

The music moves quickly into harmonically distant zones, but unlike the development, does not manage to stay away from the tonic for long, arriving instead at a dominant pedal, starting in measure 401 in the winds. The bass hovers around the tonic sixth chord, then rises to the dominant in measure 427, but avoids arriving at the tonic in root position until measure 442. Several more dominant/tonic alternations finally close the movement.

As is often the case with a separate coda, this final section becomes the most powerful climax in the movement, owing mainly to its sheer length (mm. 389–450, for a total of sixty-one measures). It is in effect a giant cadential progression, starting very far away from the tonic and very gradually returning to it. As it gradually moves closer and closer to home, it creates enormous suspense.

This coda has begun quietly, but starts a crescendo in the winds in measure 409. The culminating *ff* arrives in measure 423 and perseveres until the end. The highest note in the coda, the top A in measure 446, also provides a sense of culmination, a feeling that one cannot go any higher, because we have finally arrived at the long-expected tonic in both the melody and the bass, supporting a root-position triad. The dotted-note motive, which has been omnipresent in the entire movement and which was heard at the start of the coda, disappears for a while in measure 401, only to return in measure 423. From there to the end, the insistent repetition of this motive adds increasing force to the conclusion.

As we can see, Beethoven combines several different processes to create a maximum of energy here.

Another very effective coda section is that from the last movement of Brahms's Violin Concerto, Op. 77. By measure 265, the imminent short cadenza has been well prepared by a long dominant pedal. When the orchestra re-enters in measure 267, the dominant pedal is still present; the cadenza has been, in effect, simply an elaborate prolongation of the dominant harmony. What is different, when the dominant returns in the bass of the orchestra, is the faster tempo. Casting the coda in a quicker tempo creates greater momentum toward the end. This is of course a fundamental goal of any coda section: making the ending feel more inevitable.

The harmonic structure of this coda, as in many others, essentially consists of repeated cadences, which are always avoided or somewhat weakened at the last moment, resulting in an ever-more powerful drive toward the tonic, since the listener is constantly being frustrated, with unfulfilled expectations. To see this process in action, we will examine measures 292–300 in more detail.

Measures 292–98 take place, like the earlier passage, over a dominant pedal, underlying a rising scale in the solo violin, which is ornamented in virtuoso fashion. At the peak of the solo line, the bass, instead of finally rising to the tonic, descends stepwise: this mitigates the force of the V-I cadence. When the tonic does arrive in the bass, in measure 300, it turns out to support a IV6/4 chord, as though the upper parts still do not agree that it is really time to end.

After several such processes, which always avoid the final destination at the last minute, the violin finally arrives on the dominant once again in measures 337–38, with a fast scale rising to the instrument's highest register and then hurtling into what seems to be the inevitable final tonic. And so it is, but the loud dynamic is interrupted by a surprising *fpp*, which yet again undermines the harmonic feeling of finality. Then the violin starts a calmer, diminuendo descent (mm. 339–45). The movement, unexpectedly, seems about to end quietly. But then three final loud chords, tutti, suddenly arrive in the last two bars. In effect, that *fpp* is the dynamic equivalent of a deceptive cadence, serving ultimately to make the final sense of arrival even stronger.

An even larger example of such a surprise ending is the conclusion of the second act of Wagner's *Meistersinger*, discussed in chapter 13. After the huge climax of the riot scene, the music gradually dies away as the lovers are left alone during Beckmesser's painful flight. However, at the very end, when we expect nothing more than a gentle, soft cadential chord, Wagner surprisingly bursts in with a sudden explosion, tutti. Note that this gesture would not have been effective without the build-up heard beforehand: ending a movement that is quiet overall with a loud chord like this would usually just sound like a mistake. The climax mentioned above helps to prepare it in advance.

The most important conclusion to be drawn from all these endings is that the composer must find some way to make the last moment very special, crowning the overall experience of the work. It should stand out vividly in the listener's memory.

## EXERCISES

**1** Experiment by recomposing endings of various large movements in pieces from the standard repertoire. At what point do we have the sense that we really are approaching the end? What harmonic means does the composer use to make the listener feel the need for the final cadence? Apart from the harmony, what other aspects of the music are involved in making the ending special? After determining what contributes to making the ending strongly conclusive, try to weaken it by attenuating various aspects of the music. If in a classroom setting, compare versions with those of other students, discussing which elements contribute the most to the impression of finality.

**2** Using the ternary form composed in chapter 8, write a second ending, to be used only after the return of the first section, which makes that (final) ending more conclusive. This new ending should be longer than the first one.

**3** Add a short coda to the rondo project composed in chapter 14. Using familiar material, try leading it toward various kinds of deceptive cadences. Find a way to increase momentum toward the end, perhaps by diverting the listener's expectations at a key moment.

**4** Write two versions of an ending for a video game or for a section of a video game. The two versions should use the same thematic material, but one should be a triumphant "win" and the other a dejected "lose." The endings should each last ten to fifteen seconds. Distinguish the "win" from the "lose" through dynamics, harmony, orchestration, register, articulation, and so forth.

# 19 SONATA FORM

Our final project in this course will be the composition of a sonata form on the Classical model. Historically, this form has been the basis for an overwhelming majority of the largest, most impressive pieces of absolute music in the western tradition. Especially in multimovement works, the sonata-form movements are usually the site of the most intense contrasts of musical character.

As in our previous projects, we will use one specific model of the form as a template. In its real-life applications, sonata form, like all the other common forms, appears in countless individual variations.[1]

The reasons sonata form has been so useful to composers wishing to express dramatic confrontation lie in its combination of major contrasts, the suspense that comes from leaving various tonal and/or thematic issues unresolved for long periods of time, and, ultimately, the presence of a large-scale recapitulation to achieve formal balance and resolution.

Let us look at each of these elements in more detail.

A sonata form begins with an exposition of its thematic and motivic material. Normally this breaks down into a first theme, or group of themes, in the tonic, followed by a modulating transition, which leads to a contrasting second theme, or group of themes, in a closely related key, usually the dominant (or, in minor, the relative major).[2] The transition between them may itself propose new material or else can use material already presented.

After the second theme(s) there is a very strong punctuation of some sort, which creates a kind of interruption: both tonally and thematically the listener has now left home and will not return there in any substantial way for quite some time.[3]

After the end of the exposition, there arrives a section of exploratory development. Frequently the beginning of this new section will propose a surprise of some sort, letting the listener know that things will no longer move on in a smooth continuation of the exposition. As discussed in chapter 16, phrase structures here are often very unstable.

The development as a whole will explore some or all of the preceding material, occasionally even introducing new ideas. Juxtapositions of ideas can now be much more abrupt, since they are familiar to the listener by this point. Harmonically, the pace of modulation picks up, which also contributes to the general intensification in this part of the form. This all normally leads to some sort of climax, as the music finally turns homeward, often over a dominant pedal.

Now comes a substantial recapitulation of the exposition, but with the transition between the first and second groups of themes rearranged so as not to ultimately leave the realm of the tonic.[4] The transition is also a moment when the structure can again temporarily become somewhat more unstable and exploratory, especially considering that the listener has developed specific expectations from hearing it twice earlier (because of the standard repetition of the exposition).

The material of the second group, originally presented in the related key, now appears in the tonic key, so that the movement as a whole can end without leaving home.

In the older versions of sonata form, the development and recapitulation were usually repeated as well. By mid-Beethoven, this repeat usually disappears, perhaps because literally reiterating a dramatic development can seem rather anticlimactic.

We can see that this structure lends itself well to conflict, suspense, and ultimately resolution. Indeed, it is hard to imagine a very different form that would meet all these needs at the same time. After all, contrasting ideas must be presented, connected, developed, and then somehow brought back for overall formal balance.

There are also optional elements in sonata form: an introduction and a coda. We have already seen several examples of these in chapters 15 and 18, on beginning and ending.

For our first example of sonata form, we will look at Mozart's Piano Sonata in A minor, K. 310. Figure 19.1 is the opening idea, presented over a tonic pedal, in the form of repeated chords. This phrase arrives at a very mild punctuation in measure 5, where the pedal point disappears. The answering phrase places more emphasis on the appoggiaturas already present in the opening, but now in longer durations, and then we arrive at a weak punctuation, in measure 8.

Figure 19.1. Mozart, Piano Sonata in A minor, K. 310, opening of the first movement

Having firmly established the tonic, Mozart now begins the transition, which is based on slightly ornamented material from the first idea. However, the music now begins to modulate, creating tonal instability. The bass descends to D in measure 14, harmonized by V/V of C, which is our goal: the relative major. In measure 16 the bass arrives at G, the dominant of C major. However, the music takes a detour to C minor, using the opening material once again, now over a G pedal (V of C). Repeated cadence formulas in measures 20–21 lead to an impressive stop in measure 22, still over the G in the bass, awaiting a clear resolution to C major.

That key arrives definitively with a new theme in measure 23, which is characterized by a quicker sixteenth-note figure (Figure 19.2). The use of C minor just before the second theme makes the change of mode to C major here even more striking, and thus heightens the contrast between the earlier minor theme and the new major theme. On the other hand, the repeated notes in the accompaniment figure of the second theme create a mild association with the first theme.

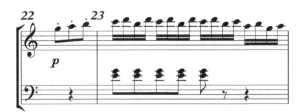

Figure 19.2. Mozart, Piano Sonata in A minor, K. 310, first movement, C-major theme

This is presented over a tonality-defining harmonic progression (I-II-V-I) that effectively installs the new key. The answering phrase, which starts in measure 27, is expanded until measure 34, where it seems prepared to cadence firmly in C. But the melody suddenly leaps an octave higher and picks up again with the same material. It seems to be leading once more to a cadence by the end of measure 39, but, as before, the cadence overlaps with a new phrase, an inverted repetition of measures 34–35, with the material now exchanged between the hands. This time the continuation is different, as imitation in the right hand, in measure 42, eventually pushes upward and then drops to a stronger cadence in measures 44–45. This cadence is elided with the beginning of the last phrase of the exposition, wherein the right hand refers back to the dotted-note motive of the first idea, and the left hand outlines the main harmonic reference points, using figuration loosely derived from the second theme. Measure 49 offers the first unequivocal rhythmic stop so far in the piece, ending the exposition.

The development begins with the first theme, returning now in C major. However, the harmony is quite unstable: by measure 53 there are hints of F minor, and then the perceived dominant of F minor enharmonically becomes the augmented sixth chord of E minor. This is harmonically by far the most dramatic thing that has happened so far in this movement. Over a constantly active pedal on B (V of E minor), we hear the dotted-note motive from the first idea for four bars during measures 58–61, first in the form of repeated notes, as at the start of the movement, and then with the dotted-eighth-sixteenth motive in imitation between the two upper parts. This is sequenced twice, a fourth higher each time, in measures 62–69. Mozart uses the dynamics to greatly intensify the drama here, by alternating *ff* and *pp* between successive steps of the sequence. Having moved up four steps in the circle of fifths, we now arrive on D major, in measure 70. Here the left hand picks up the figuration already heard in measure 45, and the right hand plays a rather ornate version of the dotted-note motive, recalling measure 42. Starting in measure 74, the harmony circles around the dominant and tonic of the home key, A minor, and then finally settles down to alternations between the dominant and the augmented sixth chord, in measure 78. This marks the end of the development and leads, via a short scalar link, directly into the recapitulation, at measure 80. The chromatic scale serves to maintain the rhythmic momentum, while leading melodically back to the first theme.

Typically, the development section has been very mobile harmonically, avoiding emphasis on the tonic key. Only at the end does a clear direction emerge, pointing the listener decisively back toward the tonic. An interesting aspect of its harmonic construction, which helps to create direction, is the way the harmonic rhythm increases to two chords per bar, starting in measure 70, after the pedal points. Then, in measure 73, it increases yet again, this time to four chords in the bar, which creates even greater momentum toward the coming recapitulation.

This development has introduced no new material, apart from some stock arpeggio and pedal figures. Rhythmically it starts with regular eighth notes, but from measure 56 onward it always moves in sixteenth notes: momentum has increased.

When the recapitulation starts, these sixteenths again disappear for a while, which contributes to the general feeling of relaxation. The recapitulation is largely the same as the exposition, with only a few differences.

First, the transition (mm. 88–103) has been rearranged so as to remain in the tonic, following a different harmonic path from the exposition. Thus when the second idea returns, starting in measure 104, it is in minor, giving a new color to the material previously heard in C major. Measure 119, which corresponds to measure 38 in the exposition, now has more dynamic arpeggio figuration, and is intensified with a diminished seventh chord. The answering phrase (mm. 121–5) acts like its original (mm. 40–44), but this penultimate cadential progression is dramatically interrupted by cascading arpeggios on two successive diminished seventh chords. The expected cadence arrives in measure 128, leading to the end of the movement. These last five bars are identical to the end of the exposition, just transposed into A minor.

Overall, like most sonata movements, this one represents a voyage that starts from stability, leads to a more restless and dramatic development, and then returns to stability.

Our next example will be the first movement of Beethoven's String Quartet in E minor, Op. 59, No. 2.

This movement is slightly unusual for this period of Beethoven's production, in that it preserves both the repeats standard in the pre-Beethoven sonata form. We can tell, however, that Beethoven does not see this as a mindless convention, because he takes the trouble to write first and second endings for each repeat: he has carefully imagined the effect of each of these transitions.

The movement begins with two loud, assertive chords: I, V6 (Figure 19.3). When a composer proposes such a very short introduction, it is worth trying to understand why. If Beethoven had started the movement with the quieter idea from measure 3, the effect would be quite different. Particularly given the strong punctuation in measure 4—a cadential V-I progression, followed by a measure of silence—this little phrase is not very energetic. By preceding it with the two loud chords, the main idea becomes not just the quiet phrase itself, but rather the contrast between the two gestures. And indeed, this contrast will figure prominently throughout the movement.

Figure 19.3. Beethoven, String Quartet in E minor, Op. 59, No. 2, first movement, mm. 1–4

The quiet phrase is then repeated over a Neapolitan ♭II harmony, followed at measure 13 by a little elaboration of a remote variant of the motives from measures 3–4 (Figure 19.4). Only the first violin part is given here.

Figure 19.4. Beethoven, String Quartet in E minor, Op. 59, No. 2, first movement, mm. 13–14

This leads to an abrupt stop on the initial two-chord idea, in measure 19. After a bar of silence, the transition begins. It is based on the motivic variants already heard in measures 13–14. The appearance of the Neapolitan harmony in measures 6–7 has already suggested that this movement will be quite rich in its harmonic scope, and indeed the transition passes through numerous tonal regions: F major, C minor, and G minor, finally coming to rest on V of G major, in measure 33. It is also notable that the transition includes several strong dynamic contrasts, which underline the at times rather brusque character of this movement.

Figure 19.5. Beethoven, String Quartet in E minor, Op. 59, No. 2, first movement, mm. 38–40

Starting in measure 35, while still poised on the dominant of G major, the cello and the first violin turn around the motivic variant first proposed in measure 13. The second theme then arrives complete, starting in measure 38 (Figure 19.5).

This idea is then spun out, extended. In measure 48 the music seems about to cadence, but the bass rises unexpectedly to E♭, under a diminished seventh chord. This harmonic subversion is not unique; a similar process recurs in measure 53. The music builds up to a local climax in measure 55, with yet another strong arrival on the dominant in the bass, supporting a tonic 6/4 chord in G. This chord typically acts like an appoggiatura onto the dominant, but the music then takes another surprising harmonic turn, descending into a series of syncopated chords, turning chromatically around the dominant.

Finally, an energetic descending arpeggio figure arrives on the cadential G-major harmony, alternating between the viola and the first violin before moving to the cello in measure 69.

It is notable how many times the music has been led up to the new tonic, G major, without ever arriving conclusively. This kind of teasing the listener repeatedly with the dominant of the coming tonality is typical in a sonata form: it comes from the need to firmly install a new key after the first one has already been solidly established. This same requirement is also a reason for the more complex phrase structures in the second theme group:

the important point is not simply to arrive at the destination, repeating it monotonously, but rather to direct the listener toward the goal repeatedly, to create a sense that it is inevitable. Thus its arrival can finally reduce the tension created by the listener's constantly frustrated expectations.

The first ending leads, as expected, back to the opening two chords in E minor. By way of contrast, the second ending, despite using exactly the same material, immediately goes harmonically far afield. The descending G-major arpeggio that leads back to E minor in the first ending now becomes a G-minor arpeggio, which leads to the tonic and dominant of E♭ major.

The pauses from the opening idea, between the loud chords and the quiet gesture, now become more dramatic. Beethoven repeats the two-chord figure, twice quietly and then once loudly. We have arrived, via a descending bass, at B minor in measure 76. But this time something new and striking is added to the original idea: the first violin holds its top note, diminuendo, through another otherwise complete stop in measures 76–77. Then the quiet idea from the opening recurs, now redistributed between the instruments in a new way: the cello plays the first part, in eighth notes, but the second half of the phrase, in sixteenths, remains in the first violin. The combined harmony of all the instruments creates a deceptive cadence in B minor in measure 81. This measure is much like the opening of the exposition, where we heard the theme repeated on the ♭II. Here Beethoven repeats this phrase up a semitone, in C minor. But this time the phrase is greatly extended. The two parts of the quiet motive—the rising arpeggio in eighth notes, followed by the descending sixteenths—are developed, in imitation, between the first violin and the cello, as the music modulates to the dominant of B♭ minor. Now the syncopated idea, first heard in measure 58, returns in measure 93. The combination of this rhythmic tension with the restless, harmonic wandering creates great suspense: the listener is now completely lost in these elaborate tonal and motivic adventures. This, of course, is exactly the point of a development section.

Apart from the one loud explosion in measure 76, this development section has remained very quiet. In measure 93, the syncopated bass rises to G♭, which changes enharmonically to F♯, supporting a crescendo that is all the more potent owing to the preceding hush. As the F♯ turns out to be the dominant of B minor, in measure 97, the dynamics fall suddenly back to piano, while the first violin recalls the falling sixteenth-note arpeggios once again. As they did in measure 90, in measure 100 they lead to the same syncopated phrase, as well as to a similar crescendo. However, this time the harmonic destination is different: C major, now building to a full fortissimo when the crescendo reaches its peak in measure 107. This, in addition to the greatly expanded registral gap between the outer instruments, has the effect of making this passage the first true climax of the development section. The cascading sixteenths are contrapuntally combined here with the rhythm from the chordal gesture in measure 1, and then sequenced down a third to A minor. Starting at measure 117, we again hear the material from measures 13–14.

This soon gives way to more sixteenths, turning around a B♭-major chord in a textural crescendo, which culminates in measure 127 with a reminder of measures 26–27, originally part of the transition. This is repeated in sequence, over a rising chromatic bass, creating great energy and finally reaching its peak in measure 133. At this summit, all four instruments begin loudly playing in octaves, in a dramatic restatement of the second theme, originally heard in measures 45–46. The trills now sound much more agitated, given the loud dynamic and the bare octaves: there is no accompaniment or counterpoint to mitigate their harshness.

The recapitulation begins in measure 139, but this time the chordal idea and the sixteenths are combined instead of alternated, giving the music no opportunity to lose its rhythmic momentum. The dynamics alternate between *ff* and *p*, until in measures 143–44 we recall measures 3–4. This is followed by a pause, as it was in the exposition, and the continuation is the same, only diverging in measure 156.

This new continuation leads into the transition, which functions as it did the first time, but now arriving at E major instead of G major. It is notable that the long dominant preparation, originally from measure 33 to measure 38, is now extended from measure 169 to measure 178. The rest of the recapitulation follows the path laid down by the exposition, with only minor changes of scoring.

As already mentioned, this movement preserves the traditional second repeat. The shift from E major to E♭ major, where the development restarts, proves quite as dramatic as that from G major to E♭ major, although with a somewhat different flavor.

Had Beethoven ended the movement here, after the repeat, the neat symmetry would seem somewhat at odds with the many dramatic contrasts of texture, dynamics, and motives. So Beethoven adds a coda at measure 210, which starts exactly like the development, but in a different harmonic area: C major. However, the held F♯ from measure 77 has no analog here. Instead, the sequence, which by measure 222 has arrived in G♯ minor, continues a modulating dialogue around the same motive, the eighth-note idea from measure 3. This dissolves into the syncopated idea from measure 58, which in turn settles onto the dominant of the home key, E minor. This arrival corresponds with a crescendo, which culminates in a repeated V9 chord in measures 235–39. This dominant peak, however, dies down without resolving, and a little link leads to a recall of the idea from measures 13–14. This dissolves into a last crescendo, built around the same turning motive, starting in measure 245, thus preparing the movement's final climax in measure 250. A last recall of measures 3–4, now loud, subsequently descends, diminuendo, to the final cadence.

This movement is a particularly clear and potent example of dramatic exploration around the given material. This occurs not only in the development section, but in the more general sense that all the ideas return multiple times, in varying contexts. This creates a large-scale unity, while the new contexts continually enrich the meaning of those ideas, deepening the drama.

## ELABORATIONS

Even a cursory examination of sonata forms in the standard repertoire reveals great variation, both in the amount of contrast between the themes and in the possibilities for dramatic confrontation.[5]

As already mentioned, some sonata movements benefit from the addition of a separate introduction or a coda. Already by the midpoint of Beethoven's composition career, the development section is often so long and elaborate that his sense of formal balance requires a coda, which usually begins like a second development section, although eventually settling down to repeated cadences.

In twentieth-century examples of the form, both repeats from the Classical sonata are often omitted.

Some sonata forms by Mahler are gigantic, but overall they still work on the same principles described above.[6]

A common form for the last movement in a symphony or a sonata involves combining the rondo and sonata principles: the sonata-rondo form. Here, before the development, there is a reprise of the first theme, and a similar process takes place at the end, where, instead of ending with the second theme in the tonic, there is yet another return to the first. Because it increases the amount of familiar material, this usually has the effect of somewhat relaxing the tension inherent in the form. Sometimes these extra reprises are ornamented and/or varied to avoid making the overall design too simplistic. Even the structure of the reprise may be varied somewhat, as long as there remains a clear sense of familiarity. A good example of the sonata-rondo form is the last movement of Beethoven's *Pathétique* Piano Sonata, Op. 13.

The concerto is also related to sonata form, but it requires some changes to its basic design to make the soloist's appearance seem a truly integral aspect of the form. "Concerto form" refers to a formal structure that incorporates aspects of both the Baroque ritornello form and the Classical sonata. This often results in a kind of double exposition, where the orchestra first presents the main material, entirely in the tonic, and then the soloist goes over the same ground, but now modulating to the related key. Later, there may also be other extended alternations between the soloist(s) and the orchestra. Mozart's and Beethoven's many concerti provide numerous examples of this kind of concerto form. Beethoven's Fourth and Fifth Piano Concerti both begin with the soloist, immediately establishing the confrontation between individual and group as an essential dramatic aspect of the form.

## THE SONATA PROJECT

This project will be a synthesis of everything learned in the previous chapters. The goal is to write a full-fledged sonata movement for a keyboard instrument. More experienced students may wish to compose for chamber ensemble instead.

As usual, start with some sketches for the thematic material. The project needs at least two themes of contrasting character, although more are possible. Normally the amount of material will roughly correlate with the length of the movement: more material implies a longer movement. The contrast in the second theme should depend not just on the notes and the rhythm, but also on other elements like texture, timbre, register, and articulation. Changing tempo is more problematic; for a first effort, it is best to stay within a single tempo.

Experiment with various ways the themes can combine with or succeed one another, taking note of the more dramatic confrontations, for eventual use in the development section.

Work out the first theme in detail, adding introductory material as needed. The structure should be fairly simple and stable. However, the final cadence may be slightly weakened, so that the music does not come to a complete stop.

The transition should begin with material from the first theme and then modulate toward the dominant of a closely related key, in order to prepare the second theme. The transition should either end on the dominant of the new key, or else elide directly into the new theme. It is also possible to add new material during the transition, but be careful to ensure that the harmony remains typical of a transition, not staying for too long in any one place before the final destination.

Work out the second main idea in detail. The phrase structure of the second group should not be identical to that of the first. The second group should be longer than the first, and it will probably need several cadences in the new key to firmly establish the new tonic. Seeming to approach a cadence, but avoiding it at the last minute, is often a potent way to lengthen the structure, and to make the listener feel the cadence's eventual arrival as more inevitable. The end of this section should be a very firm full stop in the new key.

Begin the development with some sort of surprise: a more distant modulation, a motive that has not been heard in a while, or a familiar motive with a very striking change of character. The development should be generally unstable in structure, modulating frequently, and not staying very long with any one idea. It is generally a good idea to avoid emphasizing the home tonic during the bulk of the development. Aim for dramatic confrontations between motives, including more distant variants. Use register, dynamics, and texture to reinforce the contrasts. Near the end of the development section, direct the listener toward the home dominant, either with a pedal point or with repeated harmonic approaches leading up to it. There should also be a clear climax near the end of the development section. (However, if the movement as a whole ends loudly, the climax at the end will need to be even stronger than this one: keep something in reserve.)

Now restate the first theme, keeping the structure the same as in its first presentation. It is possible to ornament or lightly vary the material, as long as it remains clearly recognizable. Rearrange the transition so as to end up in the home key, then recapitulate the second theme. The latter may also be varied, so long as the listener is left with a clear sense that the experience, as a whole, is familiar and relatively stable.

Listen to the whole movement and adjust as needed. More advanced students may want to add an introduction and/or a coda.

# 20 REFINEMENTS

We have now covered the essential skills that a beginning composer needs. But there is still much more to learn. In this chapter we will look at three principles that begin to go beyond basic craftsmanship, leading us toward a more artistic level of musical composition. These principles are all derived from the practice of great composers; there are many more such ideas for students to find on their own.

## ANNOUNCING

Part of the composer's job lies in preparing the way for what is ahead in the music. If the composer fails to keep the listener alert, curious, and expectant, many possible deeper reactions to the music fall by the wayside.

We have already noted that any musical form will have some special, important moments that need to be underlined and prepared; here, in two masterful examples, we will see how this can be accomplished. The key to accomplishing this is to have a clear idea of where the important event will occur, and then to find a way to make the listener feel its necessity.

Our first example is from Bach's Fantasia and Fugue in G minor for organ (Figure 20.1). We will examine the first three entries of the fugue.

Since a fugue normally brings in one voice at a time, the successive entries create a natural crescendo of textural intensity. Here Bach shows us how to keep the momentum of the fugal exposition going, creating a sense of inevitability about each entry.

Between the first and second entries there is no pause; all that is needed is to keep the sixteenth-note momentum going. But after the second entry, Bach inserts a short episode (mm. 7–9) that serves several purposes. First, it allows for a more leisurely modulation from the dominant, where the sec-

Figure 20.1. Bach, Fantasia and Fugue in G minor, BWV 542, beginning of the fugue

ond entry took place, back to the tonic, for the third entry. It also gives the exposition some breathing space, appropriate to the scale and richness of the subject. This episode, like most fugal episodes, is constructed around a sequence. What is special about this one is the way, in measure 9, the soprano and alto parts rise to a little climax right before the coming entry, which will be in the tenor voice. One and a half bars of build-up lead the soprano voice to a high G, which becomes a suspension whose resolution coincides exactly with the arrival of the new voice. The rising line and the suspension lead to very specific expectations—a peak and the resolution of the dissonance—but Bach uses the excitement this creates as a pretext to bring in the new voice. In other words, the listener feels the need for some sort of culmination and resolution, creating a "question" to which the entry replies. Announced in this way, the entry has a kind of inevitability that makes it much more convincing.

Another powerful example of announcing is the passage just before the first entry of the solo violin in Brahms's Violin Concerto (Figure 20.2). In any concerto, the first arrival of the soloist is an important moment. Brahms dramatizes it here by preceding it with a six-bar passage that turns around a dominant pedal. While this rhythmically active pedal repeats in the middle register, a rising syncopated line starts in the bass and proceeds upward into the highest register. The syncopations become faster as the line climbs, eventually reaching a peak at the end of measure 89. In this way Brahms builds

**Figure 20.2.** Brahms, Violin Concerto, first movement

tension, which leaves the listener feeling the need for a resolution. As in the Bach example, the resolution coincides with the next important event in the music: the solo violin arrives with the expected tonic chord. Note the sudden change in register and the ***fpp*** when the violin enters; not only do they ensure that the soloist will be heard over the orchestra, but they also make this moment more dramatic.

This kind of build-up, used as a way to prepare important events in the form, is one of many things making the music of the greatest composers so exceptional. By announcing important moments in advance, the composer makes us experience them as special.

## ACCENTING

Music is made of sounds moving in time, and its movement needs to be sufficiently varied to remain rich and captivating. During the emotional voyage that constitutes a musical work of art, there is no interest in remaining on completely static terrain.[1] There need to be at least some moments of greater tension, just as there must also be periods of relaxation. On a more local level, there will also be moments that gain from being accented, ranging from the mildest underlining of something new to the final arrival of a huge climax.[2] Here we will look at how to create such accents and highlights. In the same way that cadences and punctuation serve to delimit the terrain, making it more memorable and understandable to the listener, here we are aiming at reinforcing moments in the music that are worthy of more attention. A good way for the composer to think about this is as searching for ways to make something special.[3] By underlining such moments from time to time, the composer heightens the focus and the interest of the music. Again, this is a way of avoiding the kind of neutral, flat surface that we often encounter in uninteresting music. A memorable example, outside the realm of music, of something important that really stands out from its surroundings occurs in the film *Schindler's List*, which is all in black and white, except for a little girl whom we see for a moment in a colored jacket. This vivid moment stays in the memory because of the sudden shift to color.

There are many kinds of musical accents, with gradations appropriate to all kinds of situations. As with climaxes (which are after all just accents on a larger scale), not all accents are equal in character or intensity. But all accents are by definition momentary events. This is why they often have a somewhat percussive character.

The key to any kind of accent is novelty: the composer must add something new that is at least mildly surprising. Often, accents involve more than one thing happening at a time, since when two or more aspects of the music change in a clearly coordinated way, the listener is more easily convinced that they are not just random events. Sometimes the accent, or novel element, makes the difference between something that would be ordinary, or even boring, like repeating a motive a third or fourth time, and something wonderful.

In a melody, the simplest kind of accent is a leap. This is because, as we saw in chapter 3 ("Singing"), vocal music is naturally conjunct; disjunct movement is not the norm. Sudden short or long notes, different in length from the notes around them, also can stand out from the rest of the line.

Historically in western music, a very common way to create accent has been with a strong dissonance.[4] Depending on the harmonic language, sometimes just a change in the intervals being used can suffice. For example, in the midst of a passage in harmony by fourths, a well-placed second or a third will attract attention. In a tonal style, chords farther away from the tonic, secondary dominants, and local modulations can also create momentary intensification. The bass line can also be a source of accent, for example, when a bass that has been stepwise for a while finally starts to leap.

Changes of spacing are also useful for creating accent—for example, a sudden, thicker chord in the orchestra. A contrapuntal texture that is basically in two parts might expand momentarily to three or four parts for one chord. This technique is especially useful when writing for keyboards or for orchestra. Similarly, the use of an extreme register, not yet or not recently heard, can highlight the arrival of a new motive or a modulation.

Accent can also be achieved through a change in playing technique—for example, a string section suddenly playing a pizzicato chord, or a horn suddenly playing a loud stopped note. In ensemble music, adding a new, percussive timbre is a classic method of attracting the listener's attention. Examples include using a harp chord to trigger a lyrical string phrase, or adding some kind of sudden percussion, such as timpani, to highlight the peak of a phrase.

Of course, the degree of accent must be appropriate to the formal importance of the event being underlined. Once again, the apprentice composer should attempt to quantify how much accent is needed. At the very least, accents can be divided into four classes: mild, medium, strong, and climactic. Thinking in this way allows the composer to find the exact right degree of emphasis for a given situation, adjusting it according to the character of the passage and where it occurs in the form.

The most common situations requiring accent are when starting a new phrase or a new section, or when introducing a new motive at a cadence, a climax, an interruption, or a turning point in the melodic line.

In Chopin's Mazurka in C-sharp minor, Op. 63, No. 3 (Figure 20.3), the melodic line in measures 13–18 is an ornamented descent from the high B (and its neighbor note, C♯) down to E. But instead of the most direct route, Chopin takes a winding path, hovering momentarily around the G♯ in measures 16–17. Note that the first arrival at this temporary, local goal (the G♯) is

Figure 20.3. Chopin, Mazurka in C-sharp minor, Op. 63, No. 3

announced by the strong V-I (the low B-E) in the bass line in measures 15–16. What makes its recurrence in measure 17 more special is the leap of an augmented fifth in the bass line (E-B♯). This new harmonic color makes an enormous difference. If Chopin had remained on the E-major harmony, measure 17 would be musically uninteresting. With the surprising B♯ in the bass to accent it, it becomes quite magical.

Our next example is from the first movement of Debussy's Sonata for Flute, Viola, and Harp (Figure 20.4). Note how Debussy underlines the start of the flute arabesque, following the viola solo. The harp chords not only supply harmonic support, but also fill out the texture, highlighting the beginning of the flute phrase—a contrast to the previous monophonic line in the viola.

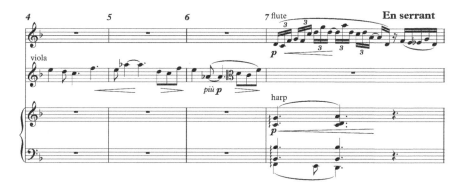

Figure 20.4. Debussy, Sonata for Flute, Viola, and Harp, first movement

In the *Rondo capriccioso* by Mendelssohn (Figure 20.5), the composer marks the peak of the melodic line—the high B in measure 6—by adding an octave doubling in the bass. Enriching the texture in this way makes the peak fuller and more satisfying.

For a more recent example, from film music, listen to "Witches, Wands, and Wizards," from *Harry Potter and the Prisoner of Azkaban*. Here composer John Williams ornaments the first attack in the woodwinds with a little

Figure 20.5. Mendelssohn, *Rondo capriccioso*

grace-note figure, creating a sort of quick upbeat. The purpose of these grace notes is to create a little rush of momentum, setting off the opening accent. This energetic trigger highlights the listener's attention.

In video-game music it is particularly important that accents arrive exactly where they are required in the animation, and also that they be proportional to their importance in the overall narrative structure.

## ENRICHING

The composer aims to lead the listener on a rich voyage of the imagination. The depth of this experience comes from many things, some of which we have already discussed: creating and playing with expectations, highlighting important moments, using surprise and contrast effectively, and so on. Another way to enrich the listener's experience is by creating multiple perceptual planes at once. This means providing not only a foreground, but also one or more background planes of tone. While the details of such planes of tone are properly the domain of orchestration, it is worth saying a few words here about their importance in artistic composition.

At times simple forcefulness can be appropriate, for instance, having the whole orchestra playing in unison and and/or octave doubling. But often the music's effect can be deepened through subsidiary layers of sound, creating richness and intrigue.

Two of the most common types of background planes of tone are movement and resonance. Movement, usually in the form of repeated notes, scales, or arpeggios, makes the texture come alive, reminding us at times of the natural world, which is never completely static. It adds life to the orchestral texture.

Resonance is the result of the sustaining pedal at the piano; in the orchestra it is accomplished through soft, sustained sounds. It creates a subtle sense that the world is somehow reverberating behind the foreground, giving the listener greater depth of perspective: there is more than just the foreground plane.

A well-known example of orchestral movement is the beginning of the third act of Wagner's *Die Walküre*, the passage commonly known as "The Ride of the Valkyries"; measures 12–13 are given in Figure 20.6. The leaping theme, which starts in the bass and is then more fully developed in the horns and the bass trumpet, suggests the fast, galloping movements of the horses. However, the background—the quick trills and scales in the woodwinds, and the arpeggios in the upper strings—adds immeasurably to the energy of the

Figure 20.6. Wagner, *Die Walküre*, act 3, mm. 12–13

whole passage. Without this magnificent rush of energy, the overall effect would be greatly weakened.

Note how Wagner ensures that this background movement does not interfere with the foreground. This plane of tone is in itself not very interesting; it doesn't distract from the leaping motive. It is in another timbre and a different register. It moves at a different speed and uses a different rhythmic motive. (Think of how much less evident the foreground would be without those dotted notes!)

Another magnificent example of orchestral movement is the "Lever du jour" (Daybreak) from Ravel's *Daphnis et Chloé*. In the first two bars (Figure 20.7), the rippling figures in the harps and in the winds create waves of color, suggesting the first awakening of the day. Shortly, after seven measures of introduction, these waves will become the accompaniment for a slowly rising sustained theme, again suggesting rising energy.

This example is also notable for its delicate resonance in the background, played by muted strings (the harmonics in the second bar) and by muted horns. Without this background sheen of tone, the movement in the winds and harps would sound rather dry. As it is, the figures in the winds and in the harp emerge as if from a mist.

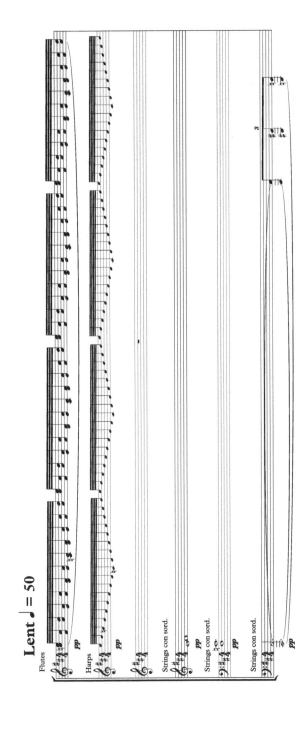

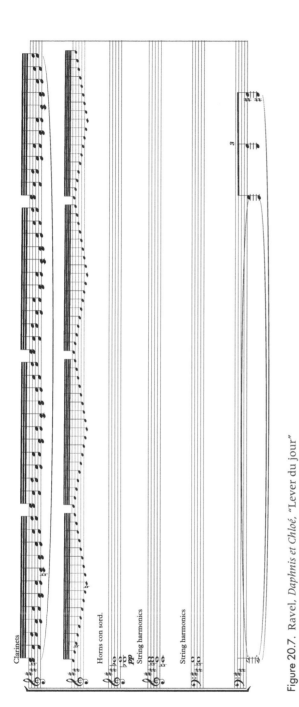

Figure 20.7. Ravel, *Daphnis et Chloé,* "Lever du jour"

In a sense, any accompaniment provides a background for the foreground. Even in the simplest piano accompaniment to a song, the piano part contributes to the atmosphere. But, especially in the orchestra, it is possible to go much farther, creating a sense of depth and intrigue.

The best composers elaborate such background planes of tone with much care and in great detail, making them rich and attractive even after multiple hearings. They are perfect examples of the great artist's desire to use every available means to create the most rewarding experience possible for the audience.

## EXERCISES FOR ANNOUNCING

**1** Look at three works from the standard repertoire and find at least one example in each of an important moment, prepared by a build-up of tension. Explain how it works. How does the composer intensify the listener's expectations before the moment in question?

**2** Look back at the rondo and sonata projects (chaps. 14 and 19) to see if, and how, important moments could be enhanced. Quantify them: the amount/length of preparation should be proportional to their importance in the form. More significant moments will need longer preparation.

## EXERCISES FOR ACCENTING

In the accompanying phrases, change the music to add an appropriate amount of accent at the moment indicated by the X.

**3** Figure 20.8 is a model example; note that it could also be realized in other ways.

In the fourth bar of the phrase, the motive from the third bar is repeated. The slight change of harmony in the left hand, however, does not sufficiently accent

Figure 20.8. Exercise 3

the repetition, which needs more emphasis. Therefore we will underline this moment with the orchestration. Figure 20.9 shows one way to achieve this.

Thickening the pizzicato texture in the accompaniment going into measures 4–5, by having the bass leap back down into the lower register, creates a gentle accent.[5]

Figure 20.9. Exercise 3: a model solution

**4** Figure 20.10 shows two more phrases to be treated similarly. In each case, find a way, or ways, to underline the indicated special moment, marked by the X, with an appropriate degree of emphasis. The student should first appreciate why the given moment needs to stand out. What is it that merits a stronger accent? Then quantify how much accent is needed.

Figure 20.10. Exercise 4

# CONCLUSION

## FROM THE CRAFT TO THE
## ART OF COMPOSITION

The bulk of this book has focused on the craft of musical composition, and the student has been working to acquire the basic skills necessary for a composer. How to present the musical material in a memorable way, how to build up a climax, how to connect contrasting ideas—these and the other subjects we have discussed here are everyday tasks in the life of a composer. Without this kind of technical know-how, it is impossible to work efficiently, and the result will inevitably sound amateurish.

However, the previous chapter began to approach the more artistic side of composition. In fact, craft, when explored over a sustained period of time in an open-ended way, becomes indistinguishable from art. If the aspiring composer aims to become more than a good craftsman, the deeper and more artistic side of musical composition will begin to emerge. The boundary between craft and art is the subject of this chapter.

Another way to think about this subject is as the development of a constantly more elaborate list of criteria for artistic excellence. These criteria emerge from looking at many works by great composers and simply asking, what makes them great? The young composer should make a habit of exploring the music that seems most powerful and expressive, constantly seeking to find out how the effects in question are achieved. Why does a certain contrast seem to fit so well? What makes a given climax so potent? Why is the ending so unequivocal and convincing? What, specifically, did the composer do to make the music speak so eloquently?

The core of a composer's art lies in the innumerable decisions that, ideally, are made for expressive reasons. A serious composer aims for emotional force; no composer wants a tepid response to his or her music. This is just as true in film or video-game music as it is in concert music. The music's main task, in all these situations, is to quickly and powerfully evoke a certain emotional state in the viewer.[1] When this is accomplished, we move closer to high art.

## THE COORDINATION PRINCIPLE

We have already mentioned what I call the coordination principle, the idea that no single dimension of the music can create a really convincing result by itself. A single high note in a phrase, unprepared and unsupported by any change of harmony, texture, orchestration, or dynamics, will just sound like a mistake. A change of orchestration in midphrase, with nothing else changing at the same time, will sound like a wrong entry. A good composer wants first to avoid sounding arbitrary, to convince the listener that the music is intentional, and then to make the expressive intention as clear as possible. Once the composer has a clear idea of the musical character desired, the next step is to ask what each element of the music—line, harmony, timbre, and so on—can contribute to evoking it.

Of course, not every moment in a piece calls for the strongest emotional impact. The coordination principle does not mean that all the aspects of the music must progress in the same direction and to the same degree at all times. On the contrary: controlling the many interactions of the various musical elements with sensitivity is what allows for fine adjustments in the emotion and mood. Only at a major climax or an ending will all aspects of the music normally point in the same direction. However, the other extreme, no coordination at all, is a guarantee of ineffectual results.

The coordination principle gives the composer control over expressive force. It also contributes to achieving another important goal: wide emotional range. Looking at the greatest composers, one is struck by the emotional richness and variety of their work. The Beethoven examples discussed in chapter 16 ("Exploring") all have in common that they greatly increase the range of character in the work in question by coordinating many aspects of the music, including several that were seldom explored before Beethoven. As an example, think of his use of sudden dynamic changes to dramatize certain moments.

## FORMS AND FORMAL PRINCIPLES

For reasons explained in the Introduction, a good part of this book has centered on practice forms: these are necessary to gain control of the tools of the trade. However, as we have frequently mentioned, these pedagogical forms are not necessarily typical in any statistical sense. In fact, it is often quite hard to find examples in the repertoire of these forms, at least in the somewhat simplistic variants presented here. This is because in a mature composer's work the form is not a rigid container into which one pours the content, but is itself an outgrowth of the musical ideas.

This is why the mature composer thinks not in terms of standard *forms*, but in terms of formal *principles*. Our practice forms should ultimately be seen as basic examples of fundamental formal principles at work. It is impossible to write any serious music at all without thinking about coherence, contrast, development, and balance. Applying these principles is part of any act of composition; that is why the chapters presenting them have all been named as verbs. They are things that must be achieved in the music.[2]

As we have seen, the core idea behind this approach is that the parts of a musical form are not interchangeable. Even when a given passage returns identically several times, its meaning will change, owing to the functioning of the listener's memory and its effect on the listener's expectations. Also, context affects perception: what we expect at the start of a piece is not the same as what we expect at the end.

Given the fact that music is a temporal art, we can distinguish a minimum of three basic challenges the composer must address in any piece: beginning, continuing, and ending. We have referred to this fundamental structure as the musical frame.

Several other general principles, for example, concerning punctuation and transitions, have also been explored here. These principles have been discussed independently of any single musical form, since they apply to all music meant to be listened to with full attention.

There are many things to be gained from approaching musical form in terms of these general principles. Understanding them on a deep level is a necessity for a composer who is trying to find the right form for a new piece that for one reason or another may not fit into a familiar mold.

Another major advantage of this principle-based approach is that it is style-neutral. While many of the examples in this book have necessarily been taken from the standard repertoire of tonal music, the question of what makes an effective beginning or a smooth transition, for example, is just as relevant in most other musical languages. It is very helpful for the novice composer, who is just beginning to find a personal voice, to feel that what has been learned up to this point does not suddenly become totally irrelevant.

Beyond these basic formal processes there are several other overall criteria that an experienced composer applies to a work in progress. For example, apart from its expressive force, a well-designed work should feel balanced. Somehow the parts of the work must seem to be in harmony, with each in the right proportion to the whole. Examples of unsatisfactory balance include things like a feeling that one section is too long or too short, a sense that the intensity of a given climax is inadequate for the context, or the impression that a given contrast does not renew interest as vividly as it should.

Here once again it is always worth studying the masters, since a big part of being a great composer lies precisely in consistently getting these things exactly right. One method for exploring this kind of refinement is to play with the timing of important musical events in familiar music. Take an admired piece by Debussy, Bach, or Wagner and experiment, changing the timing of a key event: subtract one bar from the build-up to a climax, add one bar to a transition, and so forth. This kind of experimentation very quickly reveals the enormous importance of perfect timing, and it is an excellent way to begin developing a sense of it for oneself.

Another issue that comes to the fore in a longer piece is the need for structural variety. It is not enough to present contrasting musical material; the context in which it appears needs to change as well. Stable phrase structures that are appropriate for the beginning of a piece can drag the music down if used later on in the wrong place. Similarly, many juxtapositions of ideas that would be perfectly appropriate in a developmental passage would sound incoherent at the beginning of a piece.

For a fascinating opportunity to see such advanced criteria applied in a real-life situation, Brahms's Trio in B major, Op. 8, for violin, cello, and piano, is a valuable model. This trio was published when Brahms was quite young, but he revised it much later in his life. Normally when Brahms revised his earlier work he made a point of burning the old versions, but since this one had already been published, that was impossible. So we have here a rare example of a large, finished work by a major composer that exists in two distinct versions, both complete, but different. Both versions are easily available in score and in sound. It is a very challenging but also a very rewarding experience to compare the two and to try to understand why Brahms felt the need to make the changes he did.

## A PERSONAL VOICE

We have briefly mentioned above the fact that a maturing composer will eventually aim to develop a personal voice.

Originality is often mentioned as a requirement for a major composer. What is especially rare is what I call expressive originality: finding new paths not just for the sake of superficial novelty, but because they are genuinely emotionally evocative and convincing. Such discoveries are often the result of feeling one's way toward a new response to an expressive need. The great originals in music history, like Beethoven, Wagner, and Stravinsky, had expressive ideas that could not be adequately realized with the existing tools, which led them to find new paths to musical communication.

It is normal, and even sometimes desirable as a learning strategy, to imitate those we admire, especially at the apprentice stage. But at a certain point, once the basics of the craft have been mastered, a mature composer will find that such imitation no longer suffices. This is the time when the composer will feel the need to apply a new, more demanding standard: even if it is well made, if the music sounds too close to a given model, it needs to be recast in a more personal vein.

Ultimately, finding a personal voice means to make one's own what one loves most in other music. Most great composers are quickly recognizable in even a short excerpt from their music, through their preferred harmonic style, their favored orchestration, their feeling for pacing and form, and so on. While one may share certain predilections with others, a mature composer at some point will emerge with a combination of preferences that resemble no one else's. Usually this will only develop gradually, over a series of different works.

There is also no shame in being "only" a fine craftsman; not everybody can become a great composer. But the composer who has absorbed and applied the criteria discussed here is already on the way toward becoming an artist. And the generous attitude of a great craftsman, for whom no amount of effort is ever too much to achieve the best possible result, is very close to that of a great composer.

# APPENDIX A
## SKETCHING

Student composers often ask how exactly to go about composing a large piece, above and beyond academic projects of the kind we have seen in this book. Often they wonder if there is some kind of formal plan one can make in advance, and how to go about realizing it. This appendix is about sketching and, in a larger sense, how to go about composing.

Obviously, if the music to be composed is a commission, the first step is to think about the framework imposed by the commissioner. Music for a film or a video game will of course have timing and other structural constraints, and indeed many of the main formal decisions may actually lie in the hands of the producer. However, these latter situations go beyond the scope of this book, where our main focus is on concert music, which is meant to be listened to with full attention and with no need for visual support.

But even concert music still imposes a framework: a commission is normally for a given performer or ensemble, and usually at least an approximate duration is specified. Sometimes the premiere event may also impose certain constraints; for example, the new work might need to be the last one on the program, or thematically related to other music being played in the same concert. The performer(s) may also have specific requirements, for example, that the work should display a certain level of virtuosity.

All these things need to be considered before starting the actual composition. In chapters 3 and 4, on singing and playing, we discussed various limitations and possibilities imposed by the choice of instruments and/or voices, so there is no need to repeat those points here. But once all these preliminary limitations have been taken into consideration, how is one to get from such relatively vague first intentions to a finished piece?

In all but the shortest works, the process of composition is normally a progression from fragmentary sketches to fully worked-out music. Only the most experienced composer would embark on a large orchestral work simply by working from the first bar to the end; even then, most would start with a reduced version as a sketch. It is simply too demanding to attempt to imagine multiple ideas, the way they are worked out in the form, and the orchestration all at once.

The most common procedure is to roughly sketch out the ideas that are to become the basic material first, and then gradually to work out how to elaborate them and combine them into the final form. And even then there will still be more to do: the composer must eventually fill in all the details of texture and the orchestration, and then finally produce a fair copy, ready for the performers.

A useful method for working with rough ideas is simply to jot down scraps of music, preferably with only one idea per sheet of paper. If the composer prefers to record an improvisation, for example, at the keyboard, it is a good idea to make each idea a separate sequence or file. This allows for maximum flexibility in their subsequent arrangement, during the working-out phase.

These rough ideas are by definition provisional: they need not be perfect, nor will they be well developed as yet. What matters at this point is simple quantity. It is also good practice to make more sketches than necessary. If the goal is ultimately to produce really refined work, having extra sketches available leaves more room for choice.

During this initial brainstorming, while inventing ideas, composers will often be in love with the first results; indeed, if there is no pleasure involved, the ideas are not likely to seem worth the trouble in the first place. However, at a certain stage it is necessary to become more objective and critical; this is when having multiple options is very useful.

These initial sketches will usually be very short, sometimes consisting of just a motive, perhaps a phrase or two, not more. Of course, if the idea that comes out is somewhat longer, that is not a problem; the essential point is to keep the creative momentum going, rather than holding back to work out the details. Often it is a good idea to start sketching one day, intentionally leaving some things incomplete, and then to continue over the next few days. This is an excellent way to get the musical subconscious working. Many creative artists have had the experience of going to sleep pondering a problem, and then waking up the next morning to find it solved.

Once the composer has accumulated a pile of sketches, the next step is to work on them individually, for improved expressive focus. Within a phrase there may be parts that are less interesting or less personal than others. Experimenting with the details, so as to bring out what is best and to minimize the less promising parts of an idea, will eventually lead to a superior final result. The goal should always be to create strong musical character. Concert music is the opposite of background music: it should never go unnoticed!

Once the initial ideas are well focused, the composer can begin to imagine what they will eventually become over longer stretches of time. How they can be developed?

One useful way to think about this is to imagine each idea as a character in a novel. At a first presentation we will necessarily see only one side of the character, but as the novel goes on, what other aspects will emerge? A lyrical idea for solo oboe might come back as a very assertive tutti. Perhaps a playful theme will eventually take on a melancholic tinge. In chapter 1, on motives, we discussed closer and more remote variants of a given idea. This is the moment where we may be looking for motivic variants that are more on the remote side, since they can be useful as contrasts later on in a larger form.

This is another reason for our initial suggestion to keep each idea in a separate file or on a separate sheet of paper. At last some of the original single ideas, if not all of them, are now going to become groups of related ideas.

As the more promising aspects of the material emerge, it is time to begin to try to imagine the context for their arrival in more detail. To carry the above example a little farther, what kind of context would throw the oboe idea into best relief when it becomes the assertive tutti? Should it arrive as an abrupt explosion? Or should the music gradually evolve from lyrical to assertive?

This is a critical phase in developing the musical form. Although we are still working within the variants of one idea at a time, now we are beginning to seek out its long-term potential in a larger context. Perhaps the oboe idea should occur two or three times in its first, lyrical character, and then, as a final surprise, it could arrive as an explosion, with tremendous dramatic impact. As we saw in chapter 16 ("Exploring"), in our discussions of Beethoven's Fifth and Ninth Symphonies, sometimes an idea at first presentation turns out to be only a seed whose eventual germination will become a major turning point in the form.

The next step will be to take each idea and to elaborate it into a longer structure, usually several phrases long. Although the final shape of the piece may not yet be obvious, simply extending the ideas in this way will already begin to expand the form.

Having explored the potential of the individual ideas in some depth, it is time to experiment with their combinations. A simple way to begin is to lay out all the sketches together, still on separate pieces of paper, and to shuffle them around in various orders. Elliott Carter recounts seeing Stravinsky's work table filled with little scraps of paper, which Stravinsky played with in this way.[1] Although this corresponds particularly well to Stravinsky's signature cross-cutting technique, this method can also be very useful in other situations.

It is important to take the time to fully explore many possible combinations of the starting sketches. At this stage the composer has not yet entirely committed to one precise overall form. Putting idea *b* after idea *a* might be only of moderate interest, but reversing their order could make a huge difference, greatly increasing their impact. Indeed, the whole reason behind this method of work is to find the best and the most forceful successions of ideas. In the process of moving the ideas around like this, some combinations will inevitably turn out to be more convincing than others. In some cases the best juxtaposition might be as a sudden contrast; in others it could require composing a transition.

This is also the point where the composer is trying to gauge just how much contrast will be needed at various points in the form, and perhaps modifying some of the ideas in order to create more or less contrast at specific places as needed, as discussed in chapters 11 ("Contrasting") and 12 ("Connecting").

By now the music will be taking shape at some length. Several entire sections will be more or less worked out, and the composer will have a good idea of what the best sequence of ideas will be. In many cases, transitions between sections will also already be at least partially sketched out.

Now it becomes necessary to take a step back, to get a better idea of the overall form. In previous chapters we have discussed the requirements for an effective beginning and for a convincing ending, as well as various techniques for developing the material. The composer should now be able to listen to long stretches of the music continuously, perhaps even producing a rough draft of the whole movement. Various formal problems may emerge. Perhaps one idea is not sufficiently developed: in context, it goes by too quickly. Perhaps another is too long. Perhaps the transition between two ideas is too slow or too sudden. Perhaps there is not enough recapitulation to balance the form. Perhaps the beginning would be more effective with a separate introduction, or the ending needs a final coda section.

These kinds of questions have as their goal overall formal balance: the piece as a whole needs to feel like it is the right length and has the right proportions for its material. If the piece is a commission with a set duration, it may now become necessary to add, remove, or modify various elements in the whole.

It can be useful at this stage to occasionally take a day or two off, and then to listen to the whole with fresh ears, trying to evaluate it as though it were by somebody else.

Eventually it will become clear that the overall design is satisfactory. Then comes the work of refining the details. Sketches may be incomplete as to harmony, texture, or orchestration; now is the time to fill in the holes. If the sketch is for an orchestral piece, now is the time to transfer it into full score, filling in all the secondary details of the orchestration.

When all this is done, the composer needs to make a fair copy for the performers, or perhaps a fully detailed mock-up for the film or the video game. These processes will be the subjects of Appendix B.

Sketching is a time-tested way to develop a large work from its basic ideas; it is especially useful to a younger, less experienced composer. It is not a mechanical method to get good results; rather, it is a way to derive the form from the musical ideas, instead of trying to fit them into some arbitrary mold. It is way of working that allows steady progress toward the final goal. As such, it is an essential tool for the apprentice composer.

# APPENDIX B
## PRESENTING YOUR PIECE TO THE WORLD

Once the composition is finished, the composer must find a way to present the piece to potential performers and to the people who arrange musical events for the public. This is normally the final goal of composition—to get the music performed. To do this effectively requires the creation of a thoroughly professional final score, and often of a convincing computer simulation of the piece as well.

### THE SCORE

Although in video games and in film scores the music may sometimes be played entirely by computer, most of the time it will involve at least some human performers, who need properly prepared scores and parts. Nothing betrays an amateur faster than inadequate performance material. When performers see something like the example shown in Figure App.1, their goodwill diminishes at an alarming rate.

Even though this part was produced with current computer notation software, almost everything here is wrong: the stem directions, the placement of the text, the clef (for the bars on the fourth and fifth systems, it should be the treble clef, to avoid so many ledger lines), missing bar numbers, and the bizarre layout on the fourth staff, which contains only one very widely spaced bar. In addition, the "pizz." indication betrays total ignorance of string writing: one cannot change from bowed to plucked strings in midphrase, with no pause. Also, slurs/ties are meaningless in pizzicato. And finally, the name of the part is not even specified.

Proper defaults in the scoring software can take care of some of these problems, but the composer needs to know what is correct in various situations, in order to be able to repair problems left by the software.

Although this is not the place to present all the rules of standard musical notation,[1] here are the basic principles. Follow accepted conventions wherever pos-

Joe Smith

Figure App.1: A poorly prepared part

sible, so that the result is easy to read, and make sure the music contains all the necessary information for a professional performance. Following these conventions and standards is really ultimately about saving the performer extra work. When musicians have to spend time figuring out what is meant by gratuitous, idiosyncratic notation, or, even worse, when they need to rework it to make it easier to read, time is lost from where it really should be spent: practicing the music. The existing notational conventions are not gratuitous; they exist for good reasons, which the composer needs to understand. This is one of several reasons why a composer who is also a performer has a definite advantage over one who is not: performers usually have a very down-to-earth attitude to musical notation.

While this is not the place to go into detail about some of the more basic errors mentioned above, it is worthwhile to set forth the norms concerning performance material.

There are two basic situations: the score and the individual parts. For the score, it is important to think in terms of the conductor's needs.[2]

## Preparing a Score for the Conductor

Conductors do not direct an ensemble with their nose in the score: most of the time they are looking at the performers. This means that the music must be large enough to be easy to see from a distance, which usually means that the score should be presented in a much larger format than the individual musicians' parts. It should include large, easily visible tempi, bar numbers, and/or rehearsal letters, placed on top of the system where they are easy to find. In standard orchestral scores, these indications also appear above the strings. Generally it is a good idea to number every fifth bar, so the musicians do not have to spend a lot of time counting bars during rehearsal.

The instruments should be ordered on the page in the standard way. An experienced conductor will be able to immediately spot the trombones, for example, if they are placed under the trumpets and above the tuba, as they should be. Since percussion parts commonly include more than one instrument, the percussion instrument that is playing at any given moment should either be labeled to the left of the system (for example, "cymbals"), or else prominently above where the notes actually arrive.

Identical wind instruments, for instance, flute 1 and flute 2, may be combined on one staff in the score to save space on the page, provided it is completely clear who is playing and when. The standard indications for this are: "1)," referring to the first flute, "2)," referring to the second flute, and "à 2," which refers to both, playing in unison at the same time.

Some conductors prefer scores where instruments not playing are omitted from each system. Other prefer to always see the empty staves.

Classical scores are always notated transposed: instruments that use transposing notation should appear in the score with the same pitches that the player will see. For complex modern scores, some prefer to write the score in C. This makes it easier to study the music, but in rehearsal it requires the conductor to mentally transpose when speaking to the player of a transposing instrument, which can be rather cumbersome. Specify "transposed score," or "in C."

Some film and video-game music is recorded with the strings divided into "shorts" and "longs" (referring to the note values). This may require having what looks like two string sections in the score, one section for each. The composer or the copyist needs to know this well in advance, since this kind of score takes extra time to prepare. Another point, when recording film and video-game music, is that action or dialogue cues very often need to be indicated in the score, so that the conductor and the people doing the mixing can find their way around without confusion.

For small chamber groups with piano, normally the pianist is the only one who sees what everybody is playing. In the piano score the staves for the other instruments will be included, but smaller, cue-sized.

## Preparing the Individual Parts

In both orchestral and chamber music, each player gets an individual part. For example, if there are two flutes in the score, each will have a separate part.

Only in the orchestral string section do groups of players normally all play the exact same music; in that case, all the first violins, for example, will have the same music in front of them. When performing, string sections normally have one part per stand; a stand includes two players. Of course, for practicing at home, every player still needs his or her own part.

The page format for the parts will be smaller than for the score. It should not contain more than ten or twelve staves per page. If the music is dense and complicated, sometimes a page may contain considerably less than that. Staves should be large and easy to read from a distance. Players of large instruments, like the trombone, may be four or five feet away from their part while performing; the music must remain easily legible. Again, it is best to number every five bars, in a large, easily visible font.

Well-planned page turns are of critical importance for parts, since a player cannot stop playing in the middle of a fast passage to turn the page. This may sometimes lead to pages containing only one or two systems, but this is still preferable to having page turns arrive at impossible places in the music.

Players who have long silences, say, more than ten or twenty bars, will need cues. While professional players are used to counting rests, cues make their life much easier. The cue should be something prominent and easily audible played by another instrument that arrives a few bars before the player's entry. Cues are normally notated with all the stems going in what looks like the wrong direction. In passages where the stem directions are mixed, the majority of the stems determine the "wrong" direction. For instance, if most of the stems would normally be up, in a cue, all the stems will go down. Cues should also be in a smaller font than the normal music, so that they are easy to distinguish from the main part.

The instrument whose part it is should be clearly indicated on top of each page. On the first page, the title of the piece and the composer's name should be displayed prominently before the first staff. This is because, during a concert, players may have several parts on their stands; they need to be able to quickly find the right one.

Figure App. 2 shows what a properly prepared part should look like.

String bowings should be included in the parts. The first player in the section is normally responsible for this, although if the composer is a string player, who can add them while making the parts, this can save a lot of time.[3] Apart from the timpanist, who normally plays nothing else, percussionists often have to play multiple instruments within one piece. They should have their parts arranged by player—Percussion 1, Percussion 2, and so on—with all the instruments to be played by that person listed clearly at the beginning.[4]

The composer should check each part thoroughly. The most important question is: would I find this music easy to read in a hurry? Rehearsal sessions with

# Symphony #23

Joe Smith

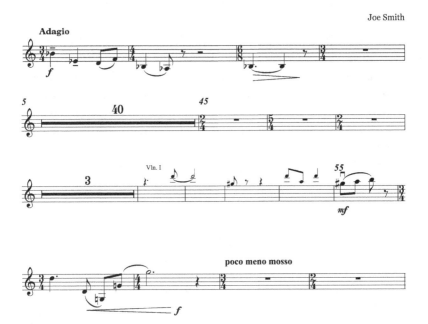

Adagio

**Figure App.2:** A properly prepared part

ensembles are so costly that even a few errors in the parts or the score can waste a large portion of the allotted rehearsal time.

All these details are indications of professionalism. Learning them is as important as learning how to compose, since without performers the music cannot come to life. Performers will always work better when they feel that the composer has done everything possible to make their job easier.

## SIMULATION

Music that stays on paper alone is meaningless. Student composers especially need to hear what they write, and in a reasonably good performance. A bad performance is worse than useless: not only is it discouraging, but it actually can teach the wrong things. However, not every student has easy access to high-quality soloists and ensembles.

Today computer mock-ups are used everywhere in film and video-game music, and when well done they can be very convincing. They have increasingly become essential tools for the composer as well as for potential performers. However, to make an effective simulation requires more than just good-quality sound libraries, important though those may be.

A sound library is only as good as the person using it. The library may have twenty violin articulations, but if the user does not know where and how to use them, the result will be at best just acceptable, and at worst completely unrealistic. Since most people looking at a new work cannot read the score fluently, remember that if the simulation is unconvincing, this will determine how they perceive the piece.

Attentive listening to students' computer mock-ups often reveals flagrant musical defects, most of which could be avoided through better knowledge of the realities of writing for instruments. This is not the place for a full course in orchestration, but here are some tips for producing good simulations.[5]

Musical scores are imprecisely notated at best. Even a score full of performance indications, played exactly as written by a computer program, will sound mechanical and unmusical. Although no human can equal a computer for sheer speed, the real goal of advanced instrumental training is much more than just velocity; it is to achieve control of the instrument in a musical way. This requires both refined musical judgment and subtle physical skills.

An instrument is an object whose design has evolved over many years to control its sound in specific, refined ways. While gross differences in timbre are audible immediately, it is the myriad subtle nuances that make a good live performance genuinely artistic. This is why musical performers spend years mastering the specific possibilities of their individual instruments.

A performing musician on any instrument always has the same basic goal: to communicate expressively. The highest artistic aim, achieved only by the best performers, is to make every controllable detail musically meaningful, underlining the music's character. As with musical composition, an artistic performance requires both a clear overall conception and the integration of all relevant details into that design in a meaningful way. Again, this requires both musical knowledge and physical mastery of the skills specific to the instrument. When developing a musical conception, the performer will experiment to find the most expressive use of the available resources, rather like an actor trying out different ways of speaking his or her lines. Details of performance left haphazard will distract the listener and weaken the overall effect.

Most of the performer's musical goals are ultimately aspects of phrasing. A phrase is not a democracy: not all elements are equally important. The performer must place the elements of the phrase in proper relation to one another, in the context of the whole piece. The performer will therefore explore several things. First, the performer looks at punctuation, finding musically meaningful subdivisions to let the music breathe and to allow the listener to make sense of the musical flow. Second, the performer looks at accent and emphasis, highlighting certain points in the phrase to bring out important moments, for instance, a melodic peak, a modulation, or a cadence. Finally, the phrase as a whole needs to be properly paced, maintaining the overall momentum while still allowing for occasional moments of relaxation where appropriate.[6]

Note that the way a clarinetist phrases is in some ways quite different from the way an organist phrases. Instruments are expressive in varying ways. No one kind of phrasing can possibly fit all instruments. Phrasing must be realized according to what the player of the acoustic instrument can control. To take an obvious example, applying vibrato to a piano sound would be completely unidiomatic.

Therefore, making good mock-ups depends a lot on detailed instrumental ear training, focusing attention on the subtleties of the instrument's tone production.

For instruments with many variables that can be controlled, there can be legitimate decisions about which one, or which combination, to use in a given situation. Should the violinist emphasize a given note by making it louder overall, by a more forceful attack, or by a faster and/or wider vibrato?

The performer must not only supply the appropriate kind of expressivity, but also in the appropriate amount. For an instrument to sound really expressive, it must allow for more than a few primitive gradations. The decisions about how many gradations to allow and how to readily control them are critical to convincing simulations. If there are not enough gradations available, the musical effect will be crude; if too many, controlling them will be needlessly complex. For example, vibrato/nonvibrato is a not a binary, on/off decision. This is why sampled vibrato is often an immediate giveaway for an amateurish simulation. Real vibrato varies in real time in depth and speed, according to musical considerations. There is also a small amount of randomness involved in any human performance.

All acoustic instruments have distinctive attacks; indeed, it has long been known that removing an instrument's attack from the recording of a note often makes its timbre completely unrecognizable. The number of useful gradations, however, varies greatly. A pipe organ allows for little or no variation of attack. By contrast, given that the piano's main tool for expressive playing is control of key velocity, a good virtual piano can require over fifty dynamic levels per note.[7] Wind and string instruments can vary their attacks considerably, both in speed and in loudness: there is a substantial range between a gentle attack and an aggressive one.

Finally, and perhaps most important, sustained notes in strings and winds are never completely static. The players may aim for smooth playing, but in practice there are often at least mild variations in tuning and in dynamics. Individual notes may be intentionally swelled or made softer. In any such variation occurring over the course of one note, many gradations will be required—enough to make the changes sound continuous rather than discrete.

In general, the more things the performer of an instrument has to control in real time, the harder a realistic simulation will be. The meaningful coordination of multiple, simultaneous elements is always a complex skill. This is why a beginner on the cello takes much longer to sound even mildly respectable than a beginner on the piano: there are many more things to learn to control. Here are some more detailed observations about instruments and their control possibilities.

The harpsichord has no direct dynamic accent for single notes. Although the player chooses when to let go of the note, the note decays at a fixed rate: beyond a certain point, there is no more sound. The harpsichord does create a very characteristic mechanical release sound as the plectrum disengages, but this is not significantly controllable by the player. So, apart from registration, which cannot be changed from note to note, the player's control is limited entirely to rhythm.

Even for instruments that may seem superficially similar in technique, like harpsichord and organ, there are often important differences. The organ's sounds do not die away, and therefore an overlapping legato can be annoying. On the harpsichord, such a legato can be a useful option, since it allows the player to somewhat camouflage the release sound of one note with the start of another. On the other hand, harpsichord chords are commonly slightly rolled, to make the attack richer and less percussive. On the organ, this is not at all common.

The string player can control many more aspects of the sound. Many are intimately related to decisions about bowing. First, on what string should the notes be played? Then, what should be the exact pitch of each note (the intonation)? Should the pitch change somewhat during the note? This includes decisions about vibrato, which can vary in both depth and speed. What is the dynamic shape over the whole note? What kind of attack is appropriate, soft or abrupt? Should there be crescendo and/or diminuendo during the note? Should the release be gentle or sudden? Should there be pitch movement between the notes, that is, portamento? How fast should it happen? Also, string players can play chords in various ways, and can also play pizzicato, col legno, and so forth.

Turning to wind instruments, the most important element in any wind instrument's natural sound is: breath. Although players aim at evenness, a wind phrase is naturally shaped by breathing. The feeling is entirely different from keyboard playing, where fingering and arm movements create grouping, and from string playing, where more or less symmetrical, alternating bow movements create a physical, rhythmic sense. In addition, tonguing controls subtle articulation in winds, rather in the way various consonants punctuate speech. A good wind player has various degrees of tongue articulation, ranging from a hard attack to a soft one. Apart from breathing and articulation, wind players also have some real-time control over intonation. They may also use vibrato in varying degrees. The flute and the oboe, for example, are virtually always played with vibrato; other winds can vary substantially in this regard, according to the style of the music, and even to some extent according to the nationality of the player.

Things that are very noticeable in a soloist's performance sometimes lose their importance in a group. For example, a solo string player's legato is very complex, since it is affected by string choice and bowing technique. However, sixteen violins playing a legato line in unison will always overlap a bit, since no two will ever attack or release a given note at exactly the same time. The same is true of vibrato. Likewise, a fast run by a group of instruments in unison is always slightly blurred. Therefore, successfully simulating a section of violins dictates a somewhat different approach from simulating a soloist. In a real orchestra the result of divisi writing is that fewer instruments play per note. For example, a section of sixteen violins divided into four groups gives four violins per note. Composers often use such divisi to create a thinner, more transparent sound. Simply playing the chord using samples of a string section with sixteen players gives a total of sixty-four (four times sixteen) notes, which is not at all the same sound. By the same token, when a string section does play chords (multiple stops), the attacks of the notes are never precisely together, either for the individual instruments or within the whole group. This creates an unusually rich attack. When real instruments play together in unison, they are also never totally in tune. Further, the intonation evolves subtly even within a sustained note, as the players try to adjust to each other. In the same manner, there is a constant subtle balancing of loudness and tone going on in a good orchestra, where the players are always listening to each other, and where the conductor makes continuous adjustments. Such details may sometimes sound mildly random, but usually they tend toward more refined intonation, tone, or balance.

For sampled instruments, dynamics can create special problems. Acoustic instruments each have a natural dynamic curve, which varies according to register. For example, the flute is always softer in its low register than in its high register. While the specifics vary for each instrument, it is important to realize that sampling technology can have the effect of eliminating or minimizing the normal dynamic differences between instrumental registers.

The composer needs to learn to hear all these things. Working to achieve good mock-ups can be an excellent opportunity to get to know more about instruments and performance. Since composition involves all the elements of music —melody, harmony, counterpoint, and orchestration—a composition course is an ideal place to integrate this knowledge.

# NOTES

## INTRODUCTION

1. Although not the focus of this book, there is also the whole category of interactive composition. For more information about this genre, see V. J. Manzo and Will Kuhn, *Interactive Composition: Strategies Using Ableton Live and Max for Live* (New York: Oxford University Press, 2015).

2. Arnold Schoenberg, *Fundamentals of Musical Composition* (London: Faber and Faber, 1967).

3. One such book is Leon Dallin's *Techniques of Twentieth Century Composition: A Guide to the Materials of Modern Music,* 3rd ed. (Dubuque, IA: William C. Brown, 1974). A similar resource is *New Music Composition,* by David Cope (New York: Schirmer Books, 1977).

4. Most, but not all. This text concerns what might be called, in a broad way, traditional music, which is often, but not necessarily, tonal. Note that by traditional, I do not mean folk music, but rather music that remains anchored in the western tradition. Aesthetic points of view that explicitly aim to leave this tradition behind can be of interest, but they will not be addressed here.

5. The first chapter of Edward T. Cone's *Musical Form and Musical Performance* (New York: W. W. Norton, 1968) provides a stimulating, in-depth presentation and discussion of this notion of the musical frame.

6. This is why we will not discuss program music or through-composed music in any detail here. In the former, the music's form is suggested by an explicit story, known to the listener. In the latter, the music has no obvious repeating sections. In both cases, however, the composer still needs, once again, to provoke interest at the start, to develop the material in a coherent way, and to reach a convincing conclusion.

# CHAPTER 1. MOTIVE

1. For a thorough and fascinating discussion of the importance of musical expectations, see David Huron, *Sweet Anticipation* (Cambridge, MA: MIT Press, 2006).

2. Note that background music can tolerate much more literal repetition, since it is not the listener's primary focus.

3. Note that we are talking here about auditory recognition, not visual recognition. The two do not work the same way.

4. Unless they are unusually large and pronounced, leaps in a motive can become steps without distorting the character very much, perhaps because stepwise motion is somehow perceived as the norm. The opposite—steps becoming leaps—is a much more dramatic change. The details of the size of the leap are not as important.

5. Repeated notes, if they are present at all, immediately become a distinctive part of any motive. The one exception to this rule is where the first of the two notes is a long note, followed by a short note. In these cases, the ear will often hear the longer note as the end of a segment, and the following short note as the beginning of a new one. Since the two notes are not perceived as a unified group, the effect of changing them in a motivic variant is less noticeable.

6. Schoenberg, *Fundamentals of Musical Composition,* p. 58.

# CHAPTER 2. PHRASE

1. Even in completely tonal music, harmony alone cannot create cadence: there must always be other aspects of the music, rhythm in particular, that contribute as well. Some theorists call punctuation without a familiar harmonic cadence a "caesura."

2. I use the word *punctuation* here since the exact definition of *cadence* is not unanimously agreed upon. In classical music in particular, thematic aspects are considered by some theorists to be part of the definition; others only look at the harmony and the rhythm. Here we will consider a cadence simply as a clear punctuation in the main line, associated with some sense of harmonic arrival. There are many degrees of cadence, and subtlety in their application is a big part of the composer's craft. Again, we will have more to say about this in chapter 5.

3. Again, the exact definition of the word *phrase* can be controversial, especially if one includes repertoire outside the common practice period. For our purposes, a phrase is a coherent statement that goes beyond one single presentation of a motive, and that ends with clear punctuation. The important points for the composition student are (a) coherence and (b) knowing how to achieve various degrees of punctuation.

4. One could conceivably label these two bars as two separate phrases, but, whatever the nomenclature, the essential point is that m. 2 is heard in the light of m. 1, which defines its character more strongly, through contrast.

## CHAPTER 3. SINGING

1. Note that singing does not refer only to music for voice; an enormous amount of music for instruments also stems from song. Our musical tradition was first vocal: folk songs, Gregorian chant, popular tunes. When instruments arrived, much of the time they just played vocal lines. In Renaissance music it is not uncommon to see music designated as "for voices or viols," as though there were no difference—despite the fact that viols definitely do not speak in words! Only in the Baroque era do we observe the development of distinct instrumental styles, where instruments begin to specialize, so to speak, using techniques not possible for the voice. But even today, attending an orchestra rehearsal, a student is likely to hear the conductor at some point asking the musicians to make their instruments sing. Instruments can sing about our emotions, even without words.

2. A useful one, specifically for composers, is Gerald Custer and Blake Henson, *From Words to Music* (Chicago: GIA, 2014).

3. In the Classical period, arias were detached movements that could be sung separately. By the late nineteenth century, the two were usually integrated into the overall form without stopping. However, the differences in purpose and style remain valid.

4. Sometimes in Classical opera, certain numbers (arias in particular) may include repeats that are not in the text to start with. Well set, they should at least make sense with the text; otherwise the effect can be quite comic, and not in places intended to be funny. In art songs, there may be occasions where the composer contradicts or mitigates the textual punctuation for artistic reasons, for example, to put more emphasis on a key word or phrase. The important thing is that this should happen deliberately, at an emotionally appropriate moment, and not through simple carelessness.

## CHAPTER 4. PLAYING

1. Although occasionally in recent scores one sees special effects requiring the players to sing while playing, the fact is that instrumentalists are normally not trained to sing, let alone while playing their instruments. This means that such effects are hard to deploy with any subtlety. If the composer wants to use such effects, it is important to avoid the impression of instrumentalists doing badly what singers could do better. Of course, there are occasional dramatic situations where having the instrumentalists sing while playing might nevertheless be appropriate.

2. In an interesting documentary, *Maestro or Mephisto: The Real Georg Solti,* the great conductor, who was also a pianist, points out that chamber music is collaboration, whereas in the orchestra one person, the conductor, has to make the decisions. This statement comes from somebody who knew how to fulfill both roles, superbly.

## CHAPTER 5. PUNCTUATING

1. This is not to say that there are no other aspects of the music that provide important formal information, in particular, themes and motives.

2. We have already discussed the use of motives in this example, in chapter 1.

3. It is not a coincidence that strong beats are called downbeats, and weak beats upbeats; the gravitational analogy is telling.

4. The coda section has started earlier (at rehearsal 156), its arrival marked by a bell stroke. Within the coda itself, the harmony circles around the tonic several times; this last section is preceded by a final V-I. While prolonging this final tonic chord, Shostakovich uses rhythm for this last stage of the coda.

5. A common beginner's error in orchestration is to change instruments in midphrase, or worse, in midmotive, which simply sounds like a mistake.

6. Since so much of music's effect has to do with expectations and moving toward or away from musical goals, if the listener simply feels lost, much of the force of the music is sacrificed.

7. There is a good deal of legitimate discussion in theory circles about how long the phrases actually are here, as well as where the cadence actually occurs. Some might even call the whole passage one single phrase, with only one cadence, in m. 16. This has a certain logic, especially for a performer, who needs to decide which cadential moments need to be underlined. Underlining too many such moments leads to a bumpy, stop-and-go kind of performance. But a composer needs to intelligently apply many more levels of punctuation, ranging from the mildest stop in the middle of a motive to the most conclusive final cadence.

## CHAPTER 6. PRESENTING

1. Note that although there is some overlap, my use of the word "presenting" here does not have quite the same meaning as William Caplin's "presentation function," discussed in his book *Classical Form: A Theory of Formal Functions for the Instrumental Music of Haydn, Mozart, and Beethoven* (New York: Oxford University Press, 1998).

2. In reality, as with motives, there is a continuum between the most predictable combinations of phrases and the most heterogeneous and surprising ones. However, again as with motives, there is a distinct point where the listener is struck more by the novelty of the new phrase than by a sense of familiarity.

## CHAPTER 7. ONE-PART FORMS

1. There are occasional preludes that are larger and more elaborate, but the most common place to find a small form with no major punctuation or contrasts remains the prelude.

2. This is not to say there is no counterpoint in a prelude, but rather that its use is not an essential feature of the form, unlike, say, the fugue. We will not

discuss fugue here, except to mention that the general principles of progression and climax, discussed elsewhere in this book, apply there as well. (Fugue is normally studied as the culmination of a counterpoint course.)

3. Of course, when a prelude precedes a fugue, for example, in some sense the two pieces should complement each other, but the relationship between them is usually rather straightforward, a simple, vivid contrast, without internal thematic references or transitions between the two.

4. In the manuscript one can actually see Chopin crossing out the rests in the original rhythm here and substituting the quintuplets: this was clearly an enhancing revision. Note that this is still close enough to the original motive not to sound like a remote variant.

## CHAPTER 8. TERNARY FORM

1. The student may wonder why we discuss ternary form before binary form. The reason is that, despite its name, the simple ternary form is really composed of only two distinct ideas, organized into a very straightforward ABA scheme.

2. The student should be aware that academic terminology differs in regard to ternary forms, as well as the rounded binary forms discussed in the next chapter. For another point of view, see Caplin, *Classical Form*. The deeper issue here, for the composer, is that there are many factors whose interactions affect formal perception: the relative similarity/difference of material in the second section, the tonal completeness/incompleteness of each section, the presence/absence of smooth transitions between sections. Many of these distinctions are not black-and-white; they lend themselves to gradation. For example, concerning the reprise after contrasting material, just how much of the previous material is repeated? Two bars? Four phrases? The possible interactions between all these criteria become very numerous indeed, so that a really sensitive classification would require a kind of grid, with each of the criteria ranked and summed. Fortunately, for our purposes here, a simple practice form will suffice.

## CHAPTER 9. BINARY FORM

1. The main idea may contain more than one motive, but the point here is that the second section does not normally introduce new material.

2. Note that here we will look at several varieties of binary form useful to the composition student. As with ternary form, already discussed, we are not aiming at a historical survey. For that kind of information, the student is directed to, for example, Caplin's *Classical Form*.

3. This comparison need not be entirely conscious, but it should create in the listener a general sense of familiarity. Familiarity, all other things being equal, leads to psychological relaxation.

4. Some theorists would call this form a variety of ternary. The terminology is less important for us than the formal characteristics mentioned here. Again, for details of this alternative point of view, see Caplin's *Classical Form*.

5. Any really sophisticated harmonic language must allow for subtle differences in harmonic tension, to avoid monotony.

6. In our simple ternary project, as we have seen, the sections can actually exist independently; there is really no inherent necessity for the middle section, since the first section is in no sense incomplete. Here the second section cannot really exist alone: it would seem incomplete.

## CHAPTER 10. VARIATION FORM

1. Of course, one could invent a theme with an unusual form with the express intention of giving it some wonderful, long-term "destiny" over many variations, but working this out successfully would require a much more sophisticated sense of form than a student will likely possess.

2. The imitation reverses the direction of the melodic intervals: rising intervals now descend, and vice versa.

3. Invertible counterpoint is counterpoint where either part can serve as the bass. This means that what was the upper line can become the lower line, and vice versa.

## CHAPTER 11. CONTRASTING

1. Elliott Carter often referred to the most basic requirement of musical form as "convincing continuity." In other words, the emphasis is on how all the elements in a piece need to come together, creating a satisfactory musical flow.

2. Arnold Schoenberg believed that all the musical ideas in a great work were always derived from one basic source motive. While this is very debatable as a generalization, it does suggest a useful way to generate contrasting material: simply alter several dimensions of the original idea in substantial ways, at the same time. See Schoenberg, *Fundamentals of Musical Composition*, p. 8.

3. For more on this subject, see Albert Bregman's *Auditory Scene Analysis: The Perceptual Organization of Sound* (Cambridge, MA: MIT Press, 1990).

4. This is the most common reason for having a slow introduction to a larger fast movement. An excellent and very revealing exercise for the aspiring composer is to try starting such a piece minus the introduction. In a good composer's work, this kind of reverse engineering will quickly demonstrate that starting with the faster section is less compelling.

## CHAPTER 12. CONNECTING

1. Richard Wagner, in a letter to Mathilde Wesendonck, October 29, 1859; quoted in Barry Millington and Stewart Spencer, eds., *Selected Letters of Richard Wagner* (New York: W. W. Norton, 1987), pp. 474–75.

2. See (one of many possible sources) *Stress: Concepts, Cognition, Emotion, and Behaviour,* ed. George Fink (London: Academic Press, 2016).

3. An interesting work exemplifying this point is Giacinto Scelsi's *Quattro pezzi su una nota sola* (Four Pieces on a Single Note). By focusing each piece on one pitch, the composer makes other aspects of the music become much more prominent. When the central note of the piece is, occasionally, called into question, the effect is particularly strong, since there is so little pitch evolution overall.

4. Note that when this theme returns later in the movement, the chord on the first beat is included.

5. Overlapping, or elision, is a common transitional technique, but in itself it does not imply significant change of character, which is our focus here.

## CHAPTER 13. PROGRESSING

1. It is worth noting that the more static music of other cultures is usually not concert music in our sense, meaning that it is not meant to be played by itself as the center of attention. It is often functional music, created to accompany important events and rituals.

2. This is what Roger Sessions called the principle of "progression, or cumulation," the idea that over a whole work there needs to be a general feeling of intensification (see Roger Sessions, *The Musical Experience of Composer, Performer, Listener* [New York: Atheneum, 1968]). Of course, this does not imply that every work must be structured as a large crescendo, just that the listener's experience must intensify overall as the music goes on.

3. This example is nonetheless an improvement over our chromatic scale example, since the (modal) scale steps here are not exactly equal, unlike the chromatic steps seen earlier.

4. A literary analogy might be in a murder mystery, at the point when all the evidence finally points in the same direction and it becomes clear who the culprit really is. All that is left is a final chase.

5. Occasionally a composer may slow down before a climax. An example is the fugue in Max Reger's Fantasia and Fugue in D minor, Op. 135b, for organ. The end of this work is its climax, and it gets progressively slower and heavier. When the very chromatic harmony finally arrives at the tonic D-major chord at the very end, there is a sense of having achieved this culmination after overcoming great obstacles.

6. So many overtures by Rossini are organized this way that some musicians even speak of a "Rossini crescendo"!

7. Cone, in *Musical Form and Musical Performance*, p. 23, proposes the notion of an introduction as an expanded upbeat. While this passage is not an introduction in the same sense as Cone's example (the opening of Beethoven's Seventh Symphony), it does act as a kind of huge upbeat to the last movement.

## CHAPTER 14. RONDO FORM

1. The fact that this little phrase sounds cadential makes it possible for Haydn to use it both to start and to end a section. (I am indebted to Andrew Schartmann for this observation.)

2. This is a good illustration of how simply listing the motives within a section is far from sufficient to determine its character; their relative prominence is at least as important.

3. The only formal difference between the piano and orchestral versions is that the former ends loudly, and the latter ends quietly. It is an interesting question why Ravel made this change, not easily answered. The harmony and rhythm are identical in both endings. Perhaps Ravel felt that an orchestral tutti would sound too bombastic for the character of the piece?

## CHAPTER 15. BEGINNING

1. Other memorable moments are: climaxes, major contrasts, and the ending.

2. Note that although Beethoven's fugue subject will of course return many times in the course of the movement, the rhythmic gaps will from now on usually be filled in by activity in the other parts.

3. Perhaps more than any other composer, Beethoven succeeded in greatly broadening music's expressive range, over his whole oeuvre. This could not have happened just by chance: it was clearly one of his goals.

4. Evolution seems to have made us very aware of anything that seems like it's sneaking up on us: an indication of possible danger.

5. A qualification: these types of musical gestures are not limited to beginnings. An effective beginning must meet these requirements—provoking interest and suggesting potential for development—but not all such gestures are necessarily beginnings. For example, they are sometimes found in transitional or developmental passages as well. The point here is simply that a gesture that does not somehow suggest more is to follow will not likely engage the listener's interest.

6. The opposite just about never occurs, perhaps because the consequent loss of momentum would be disappointing.

## CHAPTER 16. EXPLORING

1. This chapter could also have been called "Developing." I chose the current title to avoid the possible implication that the processes here described are limited to the development section in a sonata form.

2. Although not strictly an example of the kind of development discussed in this chapter, a double fugue illustrates this principle perfectly: first we hear one idea developed at length, then another, and finally they are heard together as a contrapuntal combination. Two seemingly separate things now fit together, and thus draw the preceding, formally contrasting ideas into a larger whole.

3. We have already referred to this metaphor, proposed by Edward Cone in his book *Musical Form and Musical Performance*. In a sense, developmental structures are by nature rather like structural upbeats, creating tension over a sustained period of time. And, to follow the analogy further, they usually "resolve" into some kind of recapitulation, returning to a more stable structure.

4. Although it would be an exaggeration to say that all rising lines create tension, the association with the human voice, which rises as we become more agitated, is a fundamental one. We can say that, all other things being equal, most rising lines create a certain excitement.

5. It is worth mentioning once again the excellent book by David Huron on this subject: *Sweet Anticipation.*

6. We are not referring here to theoretical anomalies, but to something that is immediately puzzling to the listener, which can then be used later on in the piece.

7. It is worth trying to listen to this passage as though one has never heard it before. The shock is quite extreme; one really does wonder what is wrong.

## CHAPTER 18. ENDING

1. There are occasional examples of endings that leave things not quite resolved, for instance, Chopin's F-major Prelude, which ends on a dominant seventh chord. These are very rare, and it is no accident that the prelude in question is not normally played alone, but rather as part of a set. While some individual preludes can be played by themselves, it is very unlikely that a performer would play only this one.

Another well-known example of an unresolved conclusion occurs in Berg's opera *Wozzeck,* which ends with a child rocking alone on the stage, unaware that his parents are dead. But this is a dramatic work, with a story, and the horror of the innocent child who has been left an orphan is part of the force of this ending.

2. I do not mean to imply that absolute music always has a specific program or story behind it, but rather that the overall structure of any narrative whatsoever—problem, development, resolution—does indeed apply to the vast majority of artistic compositions. The deeper reasons for this lie in our human psychology, in our need to make sense of the world by connecting events into a narrative line, with causes, effects, and understandable consequences. For a fascinating discussion of this issue in literature, see Brian Boyd, *On the Origin of Stories: Evolution, Cognition, and Fiction* (Cambridge, MA: Harvard University Press, 2009).

3. Notice that although the high B in m. 27 has been heard before, it has never been so clearly and directly prepared as this. For example, in m. 7 there is not the gradually rising line leading into it that we hear in mm. 25–27.

## CHAPTER 19. SONATA FORM

1. Readers wishing more theoretical and historical detail about the Classical sonata form are directed to James Hepokoski and Warren Darcy, *Elements of Sonata Theory: Norms, Types, and Deformations in the Late Eighteenth-Century Sonata*, rev. ed. (Oxford: Oxford University Press, 2011). There is also some discussion of the post-Classical sonata form in Charles Rosen, *Sonata Forms* (New York: W. W. Norton, 1988).

2. There are examples of monothematic sonatas, particularly in Haydn. In these cases, the different tonal zones serve as the principal contrasting elements.

3. Although at first glance the conventional repeat of the exposition would seem to contradict this, ultimately it substantially intensifies the listener's impression of leaving home. Having heard the music reach the end of the exposition twice, the listener is even more strongly surprised when it takes a new turn into the development.

4. Sometimes the transition here may go toward the keys on the flat side of the circle of fifths, e.g., to IV, to balance the original transition's motion from I to V, on the sharp side.

5. The interested reader is again referred to the books by Hepokoski and Darcy and by Rosen (see n. 1 above), which discuss many possible variants of sonata form in detail.

6. A recent book by Seth Monahan discusses these works in detail: *Mahler's Symphonic Sonatas* (New York: Oxford University Press, 2015).

## CHAPTER 20. REFINEMENTS

1. Minimalist music might seem to be an exception, but all that is really happening is that the changes are much less frequent and more subtle. But the principle remains the same: something happens to intensify the listener's attention at a special moment.

2. Note that the word *accent* here is not used just in the conventional sense of playing one note louder than those around it, but rather in the more general sense of making one moment in the music stand out in some way.

3. For an interesting discussion of this idea in the visual arts, see Ellen Dissanayake, *Homo Aestheticus* (Seattle and London: University of Washington Press, 1995), especially chapter 3, "The Core of Art: Making Special."

4. Note that in a very dissonant style a consonance can sometimes have a comparable effect, as it draws attention to itself simply by its difference from the surroundings.

5. As an example of what not to do, changing the accompaniment to, say, trombones would transform a mild accent into an extreme one, far out of proportion to the requirements of the context.

## CONCLUSION

1. However, it is true that sometimes music for video games also has a pedagogical role, helping the user to learn the rules of the game.

2. A suggested method for applying them over the course of a given composition will be laid out in Appendix A, on sketching.

## APPENDIX A

1. *The Writings of Elliott Carter,* compiled, edited, and annotated by Else Stone and Kurt Stone (Bloomington and London: Indiana University Press, 1977), pp. 302–3.

## APPENDIX B

1. There are several good books presenting these rules. A standard one is *Behind Bars,* by Elaine Gould (Van Nuys, California: Alfred Publishing, 2003).

2. Works for small chamber ensembles usually do not need a conductor, but their scores should be presented like conductor scores, so that the members of the ensemble can easily verify what the others are doing in context, when necessary. However, such chamber music scores do not need to be printed as large as the standard conductor score.

3. Players often will change the indicated bowings, but, especially for situations where the correct bowing is not obvious right away, having the bowings prepared in advance is an enormous timesaver.

4. This may require consulting with a percussionist if the setup is complex.

5. Note that we will not discuss simulating the human voice here. Its problems are particularly complex, owing partly to the presence of words and partly to the much greater variety of range and timbre in individual human voices than in most instruments.

6. Even within a given basic tempo, a musician always applies a certain mild elasticity of rhythm; rigidity of tempo within the phrase is one of the most obvious defects of most computer simulations. Some programs allow for metric flexibility, for instance, jazzlike swing, but the ebb and flow of a whole phrase is much harder to automate.

7. Note that for the piano, speed and force of attack are identical: it is impossible simultaneously to attack a note very slowly and very loudly.

# CREDITS

# INDEX

balance (*continued*)
  of stability vs. instability, 118
  of suspense vs. resolution, 174, 186, 187
  in vocal music, 27, 32
Barber, Samuel, 33
Baroque era, 34, 70, 85, 196, 231n1 (chap. 3)
Bartók, Béla
  Concerto for Orchestra, Sz. 116, 157–58
  Third String Quartet, Sz. 85, 19–20
bass line, xvii, 15, 47, 72, 86, 87, 142, 146, 164, 202, 203
bassoon, 34
Beethoven, Ludwig van, 214
  *Appassionata* Piano Sonata, 54–56
  concerti by, 196
  *Diabelli Variations*, 91
  dynamic surprises by, 137, 212
  Eighth Symphony, 176
  *Eroica* Symphony, 136
  Fifth Piano Concerto, 196
  Fifth Symphony, xi, 138–39, 170, 217
  First Symphony, 156–57
  Fourth Piano Concerto, 196
  *Harp* Quartet, Op. 74, 122
  Ninth Symphony, 167–69, 217
  piano concerti by, 43, 44, 196
  Piano Sonata in A-flat major, Op. 26, 65–66, 103
  Piano Sonata in B-flat major, Op. 106, 152
  Piano Sonata in C minor, Op. 13 (*Pathétique*), 159, 160, 196
  Piano Sonata in G major, Op. 49, No. 2, 62–63
  Seventh Symphony, 82, 163–64, 182–83
  String Quartet in C major, Op. 59, No. 3, 18–19

String Quartet in E minor, Op. 59, No. 2, 190–95
String Quartet in F major, Op. 18, No. 1, 106–7
String Quartet in F major, Op. 59, No. 1, 2–3
String Quartet in F major, Op. 135, 93–95, 104
Violin Sonata in A minor, Op. 23, 149
beginnings, 151–60
Bellini, Vincenzo, 78, 79
Berg, Alban, 237n1
binary form, xii, 82, 84–90, 163, 174, 175
Boulez, Pierre, xiv
bowing, 220, 223, 227, 228
Brahms, Johannes
  Clarinet Quintet, 44
  First Symphony, 159–60
  Handel Variations, 95–102
  Intermezzi, 35
  *Paganini Variations*, 91
  Piano Trio in B major, Op. 8, 213
  Second Symphony, 124–27
  Third Symphony, 2
  Violin Concerto, 53, 183, 199–200
brainstorming, 216
brass instruments, 38, 138
Britten, Benjamin, 33
bumps, xiii

cadence, xvii, 7, 9, 19, 20, 175
  in binary form, 85
  deceptive, 52, 139, 175, 193
  dissonance before, 47, 76
  dynamics and, 49–50
  falling lines characteristic of, 45–46
  half, 61–65, 72, 79, 81, 85, 86, 87, 95, 142–45, 171
  imperfect, 60, 62
  mode or scale and, 46–47, 146

ornamentation, 10–11, 79, 95

*Otello* (Verdi), 116, 118

overlapping (elision), 51–52, 235n5 (chap. 12)

*Paganini Variations* (Brahms), 91

page turns, 223

paragraph, 62–66

parts, for performance, 222–24

passacaglia, 103

passing tone, 8, 89, 147

*Pathétique* Sonata (Beethoven), 159, 160, 196

*Pavane pour une infante défunte* (Ravel), 145–48, 150

pedals
of organ, 76, 116
of piano, 36, 72, 204

pedal tone, 53, 146, 158
Bach's use of, 3, 75–76, 86, 153
Beethoven's use of, 18, 95, 139, 182
Brahms's use of, 98, 101, 124, 126, 159, 183, 199
Chopin's use of, 72
Haydn's use of, 144, 145
Mozart's use of, 187, 188, 189, 190

perception, xi–xii, 1, 106

percussion, 135, 202, 222, 223

perfect cadence, 60, 61, 62, 63, 65, 79, 81, 99, 142, 144, 148
differing weights of, 87

performance, 220–28
parts for, 222–24
simulated, 224–28

period, 60–62

phrases, 16–24, 225
grouping of, 59–69
stability of, 59–60, 187
structure of, 17–21, 162–66, 187

Phrygian mode, 21

piano, 35–36, 39, 40, 71, 99–100, 118, 190, 239n7

Beethoven's works for, 43, 44, 62–63, 65–66, 103, 152, 159, 160, 196

Chopin's works for, 70, 71–73, 74, 77, 78–80, 202–3, 237n1

Debussy's works for, 21–22, 36, 44

Haydn's works for, 39, 102, 118–20, 141–45, 148, 149, 150, 174

Mozart's works for, 61–62, 93, 187–90

pedals of, 36, 72, 204

Rachmaninoff's works for, 70, 74–75

Schubert's works for, 60–61, 102

Schumann's works for, 85, 87–89

piccolo, xvii, 51, 106

Picker, Tobias, 44

pitch pattern, 2

pizzicato, 18, 19, 20, 51, 118, 151–52, 202, 227

plagal cadence, 99

polyphony, 44

portamento, 227

prelude, 70, 75

presenting, 59–69

principles, forms vs., 212

program music, 116, 229n6

progressing, 84, 131–40, 173

Prokofiev, Sergei, 153, 154

Puccini, Giacomo, 29

punctuation, xiv, 17–18, 79, 212, 225
in binary form, 84–85
counterpoint and, 56
degrees of, 51–56
dynamic aspects of, 49–50
excessive, 178
of grouped phrases, 59, 60
harmonic aspects of, 47–48
listening aided by, 45, 52
melodic aspects of, 46–47
rhythmic aspects of, 48–49
in rondo form, 150
silence as, 57
textural and timbral aspects of, 50–51